S0-ATQ-140

The ABBOTT & COSTELLO Story

The ABBOTT & COSTELLO Story

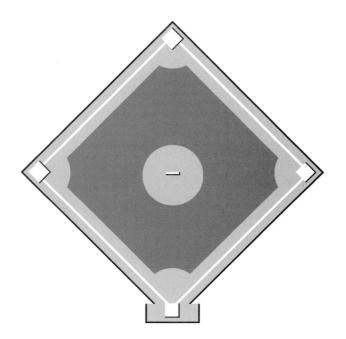

Stephen Cox and John Lofflin

Cumberland House Publishing
Nashville, Tennessee

Copyright © 1990, 1997 by Stephen Cox and John Lofflin

The original edition of this book was published in the United States of America under the title *The Official Abbott & Costello Scrapbook* © 1990 by Stephen Cox and John Lofflin.

All rights reserved. Written permission must be secured from the publisher to use or reproduce any part of this work, except for brief quotations in critical reviews or articles.

Published by Cumberland House Publishing, Inc., 431 Harding Industrial Park Drive, Nashville, TN 37211-3160.

Distributed to the trade by Andrews & McMeel, 4520 Main Street, Kansas City, Missouri, 64111.

Cover and interior design by Harriet Bateman

Library of Congress Cataloging-in-Publication Data

Cox, Stephen, 1966-
    [Official Abbott & Costello scrapbook]
    The Abbott & Costello story / Stephen Cox and John Lofflin.
        p. cm.
    Originally published: The official Abbott & Costello scrapbook. Chicago : Contemporary Books, c1990.
    Filmography: p.
    ISBN 1-888952-61-x (pbk. : alk. paper)
    1. Abbott, Bud. 2. Costello, Lou. 3. Comedians—United States—Biography.
I. Lofflin, John. II. Title.
PN2287.A217C6 1997
791.43'028'092273—dc21
    [B]   97-24295
                                                                        CIP

Printed in the United States of America
1 2 3 4 5 6 7—02 03 01 00 99 98 97

For Bernadette, Brian, and Michele,
who watched them with me on Saturday afternoons
—Stephen Cox

For Phil,
who has driven me crazy with the convoluted logic of this beauty from
Abbott and Costello Meet Frankenstein:

COSTELLO: That'll cost you overtime because I'm a union man
and I only work sixteen hours a day.
MR. MCDOUGAL: But a union man only works eight hours a day.
COSTELLO: I belong to two unions.
—John Lofflin

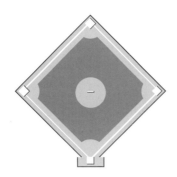

Contents

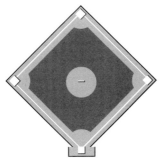

Foreword

When Abbott asked, "Costello, how did you get up in the tree?" and Costello said, "How did I get up in the tree? I sat on it when it was an acorn," that was it. Right then and there I knew I had to be a comedian.

I knew Abbott and Costello only from casual greetings time to time on Broadway and at the studio. When Lou was very ill and I filled in to make the movie *Fireman Save My Child,* Lou's stuntman, Vic Parks, came up to me.

"The ol' man wants to talk to you," he whispered. So I went to Costello's house in Sherman Oaks, California. Lou asked me, "How are they treatin' ya?"

"Real good," I told him.

"Don't let the bastards get ya down" was Lou's response.

I didn't know what he was talking about. Later on I found out how rough the movie business was and how studios could just impose their will on you. Lou always looked after his friends and family like that.

There is a LeRoy Neiman painting of Lou talking to me hanging in the den of my house in Beverly Hills. I wanted the painting—even before I played Lou's life in the movie *Bud and Lou.* It's not a flattering picture of me, but it is of Lou.

My style is a bit different from Lou's, but I've always resembled him in appearance. We've also had other similarities. Lou started out as a boxer, and I boxed, when I was fourteen or fifteen, at Coney Island for three dollars. After Lou died, his daughter Carole asked if I'd give her away at her wedding because I reminded her of her dad. I said, "Of course." I was honored when she took my arm and I escorted her down the aisle.

LeRoy Neimen painted this portrait of Buddy Hackett and Lou Costello. It hangs in the Hackett den in Beverly Hills. (Photo by Joe Wallison)

Years later I played Lou in *Bud and Lou* opposite Harvey Korman. I didn't like the part of the script that made Lou look like a bad guy. He was really a great guy. One scene was left out of the picture, and had it remained it would have given a clearer idea of what Lou was like. You'll soon read about it in this scrapbook. I loved Lou, and he was a great force in my life.

This book celebrates not only Lou but Bud as well. I must admit they complemented each other and worked together like a well-tuned machine. To really understand Abbott & Costello's relationship, you might have to be a comedian. A comedian knows how important a straight man is. Don't let anyone tell you that Dean Martin, Dan Rowan, and Peter Marshall (remember Noonan and Marshall?) weren't great too. Each was magnificent in his own right. Straight men are just as important as comedians.

And Bud was superb.

Not that I've ever had problems, but sometimes when I stand out there alone, I wish I had a straight man. The straight man makes it all come easier, and Bud did that for Lou. They fed each other. They were made for each other.

Let me leave you with this. Abbott & Costello saved Universal Studios during the forties. We're finding out now how important that was. When all the history is finished being written about the importance of comedy, Abbott & Costello will be remembered as much for their economic as their creative contributions to the industry. They'll be on first.

I'm confident that you'll enjoy this book.

Buddy Hackett

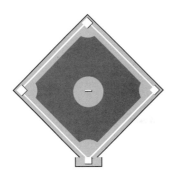

Preface

Wonderful things happen when you start looking up the folks who worked with Abbott & Costello. When we left Eddie Forman's house after a delightful evening of listening to the irascible, eighty-nine-year-old gag writer reminisce (the first thing he asked was if we knew any good agents because "you can't just sit and stare at the pool all day," and the second thing he asked was how we liked a new joke he'd just written about an elderly man who'd lost control of his bladder), he shook our hands and said, "You're a couple of right guys." Bogart couldn't have delivered the line with a more virile wink or a more knowing sneer.

We were late to interview Sheldon Leonard at the Directors Guild but still found him hospitable. We didn't know whether to laugh or say we were sorry when he walked smack into the very glass partition we'd accidentally walked into ten minutes earlier. (We still don't know if he'd seen us stumble into it and made his own pratfall to give us a laugh or if he actually didn't see the partition either.)

We sat well into the night at the dining room table of eighty-two-year-old Vic Parks, Lou Costello's double who himself had cut his teeth in vaudeville and burlesque, and listened to him do those timeless routines as if, indeed, there existed no such thing as time.

It's impossible to understand why Abbott & Costello became stars or just how brightly their stars burned without understanding how The Boys fit into their time, how the luster and joy of their movies were a godsend to 1940s America. It's impossible to understand their humor without understanding the tradition in which it was rooted, a tradition they loved and deeply respected. Even if their work is sometimes difficult to fully appreciate sixty years later, some of the routines they preserved have proved timeless.

Surely Bud and Lou had no idea of the consequences of their actions that evening of March 24, 1938. It was exactly sixty years ago that Bud and Lou first stepped up to the CBS microphone and dizzied a nationwide radio audience with "Who's on First?" It was their checkmate because, at that moment, that very instant, their career shifted into warp speed. That stumble-bumble routine, built on pure malapropism, literally catapulted them into Hollywood, into motion pictures, and into the history books.

Their work is alive today on audio- and videocassettes and on Sunday morning cable TV. A new generation heard their most famous routine for the first time in 1988 when Dustin Hoffman brought his own grating, squeaking, wandering-all-over-the-scale voice to the role of an autistic savant in *Rain Man* and won an Oscar for the portrayal. Throughout the movie his character, Raymond, chanted the dialogue to "Who's on First?" It was something Bud and Lou would have loved.

Steve Cox
John Lofflin

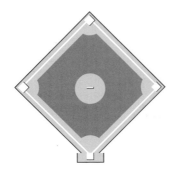

Acknowledgments

The authors wish to cheer the following pinch hitters who lent their time and efforts to make this book possible: Steve Allen, Morey Amsterdam, Joe Barbera, Julie Gibson Barton, Jerry Beck, Ken Beck, Milton Berle, Noel Blanc, Tom Brown, Susan Buntrock, Jerry and Blanche Cox, Nancy Cushing-Jones (MCA Publishing), Corin DeLuca (MCA Publicity), June Easton, Brad Farrell, Fine Arts Theater (in Mission, Kansas), Howard Frank, Tom Frederick, Joe Glaston, Rick Goldschmidt, Linda Gray, Joey Green, Hanna-Barbera Productions, Bill Honor, Gary Lassin, Gretchen Lindensmith (Columbia House Video Library), Heather Lofflin, Kathy Ehrig Lofflin, Rosalie Longo, Tod Machin, Kevin Marhanka, Tim Neeley, Sandy Oliveri, Jordan Reichek, Paul Rubin, Bob Satterfield, Ray Savage, Robert Sherman, Rob Swerdlow, Universal Studios, and Jerry Weinstein.

A special thank-you to comedy-team historian Joe Wallison, who worked as a research assistant with us on this project. Joe strived to make sure we hit a homer with this one, and was gracious enough to allow us to reprint some rare images of Bud and Lou from his private collection.

Here's the lineup of the all-star team we interviewed. A big cheer to: Bud Abbott Jr., Norman Abbott, Olive Abbott, Maxene Andrews, Patty Andrews, Joe Besser, Hillary Brooke, Helen Gurley Brown, Candy Candido, Chris Costello, Bob Cummings, Joe DiMaggio, Robert Easton, Eddie Forman, Betty Abbott Griffin, Abe Haberman, Ralph Handley, Buddy Hackett, Paddy Costello Humphreys, Stan Irwin, Sheldon Leonard, Ron Masak, Don Messick, Jim Mulholland, Lee Orgel, Vic Parks, Aida "De De" Polo, Don Wheeler, and Vickie Abbott Wheeler.

Acknowledging their contribution to radio, motion pictures, and television, Bud and Lou each have three stars on Hollywood's Walk of Fame. Look for Bud's stars in front of 6333 Hollywood Boulevard (radio), 6740 Hollywood Boulevard (TV), and 1611 Vine Street (film). Lou's stars are located at 6780 Hollywood Boulevard (radio), 6438 Hollywood Boulevard (film), and 6276 Hollywood Boulevard (TV).

For a beautiful array of photographs, we also thank: Abbott and Costello Enterprises, Archive Photos, Associated Press, Al Hirschfeld, Columbia Pictures, Duocards, Inc., Hanna-Barbera Productions, Metro-Goldwyn-Mayer, NBC, Neal Peters Collection, *North Jersey Herald and News,* Personality Photos, Inc. (P.O. Box 50, Brooklyn, N.Y., ll230), Photofest, Ralph Edwards Productions, RKO, Shanachie Entertainment Corp., *TV Guide*/News America Publications, United Artists, United Press International, Universal Studios (MCA), Warner Brothers, Wide World Photos, Inc.

Information regarding the Abbott and Costello Fan Club may be obtained by writing: P.O. Box 2084, Toluca Lake, CA 91610.

And finally, a great big thank-you to the folks at Cumberland House: Leslie Peterson, Ron Pitkin, Stephen Woolverton, and the rest.

The ABBOTT & COSTELLO Story

CHAPTER 1

Heyyyyyy Aaaaaaabbott!: The Art of Abbott & Costello

*The proof of the poet is that his country absorbs him as affection-
ately as he has absorbed it.*

—Walt Whitman

The fat little man has just seen Frankenstein's monster lift the lid on a
packing crate in an empty warehouse at midnight. He is so frightened, he
can't even whistle. He puckers up his chubby cheeks and blows, but nothing
comes out. His eyes are as wide as saucers and he's gasping for breath. He's
shaking from head to toe as though he just grabbed a bare electric wire. He's
Lou Costello, and his slick-talking partner, Bud Abbott, won't believe him
when he stammers on about the hideous goon in the packing crate.

Bud Abbott and Lou Costello made millions of dollars and millions of
laughs with routines as simple and as universal as this one. Whether you
laughed at the duo in first-run theaters on Saturday nights in the 1940s and
early 1950s, at matinees on Saturday afternoons in the 1950s and 1960s, on
television on Sunday mornings in the 1970s and 1980s, or you discovered
them in the video age, you laughed because they were masters of their craft.

If you were lucky enough to be a child in the 1950s, you know that
Abbott & Costello *were* Saturday afternoons—at the Granada Theater in
Kansas City, Kansas; the Fox Theater in St. Louis, Missouri; the U.S. Theater
in Paterson, New Jersey. Their image is stuck in with your memories of other
strange, fuzzy scenes from childhood—the bloody noses you got in fights,
the first time you got the sweet part of the bat on a baseball, the way the
leaves on maple trees turned themselves upside down just before a storm.
Your first kiss.

3

Marquee for the New York opening of Mexican Hayride *in December 1948. (Personality Photos, Inc.)*

In those days, Saturdays did indeed mean Abbott & Costello. Well, not *just* Abbott & Costello. In addition to a second-run showing of one of their features, Saturdays meant a western, several cartoons, a serial, and a news-reel. Later it meant a Disney movie too, something to do with Flubber or talking cats, if memory serves. *Chicago Sun-Times* critic Roger Ebert once mused about the contrast between the many hours we were willing to commit to a Saturday movie as children and how impatient we are today. No more triple bills. No more double bills. Even the single bills don't come with cartoons.

To understand the art of Bud Abbott and Lou Costello, you first have to drift back in time to a different moviegoing experience. The movies we loved then didn't need gargantuan budgets, undressed teenage actresses, or credits that took fifteen minutes to roll across the screen. They didn't need serious, thought-provoking messages, antiheroes, or subtitles. They didn't even need epic proportions, though many had them. It was enough, in the

Entertaining the servicemen was a responsibility Bud and Lou took quite seriously.

The famous drill routine onstage in New York, circa 1937. (Courtesy of Olive Abbott)

1940s and 1950s, if a movie simply made you laugh until you were weak. It was enough to be scrunched down in your seat, laughing and gasping and snorting until tears came out of your eyes and you thought you might die right there without ever catching your breath. And nobody did it better to you than Abbott & Costello.

Little movies were fine with us in the 1940s and the 1950s. After all, we intended to watch three or four in an afternoon, and we paid only two bits to get in, anyway. Two-bit movies didn't even have to be very good. Who cared if they stood the test of time?

Abbott & Costello made a few blockbusters—*Buck Privates, Abbott and Costello Meet Frankenstein, In the Navy*. But most of their thirty-six films were just nice little outings—seven-hit, three-run affairs, an overall 12-and-9 pitching record, perhaps. A few were stinkers, and others left a genuine sense of déjà vu because, for heaven's sake, how many ways *can* you twist the same plot and recast the same routines?

But entertainment didn't always have to be "new" then. Like jazz musicians of the 1940s, Abbott & Costello, and their public, were content to bend and twist and shape old material like so much clay. The emphasis was on performance. They created the immortal "Who's on First?" from the

Award winning director Normen Abbott got his start in the business from his Uncle Bud. (Photo by John Lofflin)

Bud and Lou are about to meet the killer . . . Boris Karloff.   Or do they?

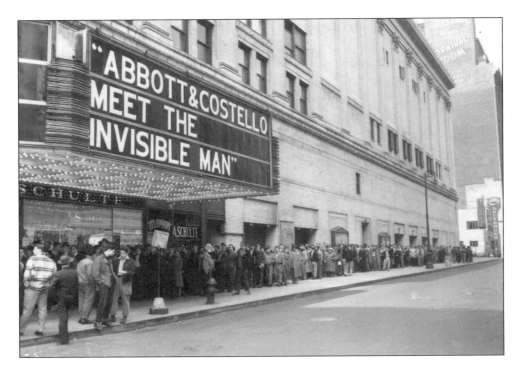

The New York opening of Invisible Man *in 1951.*

vaudeville chestnut "Baker's Dozen" the same way Charlie Parker made "Ornithology" from "How High the Moon." When it came to performance, Abbott & Costello were masters; their routines, if not original, were impeccably timed, flawlessly delivered, excitingly improvisational. So what if most of their movies were little more than vehicles for those routines? It is hard to imagine a human too jaded to laugh at the old "Pack, Unpack" bit, even if Abbott & Costello's favorite director, Charlie Barton, did manage to shame them out of using it yet again in 1948 when they filmed *Abbott and Costello Meet Frankenstein*.

"They weren't innovators," says Bud's nephew Norman Abbott, an Emmy Award-winning director and producer today. "Chaplin was a first. Buster Keaton was a first. Lenny Bruce was a first. Redd Foxx was a first. Abbott & Costello were flat-out joke men. They took existing material and did it better than anyone else."

Comics today live and die by a different set of standards. For decades, one shot on Johnny Carson's show blew a year's worth of material—forever. They might do the same pile of jokes in Minneapolis on Wednesday, Iowa City on Friday, and Las Vegas on Saturday. But heaven forbid they cast those jokes out twice in a row on national television or have the audacity to bring them back to Minneapolis, Iowa City, or Las Vegas next year. And borrow from one another? Or borrow from The Tradition? Comics would rather have laryngitis than admit to such petty larceny. That's not to say there's anything wrong with doing original material. It's just that the 1940s were a

A superimposed publicity shot for Invisible Man. *(Personality Photos, Inc.)*

Stuck in a blazing desert didn't seem so bad after all. . . . Abbott and Costello in the Foreign Legion.

different time, when being original wasn't nearly as important as getting laughs.

In the 1940s and 1950s, *Abbott & Costello* on the marquee *guaranteed* there would be plenty of laughs in store for moviegoers. An afternoon at the movies with Abbott & Costello was pure escape, something like the lazy glory of cutting school. Their movies typically had large casts and broad canvases. The Boys, as they were lovingly called, were as likely to turn up

The team play school janitors, Slats and Oliver, in Here Come the Co-eds, *the team's fifteenth film.*

on the high seas as in the desert, on Venus as at Mardi Gras. They found themselves in harems and in Hollywood; in the French foreign legion, the army, the navy, and the air force; on horses and on runaway torpedoes. They met Frankenstein, Count Dracula, the Invisible Man, Boris Karloff, Captain Kidd, the Mummy, Dr. Jekyll and Mr. Hyde, and the Keystone Kops. There were also pretty girls woven into the plots, although weaving an Abbott & Costello plot was something akin to weaving spaghetti. The pretty girls were either making a debut, as did Carol Bruce in *Keep 'Em Flying,* or unabashedly on display, as in *Abbott and Costello Go to Mars,* which included a bevy of Miss Universe contestants playing Venusian handmaidens. Bad guys such as Sheldon Leonard in *Abbott and Costello Meet the Invisible Man* were there for ballast and foil, and we cheered heartily when The Boys gave these foes what they had coming.

We weren't very sophisticated about special effects back then, and the special effects in Abbott & Costello films are, admittedly, no match for the wonders of a *Star Wars,* an *E. T.,* or any '90s exhibition. But American audiences have always been fascinated with the gadgetry of filmmaking, so Abbott & Costello movies used all the tricks at hand in the 1940s. It was often part of the Abbott & Costello formula to push the limits of the machinery as far as possible, and some of those effects were truly wonderful. The disappearing act in *Abbott and Costello Meet the Invisible Man* is terrific. (Did you notice that the ex-boxer character, Tommy Nelson, who dis-

The Denver, Colorado, premiere of Abbott and Costello Go to Mars, *April 1953.*

appears before Lou's unbelieving eyes, then strips off his shirt, trousers, and socks, is apparently not wearing underpants?) Later in the picture, Bud gets "plastered" in a restaurant, the Invisible Man in tow, and the result is equally priceless. The way Dracula dissolves into a cartoon bat in *Abbott and Costello Meet Frankenstein* seems to work even for modern audiences, providing an early example of live anima-tion à la *Who Framed Roger Rabbit,* the tech-nical wonder of 1988.

Although some of Abbott & Costello's funniest movie moments are built on physi-cal comedy—Lou Costello was, in fact, a supreme comic athlete—much of their humor was carried in rather dense comic dialogue. That mix is certainly a holdover from the vaudeville, burlesque, and radio days, during which Bud Abbott and Lou Costello learned the trade. And this blend is refreshing to modern audiences, who are accustomed to film comedy that always seems to be either physical or cerebral, but never both.

Bud and Lou had something else going for them that helped make their transition to radio in 1938 a success. They managed to salvage the great routines of vaudeville with-out the heavy sexual innuendo of the steamy burlesque house. To be more precise, John Grant, their writer, had that gift. In 1938, those routines opened Abbott & Costello's window to success on *The Kate Smith Hour* when Henny Youngman, who was the show's regular comic, left on sabbatical to Hollywood. The typical burlesque routine wouldn't have lasted a flicker on live radio. But Abbott & Costello's performance of the vaudevillian "Who's on First?" with its Dizzy Dean logic and squeaky-clean joy, lit up the switch-board at CBS and the lights on their career.

That career spanned a unique period in communications history. In less than a decade and a half, they went from the remnants of the Chautauqua circuit and vaudeville to the snowy screens of early television sets, a trek few performers were able to survive. In the middle, they made an amazingly prolific spate of films. They came into Their Era at an ideal wink of a moment—at the dawn of the 1940s, when, as comedy historian Lonnie Burr explains, Laurel & Hardy were "losing steam," the Marx Brothers were "on hiatus from moviemaking," and George Burns and Gracie Allen "lacked the physical, visual comedy for film." When Abbott & Costello's wink was over, the 1950s had arrived with a new set of comics more attuned to postwar America, comics who were both sophisticated and, like their audiences, more cynical.

Change was sudden and stunning in the early 1950s, and change was one thing Abbott & Costello had rarely been asked to do from one film to the next, let alone within a film. Character development was simply not a factor in their art. In that respect, they had much in common with more modern film icons such as Rocky Balboa or Indiana Jones, and even more in

common with every perfectly static character in television's history of situation comedies. Lou Costello had no stomach for change; he had to be convinced that every routine The Boys used was rooted in vaudeville or burlesque. The public went to the theater to see Abbott & Costello be Abbott & Costello, he reasoned, so why trot out anything else? In a few films The Boys actually did just play themselves, but even when they were Chick Young and Wilbur Grey, they were still Abbott & Costello.

Abbott & Costello were a great American comic type. Their films may have been escapist, but they weren't vacuous. The Abbott & Costello of film was based upon the straight-man/clown relationship that traveled in a dozen incarnations through vaudeville and burlesque. Their relationship was about being an underdog. It was about being an immigrant. It was about being confused and frustrated. It was also about the triumph of common sense and common men. Twain depicted this same relationship in Huck and Tom. Tom was the schemer, but Huck was the one who escaped. There was a populist feel to the humor of Abbott & Costello that de Tocqueville might have called "democratic."

In essence, The Boys' act involved a smooth-talking sophisticate teamed with a bumbling Everyman. The tension between Lou and Bud was, in fact, a self-contained affirmation of the American democratic experience. Forget any of the adversaries they faced together; within their relationship, the smooth-talking, urbane, know-it-all was consistently upstaged by his less sophisticated, less gifted friend. Abbott & Costello biographer Bob Thomas put it like this in a 1979 interview in *Films in Review:*

Looking back, it was an ideal combination for sympathy. You had Bud as the rather officious, authoritarian figure who loved the little guy, but who punished him unmercifully. Lou was the rather mischievous but bedeviled little guy, the same character played by Chaplin, Lloyd and Keaton in the silents. . . . It was a very American kind of comedy.

A decade earlier, film scholar Raymond Durgnat described their relationship this way in *The Crazy Mirror:*

Lou Costello had just the streak of Irish or Italian in him necessary to suggest the immigrant who can hardly keep up with life and has to have everything explained to him by his sharper buddy. In this sense, they were, perhaps, earthier than most comedians of their time. . . . Slapstick comedies weren't only comic, and poetic, but reflected some tensions in American society more accurately than one might expect.

The common wisdom about Abbott & Costello is that their mindless humor was a gentle respite from the otherwise hard times of the war years. That's really inarguable. But it's not the whole story. The audiences of that era must also have desperately needed affirmation—they produced it for themselves ad nauseam in every art form during that time—affirmation that virtue lies with the unwashed, the unimperial, the sons and daughters of Will Rogers, Mark Twain, and even Teddy Roosevelt. It was a powerful

An autographed portrait for Bud's sister Florence ("Babe") and husband, Jimmy Muccia. (Courtesy of Olive Abbott)

(Reprinted courtesy of Rick Goldschmidt)

mythological notion, so powerful that Harry Truman won an improbable campaign for the presidency at the height of Abbott & Costello's popularity.

It may sound crazy to talk of their films as "message" movies, but perhaps in the popular culture of their times they were. They represented the triumph of the American underdog so often that the audience waited patiently for the tonic chord, for Lou to win, knowing that no matter what abuse was heaped upon him he'd survive. There is no better example than *Abbott and Costello Meet Frankenstein*. The film, made in 1948, carries a barely veiled anti-Nazi message to an audience that had learned the hard way to fear authoritarian societies. The mad scientist here is a woman with a heavy German accent by way, naturally, of Transylvania. Lenore Aubert, playing the role of Dr. Frankenstein's former medical assistant, is the mastermind of a project to resurrect the Frankenstein monster. As she and Count Dracula kneel over the inert creature in a foggy wood, Dracula says, "This time the monster must have no will of his own, no fiendish intellect to oppose his

"I'm not asking you, I'm telling you. Who is on first." Rare candid of The Boys in Lou's backyard getting in a little practice on February 12, 1945. (Courtesy of Joe Wallison)

An early shot of Bud and Lou together with comedian Hugh Herbert and an Atlantic City, N.J. Steel Pier official, circa 1938. (Courtesy of Olive Abbott)

master." She counters that once "the chubby little fellow's brain" (referring to Lou Costello) has been transplanted into the monster's crop, "he will obey you like a trained dog." The superrace overtones could not have been lost on postwar audiences.

It's a good guess that The Boys'd be pretty inappreciative of such intellectual angst over their craft. Like good .300 hitters, they just went out day after day and made contact with the ball. Much of what they did came naturally; they never seemed to question their gifts. Lou, in particular, was gifted with more than the ability to split your side with the way he sputtered through a word like *insomnia* or *pendulum*. Lou wasn't just a bungler. He wasn't just an uncoordinated pollywog. He was a guy we fell in love with. He had the ability to make us care about him. That may be a result of Lou Costello's own dramatic ambitions—he set out to be a heartthrob, not a comic. Despite his clowning, we see a real, lovable human being in a real human drama, and that sets Abbott & Costello pictures apart from the antics of the Three Stooges, Laurel & Hardy, or even the Marx Brothers. In his ability to make us care, Lou Costello has much more in common with his hero Charlie Chaplin and, today, with Woody Allen.

There are few unhip comics today. Lewis & Martin followed Abbott & Costello in their unhip style. Red Skelton kept the tradition alive even longer. Art Carney and Jackie Gleason in *The Honeymooners* are an example from early television. That Gleason, as a hapless, besieged bus driver, simply took Costello into the 1950s is pretty obvious. But hip has ruled, from Mort Sahl and Bob Newhart to Whoopi Goldberg and Eddie Murphy. Even the gray hairs of comedy, George Burns and Bob Hope, built careers on a stately sort of stand-up delivery, wooden and purposely over-rehearsed, so that not until the very moment after they've finished the joke and they look expectantly into the camera does their humor grab us.

These comedians do nothing, of course, like Lou Costello's famous and perhaps unmatched "look" into the camera. If you wanted a laugh in the 1930s and the 1940s, you'd better have been prepared to do something to get it. The things Lou Costello did on screen were magic.

Abbott & Costello have never been taken seriously by the critics, not in their time and not in ours. When other movies of the 1940s were trotted out in college-campus retrospectives and festivals, Abbott & Costello stayed home. When the Marx Brothers and Charlie Chaplin achieved cult status, Abbott & Costello stayed in the vault. But, as *Washington Post* media critic Tom Shales has written, Abbott & Costello need no defense. Clearly, The Boys' timeless humor gives them all the staying power they'll ever need.

CHAPTER 2

A Marriage Made in Burlesque: Ya Gotta Pitcher on That Team?

Are you the organ grinder, Mr. Abbott?
                    —*Lucille Ball to Bud Abbott*

Bud and Lou always knew "Who's on First?" was dynamite. It ripped through every audience they encountered, from the Steel Pier in New Jersey to Loew's State Theater in New York. Something about the crazy nicknames of that routine's mythical baseball players, and the lovable little man who got so frustrated trying to learn them, was guaranteed to bring down the house, even if they followed a half-dozen strippers to the stage in that house.

There were other routines in Abbott & Costello's repertoire that got laughs. "Pack, Unpack" was funny. Bud and Lou could do the "Drill" routine with precision and get laughs. They also had fun with the "Lemon" bit. Lou once said they had 28,000 gags from burlesque stashed in their trunks. But nothing worked as often or as well as "Who's on First?" It was always their ace in the hole.

When they finally got to perform it for a national audience on *The Kate Smith Hour* in 1938, their lives, and the history of comedy in America, changed.

It almost didn't happen. *The Kate Smith Hour* was tightly controlled by Ted Collins, Smith's producer and mentor. Collins, never enamored of the prospect of burlesque comedians sharing the bill with his star, argued from the beginning that Abbott & Costello were too visual for radio. He hired them at Henny Youngman's urging; Youngman was the regular comic on

Nowhere Else Can You See So Much For So Little Money

BIG JULY 4th HOLIDAYS BILL

STEEL PIER

DANCING EVERY NITE

OUT OVER THE OCEAN

HAL KEMP
And His
FAVORITE
DANCE BAND
Sat-Sun-Mon July 2-3-4

Happy Felton
And His Band
July 1st to 7th

BENNY
GOODMAN
THE
SWINGMASTER
And His
BAND
SUN, JULY 3
One Day Only

ALEX BARTHA AND HIS BAND

DADDY DAVES KIDDIES REVUE
Starting Saturday, July 2nd, 11 a.m.
"LITTLE LADY MAKE-BELIEVE"

STEEL PIER

DeLuxe
STAGE SHOW

MusicHall TheatreCenter of Pier

The Original Hollywood
3 STOOGES

MOE - LARRY - CURLEY
with EDDIE LOUGTON

BARTO AND MANN
The LAUGH KINGS Comedy Dancing Stars of Vanities

THE FOUR ALLENS
4 Youthful Stars of Steps and Tunes   OTHER ACTS

STEEL PIER

Modern
MINSTRELS

MUSIC HALL   CENTER OF PIER
"THE NUT HOUSE"

Presenting

BUD ABBOTT
AND
LOU COSTELLO

The Comedy Stars of
Kate Smith's Program
Courtesy of TED COLLINS

BEN YOST AND HIS SINGERS

Ed KAPLIN - Geo. HAGGERTY
Bobby BERNARD - Paul MOHR
ALFRED LATELL'S "BONZO"
Albert RICKARD - Jerry DUGAN
Jimmy Jones Steel Pier Orchestra

STEEL PIER

Variety
Show

A 1938 Steel Pier handbill featuring two greats, The Three Stooges and Abbott and Costello. Stooge leader Moe Howard noted in his autobiography years later, "...when we were starring at the Steel Pier in Atlantic City, Abbott and Costello were appearing there in a minstrel show, and at every opportunity, they would come backstage and watch us perform from the wings. I always felt there was much of Curly—his mannerisms and high-pitched voice—in Costello's act in feature films." (Courtesy of Gary Lassin)

A publicity photograph for the young comedi- ans' appearances on The Kate Smith Hour *in 1938. (Neal Peters Collection)*

The Kate Smith Hour, but he was off to Hollywood for a screen test. Lou said Collins refused to give Bud and himself a contract before their first perfor- mance on the assumption that they would fail. That was a distinct possibli- ty because they had no script to work from; their routine was totally impro- vised.

The Kate Smith Hour competed with Rudy Vallee at 9:00 P.M. on Thursday nights, and was losing. Abbott & Costello's first performance on the show was adequate but did little for the ratings. Collins, it seems, was reluctant to put "Who's on First?" on the air. It was funny, he admitted, but he felt it was too complex for the at-home audience that had just the lighted dial on a radio console to watch. They'd never be able to tell Bud and Lou's voices apart, he reasoned.

Collins did bring The Boys back the next week. Even without their doing "Who's on First?" the radio audience loved them. Lou worked on raising his voice a notch to distinguish it from Bud's and added his characteristic whine for good measure. Abbott & Costello went on to do ninety-nine weeks of the show, and their salary went from $350 for the first engagement to $1,250 a week when they left. In the process, *The Kate Smith Hour* soon overtook Rudy Vallee's program.

Helen Hayes, Kate Smith, Bud, and Lou clown for the studio photographer in 1938, the year Abbott & Costello debuted on radio. (Courtesy of Olive Abbott)

Kate Smith with her mentor, producer Ted Collins—the man who thought Abbott and Costello would not be funny on radio. Bud and Lou were forced to trick Collins into getting "Who's On First?" on the air.

Before appearing on Kate Smith's show Bud and Lou had spent two years together perfecting the classics of vaudeville and burlesque. "Who's on First?" started life as "Baker's Dozen," says Lou's daughter Chris Costello. It was a well-traveled routine, although Abbott & Costello were the first to set it to baseball the way a catchy lyric is sometimes set to an existing piece of music. It wasn't originality, however, that enabled Abbott & Costello to emerge from burlesque. It was, she says, "a certain magic, a chemistry" The Boys had that brought shopworn burlesque routines to life.

Timing and precision were everything in delivering those word-heavy sketches. It was their mastery of the material that later made it possible for Abbott & Costello to pick up a dropped line and still survive, or to improvise almost at will and rejoin the routine at the proper instant. Now, as the 1930s drew to a close, that work paid off. Not only were they doing *The Kate Smith Hour* once a week; they were also doing *The Streets of Paris,* a Broadway revue resettled at the New York World's Fair, and a weekly nightclub gig. The work netted them a neat little bundle— more than $3,000 a week near the end of their run.

That, of course, was pin money compared with the $1.75 million a year they averaged in Hollywood in the early 1940s. But it took Lou's immeasurable chutzpah to get "Who's on First?" on *The Kate Smith Hour* and make

Looking dapper in a portrait taken for a New York stage show titled Social Maids. *(Courtesy of Olive Abbott)*

those Hollywood paychecks a reality. Chris calls Lou's ruse "a truly beautiful scheme." Frustrated that he couldn't convince Collins to let the team do their ace routine, Lou decided it was time to play a little high-stakes poker. All week during rehearsals, Lou told Collins that he and Bud were out of routines for the Thursday-night performance. By Thursday he had Collins where he wanted him.

Five minutes before airtime, Chris says, Collins asked again what routine Abbott & Costello had ready for the show. Lou made it clear he had nothing in mind. "I guess we can't go on tonight because we've done every routine we have," he told Collins. Collins remembered the baseball routine they had been begging to do. "Do anything, do anything," he shouted at Lou. "Do that routine, what do you call it? 'Who's on First?' Do that!" Lou's gam-

Bud Abbott's grade-school graduation portrait. He attended St. Paul's in Coney Island. Bud is in the front row, third from left. (Courtesy of Olive Abbott)

ble had paid off; Collins wound up ordering them to do "Who's on First?" that night.

The routine had precisely the impact The Boys knew it would. On the evening of March 24,1938, the switchboard at CBS "lit up like a Christmas tree," Chris says. Bud and Lou's salary was immediately raised from $350 to $500 a week, and the "Who's on First?" routine became a mainstay of the show.

Even before *The Kate Smith Hour* sealed their fate, it was obvious that Bud and Lou were meant for each other. Abbott & Costello biographer Bob Thomas tried once to put Bud Abbott's contribution to the team in perspective. Without Bud, he said, Lou "might not have lasted as long as he did. He might have been too overpowering, too undisciplined, so that he would have worn out his audience too soon."

Indeed, it was Bud's presence—on film, or radio, or stage—that held Lou on the ground, that made him human and accessible. Listen to them work through a routine, "A Day at the Races" for instance, on their radio show. Lou gets more and more excited; his voice begins to quiver at the top of its range. You can almost *see* his flesh shake. Just when he begins to sound like, well, Jerry Lewis after eighteen hours on the Labor Day Telethon, when he starts to sound as if at any minute he'll just explode, Bud's calm, cultured voice, the suave voice of reason and intellect, the smooth voice of the city

Betty Abbott Griffin, Bud's niece, has only the fondest memories of her uncle. Currently, she lives in southern California and has worked for years in the film industry as a script supervisor. (Photo by John Lofflin)

Olive Abbott, Bud's sister, still spry in the 1990s and in her nineties. (Photo by John Lofflin)

slicker with just a touch of con artist, soothes the listener's nerves, brings Lou back into the routine, and then brings it all home.

That was Bud Abbott's job—to sound, perhaps, like a university professor gone bad, a university professor turned to selling encyclopedias door-to-door, or real estate in Florida. What an irony that William Alexander Abbott, born in a circus tent in Asbury Park, New Jersey, on October 2, 1895, and an eighth-grade dropout, would make millions by sounding to all the world like a smooth-talking Harvard graduate.

All Bud Abbott really lacked in that regard was the Harvard degree. He was soft-spoken, graceful, and introverted. He slapped Lou around on the screen and stage, but in private he was passive, preferring yes to no and good feelings between folks to bad. Many say he would have been as happy to stay in burlesque as to fight the tigers of Hollywood. In fact, he left the fighting to Lou. When the team's popularity sagged briefly in the early 1940s, Bud said, "We started out living in theatrical trunks, and we've still got those trunks."

His life was destined to be spent in show business. Bud's father, Harry, was an advance man for the Barnum and Bailey circus, a twenty-four-hour man who traveled a day ahead of the show making hotel and food arrangements, scouting for a locale, arranging for advertisements, and performing other tasks.

Bud's mother, the former Rae Fisher, rode elephants in the circus but retired to raise a family. In addition to Bud, there were his older brother, Harry Jr.; Olive Victoria (named after Queen Victoria—"Poppa" Abbott was in England when she was born); and Florence, always known as "Babe."

When Bud was young, his family lived in New York City, then moved to Coney Island. He was an average student but not very interested in school. Nor was he enthusiastic about his father's line of work.

"No one thought Bud would go into the business," says Olive Abbott, now one hundred years old and living in southern California. "But he would do things that made you figure he should be in show business some day. He was a teaser.

Bud and Betty had a collection of miniature brandy mugs which represented likenesses of American presidents.

"One time when my dad spanked him, Dad yelled, 'Oh, my hand!' Bud had a board in his pants. He was a little, you know, a vixen. An imp. He was full of fun," she says.

At the tender age of fourteen, Bud quit school despite his parents' protests.

"When Bud was sixteen years old, he was shanghaied on a ship going to Norway," Olive Abbott says. "He signed up as a cabin boy, but when they got him out in mid-ocean they put him down in the stoker. He was gone for one year. My mother cried that whole year. When he came back, his hands were just one mass of calluses. That was a rough one."

When Bud returned, he landed a job as a candy butcher in a carnival, and eventually another as the treasurer of a theater. He traveled the circuit, taking work where he could and watching the performers out of the corner of his eye.

Then, when he was nineteen, Betty Smith came into his life. "They got married in Baltimore on a boat," remembers Olive. "My father was on the boat with them, on the Potomac River. Years later they were remarried in the Jewish religion by a rabbi because Betty had converted to the Jewish faith."

There are conflicting stories about how long their engagement was. By some accounts, it was less than four hours. Others say it was less than twenty-four hours, and some say less than a week. Olive says she's not certain, "but it was short, I can tell you that."

During the early years of their marriage, Bud and Betty did a few comedy sketches together, he as the straight man and she as the comic, and they even went on the road playing vaudeville houses. They were in love, broke but managing.

Betty Abbott knew she did not want to stay in show business. Bud thus teamed with comic after comic and was very much in demand in the straight-man role. "He was always a natty dresser," says Olive. So was his father, who had a pedicure in the hospital on the day he died.

Bud did more than dress the part of the straight man. He perfected it. Insiders considered the straight man the linchpin of a comedy team,

"Bud was always a natty dresser," said his sister Olive. (Courtesy of Olive Abbott)

although audiences didn't see it that way. Mel Brooks once told an interviewer that Bud was "a genius." Writer Jay Grossman says Groucho Marx called Abbott "the greatest straight man ever." A half-dozen others, however, described him simply as "a good, solid straight man."

Lou Costello; on the other hand, was born to roll his eyes into the back of his head, shiver in fear, fall flat on his nose, and trip over his own feet just to be funny. His daughter Paddy Costello puts it this way:

My gut feeling is that my father knew from a very early age what he was put on this earth for. He had a gift for making people laugh. I have a lot of admiration for people who realize at an early age what they're cut out for, what they're here for. There was no other way for him to go. There was nothing else for him to be. He got such joy out of making people laugh that I don't think there was any doubt in his mind at all what he was going to be.

Charles Boyer, Micki Leemen, Bud and Betty Abbott, and Olive Abbott. (Courtesy of Olive Abbott)

Vaudeville duo Olson and Johnson pose with some of the Abbott family at Universal Studios. Errol Flynn is in back, third from left. (Courtesy of Betty Abbott Griffin)

Pair of classics: Lou Costello always adored the genius of Charlie Chaplin and finally played host to the motion picture pioneer at the Costello home in May 1942. (Personality Photos, Inc.)

Louis Francis Cristillo came out of Paterson, New Jersey, fighting. His father, Sebastian Cristillo, was an Italian immigrant. His mother, Helen, was Irish Catholic. That good ethnic amalgam made kids who were full of spunk. While Lou was still shagging flies and shooting the bottom out of the basket in high school, his brother, Pat, packed up his sax and lit out for New York City's famed jazz haunts.

Born March 6, 1906, Lou was at a prime age to fall under Charlie Chaplin's celluloid spell. He watched Chaplin films at the U.S. Theater in Paterson during his adolescence. In her biography, *Lou's on First,* daughter Chris says he actually saw Chaplin's *Shoulder Arms* two dozen times there, and that's where the idea to jam a cigar in his mouth originated. And, Chris says, he topped off this gesture by executing a classic pratfall as he walked across the stage to get his high-school diploma. He was agile, built much leaner than in his show-business years, and he even tried his hand at boxing until his father found out and put a stop to it.

Pat Cristillo had a jazz band in New York—Pat Cristillo & His Gondoliers. Pat claims he was the first to eventually change the family name, making it *Costello,* three syllables New Yorkers could pronounce more easily. (However, when honored on Ralph Edwards's *This Is Your Life* television show on

Lou Costello in his mid-twenties. Lou was always lean as a young man and quite an agile sportsman. (Courtesy of Chris Costello)

Young Bud poses with fellow funnyman Hugh Herbert at the Steel Pier in New Jersey.

November 21,1956, Lou Costello said that *he* had altered the name while working at MGM in the 1920s, inspired by the name of one of his favorite actresses, Helene Costello.) In 1927 Lou finally got up the courage to speak to his father about going to Hollywood to get into pictures.

Across this entire century, young men and women—some just boys and girls yet—have dreamed about taking that trip west to films and fame. Why some just dream and others go is hard to determine, but, like Pat, Lou had plenty of gumption. His journey to Hollywood has been chronicled a dozen ways. The United Press International obituary for Lou says he saved $200 from a stint in a hat store and spent it on a $125 Model T Ford for the trip. Another story has him renting a limousine for the last few miles of the journey into Hollywood so he could arrive in style. But Chris Costello says Lou's father borrowed $200 from the bank and gave it to him for a bus ticket. Lou hitched a ride instead, saving the money for a "stake" once he arrived on the Streets of Gold.

Lou (bottom right) in a 1923-24 team photograph for the DeGise Silk Five. (Courtesy of North Jersey Herald and News)

Naturally, all the gold was *in* the hills. So Lou worked as a laborer on the lot at MGM and wrangled a few stunt jobs on the side. In one film he actually doubled for Dolores Del Rio. Another of those stunt jobs is built into a hilarious barroom sketch in *Abbott and Costello in Hollywood.* However, Lou's first trip to Hollywood was much more difficult than that portrayed in the 1945 movie version. As a stuntman, he just wasn't able to make a go of things, and soon he was headed east again.

Over breakfast one day in St. Joseph, Missouri, Lou glanced in the local newspaper and discovered a want ad for a Dutch comic at a nearby burlesque house. He got the job, despite having no Dutch accent. St. Joe was a good show-business town in those days. Big bands played at the Frog Hop on the outskirts, and sixty miles south, in Kansas City, jazz and the nightlife were on fire. Latching onto a steady job in the business, as he did at that moment, may have been critical in Lou Costello's development as a comedian. It certainly gave him a "woodshed," a place out of the limelight where he could learn the trade without being devoured by the critics.

Lou stayed in St. Joe about a year, then shoved off for New York City. He was billing himself as Lou Costello by then, and over the next seven years he slowly built a reputation in the city's burlesque and vaudeville houses. He thus was already rooted in the straight-man/comic motif by 1936, when he and Bud Abbott discovered each other.

Lou meets Marlene Dietrich on the set of her Universal picture, Pittsburgh *(1942), and tries to best the beauty by revealing some leg before she does.*

Lou fires up with W. C. Fields, who was making a cameo appearance in the feature, Follow the Boys, *at Universal.*

There are several accounts of how Bud and Lou became a team. In a 1941 interview with *Photoplay*'s Ida Zeitlin, Bud and Lou told it this way:

> "My straight man doesn't show up," said Lou. "So I walk into the box office—"
> "To borrow a couple of tickets—" It was Bud interrupting.
> "'Wanna be an actor?' I said. At the time, he appealed to me. Later I found out different—"
> "I jumped in to save the guy," Bud said. "The customers were throwin' eggs at him to make ham and eggs—"
> "You're gettin' the story wrong, honey."

Actually, it's difficult to tell if Bud was getting the story right or wrong. Several versions exist in the Abbott & Costello mythology. One has Lou working with straight man Joe Lyons at the Eltinge Theater on West 42nd Street, where Bud is taking tickets at the time and billing himself as treasurer. Lyons doesn't show up. Bud agrees to fill in, and the rest, as they say, is history.

That's the story Bud and Lou seem to be telling *Photoplay*. But it is curiously similar to a story the veteran comic Billy Gilbert told, just before he died in 1971, about *his* teaming up with Bud. By Billy's account, Bud, then nineteen, was the ticket taker in a theater Billy was playing. His straight

Abbott & Costello are Lost in a Harem.

man didn't show up one night, so he sent for "the bright kid out front." Bud, he says, was so good that he kept him in the show.

In fact, Bud corroborates that account with an item in his official studio bio about how he entered show business. But in 1941 Hugh Roberts interviewed The Boys for a movie-fan magazine and came away with this story about the way Bud and Lou met:

> It was time for the curtain to go up on [Lou's act]. The leading lady had just discarded her modesty. And now it was time for comedy.
> Lou Costello was waiting for his straight man, his other half, his joke feeder. Then at the last moment, word came through that the straight man was ill with a mild case of leprosy or hydrophobia. The Boys don't remember today which it was. But here was the curtain going up and here was Lou Costello without a partner. Then the inspiration was born. He remembered playing

The talent behind the team: Writer extraordinaire John Grant followed The Boys from burlesque into radio and motion pictures. Grant officially began writing for Bud and Lou on the Kate Smith radio show, which sparked an auspicious seventeen-year relationship. Bud and Lou placed nearly unconditional trust in his judgement with their scripts, gags, and routines. Photo circa 1938. (Courtesy of Olive Abbott)

rummy with the dour theater cashier, that guy Bud Abbott. They'd always fought. Always tiffed. Good naturedly, of course, but everyone thought it was funny.

Lou Costello sent an SOS to Bud Abbott. And in answer, Bud Abbott left his box office forever, went on the stage with Costello and, without a line rehearsed, rolled the audience in the aisles and draped them over their seats.

However great the prose, Roberts couldn't resist this punch line:

And so, after the show, the manager came up to the two of them and he said, in [the] words of the Good Book:

"Mr. Abbott, Mr. Costello. What God has joined together, let no man tear asunder. . . . I now pronounce you clown and straight man!"

Lou is the reluctant boxer in Buck Privates. *(Personality Photos, Inc.)*

A 1947 *Colliers* account of their meeting went this way:

One shudders to think what might have happened to American culture if Abbott had not caught Costello doing "Who's on First?" . . . with Jimmy Francis, an old-timer, at the Eltinge Theater in New York one night in 1936. Abbott saw interesting possibilities in the kid and teamed up with him in "Life Begins at Minsky's," a road show that went on tour for a year.

Bob Thomas offers a less dramatic account in his book *Bud & Lou.* He has Bud leaning on an ivory-handled cane in the wings of the Eltinge Theater, watching Lou and Joe Lyons do the "Lemon" routine. Bud, Thomas says, knew he could do the classic shell game much better than Lyons.

Thomas says Bud and Lou shared the same bill for several weeks at the Eltinge before inviting each other out, with their wives, for sandwiches at Reuben's in Manhattan. That's where Lou popped the question, Thomas says, and Bud agreed. According to Thomas, they didn't actually take the stage together for another month.

Chris Costello, too, has Lou teamed with Joe Lyons and Bud with Harry Evanson at the Eltinge. But she says Lou and Bud eased into their partnership, often practicing routines backstage and filling in for each other's counterparts. She says Bud wrote Lou, who was on the road with Lyons, about joining forces.

Original publicity art-work for Who Done It?

Chris cites Bud Abbott as one of the main reasons the liaison worked. "To me," she says, "Bud Abbott was one of the world's greatest straight men. He was totally shoved under the carpet later. Of course they're going to go for Dad because of his kind of character, but very few people understand that you didn't have an Abbott without a Costello and vice versa. Abbott was a magnificent, polished, on-the-dime straight man. Anybody who could do a routine and literally bring my father back into that routine at the point of departure, with the audience never knowing what was happening . . . I mean, he was brilliant.

"The chemistry, the rhythm they had. In their routines, you drop one beat, you're off. Read the script to 'Who's on First?' and it's not really that funny," Chris says. "But it's what you do with the beat, the rhythm of that

Bud is surrounded by beauties in Rio Rita, *the team's first film at Metro-Goldwyn-Mayer. Left to right: Bobbie Anderson, Wanda Perry, Yvonne Bowman, and Sally Cleaves.*

routine, that makes it so funny. The little nuances, the facial expressions, the exasperation in my father's voice."

Once Abbott & Costello got rolling, what was left of vaudeville and burlesque was theirs. They toured the country with the Hollywood Bandwagon, which is where Vic Parks first met them. Parks says he often joined them onstage, especially to help with the "Drill" routine they made famous later in *Buck Privates.* The routine left the audience weak from laughter, he says. He still knows the routine by heart, and he can still hear the laughter when he shuts his eyes tight.

When they returned to New York, The Boys played Billy Rose's Casa Mañana, knocked the crowd out, then went back on the road. They owed many of their great bookings, including *The Kate Smith Hour,* to a fellow they picked up in 1937 to be their manager, Eddie Sherman. One of the first jobs Sherman got them was at an amusement park, where they blew the twenty dollars they made on roller-coaster rides. Sherman, however, had much bigger plans in mind.

That same year, he helped them pick up another unseen member of the team—John Grant, a writer who helped make possible everything that would happen in the next decade. While Sherman knew how to handle The Boys' theatrical affairs, Grant knew how to handle their comic affairs. The Boys rarely opposed either in those early days. Their relationships wouldn't

Boys rarely opposed either in those early days. Their relationships wouldn't always be so affectionate, however.

Norman Abbott, Bud's nephew, was too young to see the team play vaudeville and burlesque, but he spent many hours watching them work theater audiences. "You never heard laughter like that in a theater in your life," he says. "They would just rock a theater. They just knocked the critics on the floor. It was amazing. A miracle to watch."

After Abbott & Costello did "Who's on First?" on *The Kate Smith Hour* in 1938, the whole entertainment world knew the laughter they could incite. It wasn't lost on Hollywood either, where film comedy was waiting for its next big stars. Chris Costello says the reaction to that radio performance was swift.

"Universal wired them," she says, "and asked them to come out and do a test film. It turned out to be *One Night in the Tropics*."

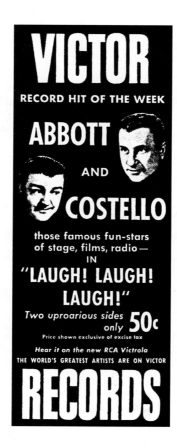

CHAPTER 3

Buck Privates: The Rookies Get Some Solid Hits

One *Night in the Tropics* was never meant to be an Abbott & Costello vehicle. For them it was a Grapefruit League exhibition game, a chance for the coaching staff to see the rookies in action and for the rookies to see a few major-league curveballs. It's a good thing for The Boys that nothing else was on the line, because *One Night in the Tropics* fell flat on its face.

Robert Cummings costarred with Allan Jones in the 1940 soft-focus romance. The love interests were played by Nancy Kelly and Peggy Moran. Cummings says the picture was actually finished before The Boys were hired to make their debut.

"We had finished the picture, and in fact Universal had previewed it," Cummings said. "They hired these guys just on the strength of that one routine—'Who's on First?' They brought them out and worked them into the plot. So we went back to reshoot some new scenes, which were later woven in.

"The producers were so enamored of them, they pushed Abbott & Costello into the picture," he continued. "Allan Jones was saying, 'What the hell are they doing?' I was under contract, so I didn't say much. Allan wasn't under contract, so he spoke up. He wasn't very happy about the situation.

"The Boys were of a different school of show business than me, very much vaudevillians and from burlesque. But for their first film, they seemed to fit in well. They knew what they were doing. At least it seemed like it. They both had quick minds and didn't need any help," said Cummings.

At least they didn't need any help with the dialogue. For the most part, they were comic relief, sticking to a handful of their best routines, established pieces that would recur in an array of incarnations across their entire

One Night in the Tropics *was Bud and Lou's entrée into motion pictures.*

careers. They did the "Mustard" routine, which essentially involved Lou being shamed into something—buying mustard for his hot dog, in the original—by Bud, who heaps tons of "logic" on him. They did a money-counting routine that would be reborn practically every time they would exchange a dollar bill on the screen. And they did a routine where Lou tries to tell a story and is interrupted to distraction by a series of trivial questions. In *One Night in the Tropics* Bud does the interruptions. In *Abbott and Costello in Hollywood* it's a classroom of children who interrupt. And, of course, they did a version of "Who's on First?"

Jerome Kern, who scored the film, was not amused. Burlesque comics weren't his cup of tea, especially in a romance with his name on the bill. Only the audiences were laughing, a fact critics noted even while panning the film. But Universal wasn't as perceptive. The film didn't make money, so the studio was in no hurry to get The Boys into a starring vehicle.

Again Lou's quick mind, boundless ambition, and, believe it or not, poker face prevailed.

Accounts differ on whether he met Universal executive Matty Fox in New York or Los Angeles. But east or west, he had a surprise in store for everyone at the meeting, including Bud and manager Eddie Sherman.

Lou told Fox the meeting had to proceed quickly because the team was expected in the office of another studio—Paramount or Warner Brothers, depending on who tells the story—to discuss a couple of starring films. Bud and Eddie Sherman sat stone-faced. Throughout The Boys' battles with directors and studios, Bud trusted Lou to do the talking and to handle the negotiations, always nodding in agreement as Lou huffed and puffed. If Lou said, "Come on, Bud, we're leaving," Bud followed.

Fox called Lou's bluff. Just what sort of pictures did the other studio have in mind? he asked. On the spot, Lou improvised the plot of a movie that resembled *Buck Privates*. He got Bud up to do the "Drill" routine for Fox. Then he improvised one that would later be included in the film *Lost in a Harem,* leading Bud through "Slowly I Turned," another vaudeville standard.

The ploy worked, and Universal gave The Boys a contract to do a picture with a military draft theme. World War II was in the wings, and the draft

Buck Privates, *a modest film thrown together for a little more than $200,000, unexpectedly grossed over $4 million at a time when a ticket to the movies cost 25 cents. (Personality Photos, Inc.)*

was at center stage. Everyone concerned thought it might be possible to capitalize on these events and get some laughs at the same time. But Universal wasn't ready to spring for a major film.

The entire budget was just over $200,000, half what even a B-movie cost in 1940. Built into that figure was the $50,000 Universal offered to pay Bud and Lou per picture, four pictures per year for seven years. Fortunately for them, Eddie Sherman wasn't too bad at the shell game either.

Sherman made a counteroffer to the studio: either $60,000 per picture or $50,000 and 10 percent of the gross. The studio executives went for the second option and signed the deal. They didn't realize how stupid their choice was until the receipts from *Buck Privates* came rolling in. The film they spent $200,000 on grossed $4.7 million, and The Boys were on the way to becoming the first major actors to receive residuals on their pictures.

Buck Privates is an eighty-four-minute slice of American history. It opens with grainy newsreel footage of Franklin Delano Roosevelt signing draft legislation, and then the actual conducting of the draft lottery. Although Abbott & Costello are the stars, they aren't yet at the center of the action. The plot is built on a simple, undisguised democratic theme you recognize the instant a mother asks the sergeant, "How can you make a Yale man a private?"

The Yalie, it turns out, has been drafted right alongside his valet. The valet is adept at making his own bed; the Yalie isn't. Both are crack shots,

Nat Pendleton, Lou, Bud, Lee Bowmen, and Alan Curtis in the box-office smash Buck Privates. *(Courtesy of Universal Pictures)*

although the Yalie complains that the stationary targets are too easy. Skeet is more challenging, he says. The valet and the Yalie both fall in love, naturally, with the same girl, Jane Frazee as Judy Gray, who does her part as a camp hostess to cheer the tender draftees in boot camp. Her father, she lectures, "always says it [the army] is the great leveler. It doesn't care how much a man has in the bank or how little."

Neither does Judy. When the Yalie schemes to be alone with her while his former valet is otherwise occupied and the scheme backfires, affecting the other boys in the platoon, Judy declares: "There's no price tag on loyalty or friendship. After what you did today, the only friend you'll have in camp is the guy who looks at you out of the mirror."

"I didn't ask for this uniform," the Yalie replies, echoing the doubts of a nation of draftees. "Why should I take it seriously?"

The Andrews Sisters had already provided the answer in song at the start of the film. Through the train station where the draftees are saying their good-byes, and down the aisle of the train as it rolls off to boot camp, they sing "You're a Lucky Fellow, Mr. Smith," a tune that reels off chorus after chorus of American virtues. Ironically, the scene contains an embarrassing

continued on page 56

A posed publicity shot of Bud playing the piano, with sheet music to "Boogie Woogie Bugle Boy" and a song called "I'm a Bad Boy" displayed.

The Andrews Sisters on Abbott & Costello

Bud and Lou's first motion-picture hits contained three important features: Patty, Maxene, and Laverne. Known as the harmonizing Andrews Sisters, the famed trio is now almost synonymous with the career of Abbott & Costello.

The girls' second film was *Buck Privates.* "We'll forget about the first," joked Maxene Andrews. It was a film called *Argentine Nights,* costarring the Ritz Brothers, and it can still probably be seen at 3:00 A.M. on a cable station, if you're lucky—or unlucky. Abbott & Costello's films boosted the girls' careers, making them the most popular female trio of the 1940s. They made three films with The Boys and continued a successful career, recording more than seven hundred songs in a tumultuous twenty-year span. During those years, which included a few breakups and reunions, the trio enjoyed a now-legendary success.

"We made two films with The Boys," says Patty Andrews, *"Buck Privates* and *In the Navy.* But for the third film, *Hold That Ghost,* the producers got a lot of resentment that we were originally excluded. Then they called us in from New York, and they stuck us in at the end of *Hold That Ghost.* We performed the song 'Aurora' in that picture."

The sisters first met Bud and Lou around 1938 at the Steel Pier in Atlantic City. They were on the bill with the comics. Eventually they were cast in The Boys' films and soon became very close to Lou Costello,

explains Maxene. "Bud was kind of in a world of his own," Maxene said. "We were quite close to Lou and Anne and the kids. We'd go over to their home on many weekends. None of us

The Andrews Sisters are visited by Bud and Lou on their CBS radio show, The N-K Musical Showroom *in November 1945. (Courtesy of John Burger)*

could afford a swimming pool, so we'd use theirs . . . oh, and the good food they would put out for us! When you get around Italian families, honey, mostly they're full of love— they're very tactile—and they love to feed you."

The sisters and their parents became friends with the Costello clan and visited often during filmmaking. "Bud and Lou always gambled," says Patty Andrews. "They had a place on

Patty and Maxene Andrews observe Lou's attempt at knitting during a break from In the Navy. *(Courtesy of Maxene Andrews)*

Lou with the Andrews Sisters in Hold That Ghost *(1941), where the harmonizing trio performed one of their most popular tunes, "Aurora." (Courtesy of Maxene Andrews)*

the set just to gamble. They just played cards all the time."

Maxene, one of the overseers of the legendary poker play-offs, recalled, "The boys would play with their friends Mike Potson and Alex Gottlieb. They had wild games. As far as I know, I was the only girl ever admitted in to watch those games. My eyes were open so wide at the amounts of money on that table. It was nothing to play for thirty, forty, and even fifty thousand dollars a hand. These poker games went on practically every day we worked."

When the Andrews Sisters' professional association with Bud and Lou ended, their personal relationship did not. The sisters kept in touch—mainly with Lou—and saw the team as much as they could. "Lou had a dominating type of personality" says Patty. "And Bud was the second banana, as far as Lou was concerned. They were not like their on-screen personas at all. Anne, Lou's wife, was just a lovebug."

Of Costello, Maxene observed: "One of the greatest tragedies in Lou's life was when he came down with rheumatic fever. Here's a man with all of this ambition and energy and desire, and who's at the threshold of probably his greatest success in movies, flat on his back for about a year."

During his illness and recovery, the

Maxene Andrews in 1990.

girls visited Lou at home. He was in a movable bed that was wheeled around the house. "One time, while I sat and just observed him," said Maxene, "I thought, what a tragedy! We were watching some movie in the little theater in his house. And here was this little funny man laid up like this. I really had tremendous affection for that man."

Today Patty Andrews continues to perform. Laverne Andrews died in 1967, and Maxene died in 1995.

A Little Bit O' Bud

One thing is certain: Bud Abbott was an impeccable dresser, on-camera and off. He was proud of his walk-in closet full of tailored suits, and at one point, he owned more than fifty pairs of shoes. During the 1940s, he was voted Best Dressed Man in Hollywood by a couple of fan magazines that he kept in his scrapbook. "My dad loved to dress," said Bud Abbott Jr. "I don't think I ever once saw my dad in a pair of jeans."

A slick appearance was not only part of his image, an element of the act, but it was a hobby for Bud. Clothes were a necessity, but more than that, they were a passion. With his debonair pencil-thin mustache that he grew in the early 1950s for *Jack and the Beanstalk* (Bud loved the swashbuckling, Errol Flynn movies), Bud was dressed to the nines when he topped himself with a new fedora.

Whether it was out to a restaurant or roaming his beautiful two-hundred-acre ranch in Ojai, California, it was rare to see Bud dressed in anything but a suit, or at least nice slacks (always with a wad of bills in his pocket) and a perfectly pressed shirt. Bud Jr. recalled: "He'd go out with the horses on the ranch, and I'd say, 'Dad, this is a ranch!'

The Boys were stylin' in One Night in the Tropics.

"He'd say, 'Yeah, well, I gotta look good for the animals.'"

Bud Abbott also liked money. Not just spending it and generously handing it out to friends and relatives—but the actual feel of cash, the look of currency and coins. For him, there was nothing like a fresh, crisp one-hundred-dollar bill.

He owned custom-made cuff links, tie clips, and money clips made of gold coins. To friend and fellow radio star Mel Blanc, he presented a personalized leather wallet with an inscription in gold on the inside flap: "To Mel from Bud." Inside the wallet was something nice, as well.

In Bud's eclectic collection of doodads and unusual items was a framed sheet of ten uncut ten-dollar bills, a rare 1891 dollar bill with Martha Washington's portrait, and a signed dollar bill from U.S. Treasurer Ivy Baker Priest. At home, Bud flicked the ashes of his cigarette (always using a cigarette holder) into his favorite, three-foot standing ashtray, which was lined with loot under the glass. It was a reminder of how "burning money" took on a whole new meaning for him and Lou once they hit it big.

Bud's "money ashtray." (Photo by Steve Cox)

Ride 'Em Cowboy

ABBOTT: The horse's forelegs are in front.

COSTELLO: The horse's four legs are in front? What's those things in back—crutches?

Costello was crazy about horses. And even crazier about heading to the track to bet on them. "The trouble is that I just don't get along with horses—or any other animals for that matter," he told a *New York Times* reporter in 1955.

"Let me show you what I mean about me an' horses not gettin'

Bazooka by a Nose: Lou with his Irish-bred racehorse in 1946. (Courtesy of Tom Frederick)

along," Costello said. "I gotta horse on my ranch who's nineteen years old. I bought him for my daughters and he's so old that he hasn't moved faster than a walk for the past seven years. I gotta figure that he's safe for me to ride him by now because he's much too old and feeble to object.

"My daughters can hit him and kick him and mistreat him. He loves every bit of it," Lou explained. "But as soon as I got on his back that old goat began to gallop and rear me and buck like a rodeo bronco. He throws me. But I still love horses."

Costello, at times, could actually become terrified of horses. When a steed from his stable broke loose on the ranch, it chased him. Sweating and sprinting, the comedian panicked and finally jumped into the pool, clothes and all, with his cigar still clenched in his mouth.

It was around 1940 that Lou bought his first thoroughbred from MGM studio head Louis B. Mayer. He paid $5,000 for the creature, named Flying Gloria, then took her out to a trainer for an assessment. "The trainer takes one look," Costello said, "and turns to me. 'You got stuck,' he says. He was right. She was lousy. I kept her for a pet."

Eventually, Costello invested $14,000 in a beautiful Irish stallion named Bazooka, and mated him with a Silver Horde mare named Bold Rebel. The first seven foals were kept as pets, but the eighth was Bold Bazooka—his prize steed. He did quite well racing Bold Bazooka and entered him in the Garden State Park competition in New Jersey, with hopes to continue on to the Kentucky Derby, but that never materialized.

In the mid 1950s, reporter Maurice Bernard filed a story about Lou getting almost 20-1 for his money at the Starlet Stakes at Hollywood Park, when Bold Bazooka "romped to an easy score by six lengths for a net prize of $47,200 in the Stakes that grossed $72,950 with a field of fifteen starters, all two-year-olds." Bold Bazooka set some impressive speed records for Lou, and put the smiling comedian in the winner's circle several times. Lou's love for the mighty beasts on his ranch never diminished. The irony, however, continued to confound him. "Me and animals just don't get along," he said.

The lone exception, Costello pointed out, was the original Bazooka, father of Bold Bazooka. "I think he knows what the score is. I'm sure he's trying to fix it up for me with the other horses. He'll even let me walk under him. Any other horse would kick just because it was me."

Costello recalled for the reporter a scary incident that took place years prior while filming *It Ain't Hay* at Universal. Costello was supposed to be asleep with a horse beside him in the bed. "Before I crawled in with the horse, the guy in charge studies the situation and says, 'Don't worry. He won't touch you. When the horse gets up, he'll get up in the other direction away from you.'

"Naturally," Costello said, "he gets up on *my* side of the bed, rolling right over me!"

Of course, of course.

Lou and Anne watch the horserace at Santa Anita in 1947. Lou signals here to a friend, making his choice in the next race.

continued from page 47

piece of racism. The Andrews Sisters croon to a black porter, "You should be shouting with joy," and he sings back, in classic "Yowssirrrr" style, "Yessum, that's just what I'm doin', 'cause I'm Uncle Sammy's fair-haired boy."

Nonetheless, the Andrews Sisters make the picture swing. Watching them belt out "Boogie Woogie Bugle Boy" makes you want to enlist. The musical numbers are crisp and snappy. If the movie was made on a shoestring budget, these production numbers certainly don't show it.

The plot continues with Slicker Smith (Bud) and Herbie Brown (Lou) accidentally signing up for service along with the Yalie and his valet, something that would happen to them again in *Abbott and Costello in the Foreign Legion.* Their stint, however, is chaotic, to say the least. Abbott & Costello's performance of the "Drill" routine is flawless despite an improvisation Chris Costello has caught: Lou, suddenly and for no reason, asks Bud, "What time is it?" during the routine.

Bud is unfazed. "None of your business," he replies.

Upping the Ante: Bud and Lou had an inkling the stakes might be high, and the team shrewdly made an unprecedented deal with Universal to share in the profits of their own films. Their original contract with the studio gave them 10 percent of the net—something unheard of in the 1940s.

Lou even does a musical number in this movie, one with lots of verve. Shemp Howard, later of the Three Stooges, chimes in as well. Perhaps Lou's funniest line comes when his face lands in the dirt on the obstacle course.

"Defend your mother soil," says Bob, a fellow soldier.

"Well, they don't have to feed it to me," he replies.

The Boys made *Hold That Ghost* next, but when *Buck Privates* created such a splash the studio raced back into production of another service film, *In the Navy.* Universal was hardly averse to the idea of bringing Abbott & Costello to the public in exactly the form the public seemed to want. If service pictures were the ticket, a service picture the public got.

By now The Boys were a hot commodity and director Arthur Lubin knew that Abbott & Costello weren't a new dance team. (He had complained when assigned to *Buck Privates* that he'd never worked with a dance team before.) Chris Costello thinks the real Abbott & Costello didn't emerge, however, until Lou began to take the reins. And she contends that the perfect Abbott & Costello director was Charlie Barton, who came on the scene in 1946. At that time, the team already had seventeen films behind it, having worked with nine different directors.

Abbott & Costello's work in the first half of the 1940s was airy and very much alive. Typical of that period is *Abbott and Costello in Hollywood,* which was made in 1945 at MGM. Martin A. Gosch, who directed their NBC radio show, also produced this campy little film about two barbers who sneak onto the lot at a motion-picture studio and help a good kid from the Midwest get a leading part. As usual, this film pits the solid, virtuous, salt-of-the-earth hero against the sophisticated city slicker. You already know who wins.

During the productions of Keep 'Em Flying, *a commanding officer at the Southern California Cal-Aero flight facility presented Bud and Lou with the honorary titles, "Flying Cadets, US Army Air Corps." (Courtesy of Tom Frederick)*

The plot, however, shows just how far The Boys had come since *Buck Privates.* In this film *they* are central and the romance is tangential. The plot is a gentle reworking of the Marx Brothers' 1931 hit *Monkey Business,* with The Boys as stowaways on a motion-picture lot instead of an ocean liner. In one touching scene, Lou is running from the cops and stumbles into the studio schoolhouse, just the way Harpo stumbles into a Punch-and-Judy show on the ship in *Monkey Business.* Lou's legendary love of children comes ringing through; he seems to melt as he tries to tell them the story of Little Red Riding Hood. Of course, he is interrupted constantly with trivial questions, an old routine from vaudeville. But there is so much legitimate love coming through in the moment that the camera is forgotten by both Costello and by the moviegoer, who can't help feeling something deeper than what is captured on film.

A later chase sequence is both brilliantly conceived and masterfully executed. Lou, racing through a barroom set up for a western, tries to hide in a wagon filled with wooden dummies. Naturally, the prop man grabs him, instead of a dummy, to be thrown from the balcony by a jealous cowboy. The sight of Lou being dragged by the feet up the stairs, his head banging on each step like a bass drum, is sidesplitting.

But the funniest moment involves Lou trying to get to sleep. His ability to carry a scene with just his body is truly amazing. Here he gets up from the bed, stretches sleepily, scratches his belly through his pajamas, closes

On the set of Abbott and Costello in Hollywood *in April 1945. (Courtesy of Joe Wallison)*

the window and curtain, then wheels drunkenly across the room several times. Bud, it seems, has a phonograph record that will help Lou sleep. It does. The only hitch is that before he can fall asleep, the record ends and an irritating scratching of the needle begins. The film is speeded up for Lou's last spin across the floor, and the effect is excruciatingly hilarious.

By 1945, when *Abbott and Costello in Hollywood* was made, Lou had grown into the business. "As time went on, they realized they had arrived at a point in their careers where it was their film," Chris Costello says. "My father began to see certain things he definitely wanted in a film."

He also knew the director he wanted. Charles Barton directed *The Time of Their Lives* in 1946 and The Boys' next seven films as well. But to Lou, choosing a director was a bit like knowing which bad-tasting medicine to take.

"To me, one of the greatest Abbott & Costello directors was Charlie Barton," Chris says. "He knew how to work them. He understood burlesque. He understood their comedy. He was the one who initiated the three-camera shot, using three cameras at the same time on Abbott & Costello. He realized the reaction was part of the humor, especially my father's reactions.

"Charlie said that at times Dad would buck him because Dad wanted to do what he knew from burlesque," says Chris. "He had a thing about not wanting to do a new routine unless it came from burlesque. But Charlie was very good with him. He told me, 'Even though your father and Bud had a keen sense of what would work, sometimes you had to show them that it was not a bad idea to modernize one of their routines, that you couldn't

Lon Chaney Jr. is the werewolf who nearly catches up with Lou. (Courtesy of Movie Star News)

keep doing the same routine film after film.' John Grant wrote this new routine for them in *Abbott and Costello Meet Frankenstein,* but Dad was adamant about doing the 'Pack, Unpack' routine. That came from burlesque. It was funny."

Chris continues: "Charlie said, 'I never sat down when I directed. I was always known for standing. But I pulled up a chair and I sat down, I crossed my legs, and I said, "OK, Lou, we'll do it your way."' Charlie said 'Action,' and they started doing their 'Pack, Unpack' routine. And it kept going on and on and on, and Dad kept looking at Charlie for a sign like 'When are you gonna yell cut?' And he finally tossed the clothes up in the air and said, 'When in the hell are you gonna yell cut?' And Charlie folded his arms and said, 'When you say something funny.'

"Well, all of a sudden Dad said, 'That's it, Bud, come on. We're going home.' And they left the set. Two days later they showed up with a new routine under their belts," says Chris.

The Time of Their Lives was a real twist on Abbott & Costello's formula, and in 1949 Bud wrote a short piece for *The Saturday Evening Post* titled "The Role I Liked Best . . . ," which praised the film:

Bud plays Dr. Greenway, a psychiatrist who thinks he's having a nervous breakdown in The Time of Their Lives.

In nearly all of my costarring pictures with Lou Costello, Lou is the one who gets hit by the current equivalent of custard pies and I'm the one who does the throwing . . . fans should be pleased to learn that my favorite role is one in which the parts are reversed and I take the punishment. As Doctor Greenway in *The Time of Their Lives* I was thoroughly bullied and tormented by Lou, who played a Revolutionary period ghost. . . .

I enjoyed this reversal of the usual Abbott-Costello film formula because it was a novelty and because I thought it would help us at the box office. The picture was fast-moving, with lots of laughs and some fine trick photography. . . .

There was nothing ghostlike about the most alarming scene in the picture, however. That came when I drove an automobile briefly. I had never driven before and don't intend to again. When Lou recognized me behind the wheel, he froze in his chair near the camera. I whizzed by, missing him by inches, and he had to go home to bed to recover.

Lou, Chris says, was more scared of trying new material than he was of Bud's driving. So it came as no surprise to him that *The Time of Their Lives* was not a raving success with the public or the critics. "I think he felt a little frightened if they journeyed too far away from what he knew the public wanted of Abbott & Costello," she says.

They didn't journey far again with Barton at the helm, but they did attempt to impose their formula on another film genre. In 1948 The Boys pumped new blood into their career with *Abbott and Costello Meet Fran-*

kenstein. Early in the war years, audiences seemed to crave light movies—romances and comedies in particular. By the end of the war, however, they were ready for heavies and monsters. Maybe the war experience made ghouls more acceptable entertainment.

The team played off the horror formula again in 1949 with *Abbott and Costello Meet the Killer, Boris Karloff.* In 1951 The Boys made *Abbott and Costello Meet the Invisible Man,* which attempts, with surprising success, to mix their comedy formula with both the horror formula and the gangster formula. In 1952 they turned *Jack and the Beanstalk* into a slight horror film, and they backed that up with *Abbott and Costello Meet Captain Kidd,* a combination of swashbuckling heavies and big musical numbers. But where *Abbott and Costello Meet the Invisible Man* is a tasty gumbo of styles and formulas, *Abbott and Costello Meet Captain Kidd* is more like mud pie.

There would be other horror films waiting for The Boys in the 1950s—*Abbott and Costello Meet Dr. Jekyll and Mr. Hyde* in 1954 and *Abbott and Costello Meet the Mummy* in 1955. But the excitement was gone. Whereas *Buck Privates* had spoken to the moment, much of their work in the 1950s seemed to be speaking to no one.

CHAPTER 4

The Forties: DiMaggio Roams Center Field, The Boys Make Hay

LOU: *That's it. Nobody wants me. The world's against me.*
BUD: *Aw, come over here and put your head on my shoulder. There. Now how do you feel?*
LOU: *Much better. Let's dance.*

The key to "Who's on First?" was timing. Even when Bud and Lou had absolutely no idea where they were in the routine—when Lou would scream, "I don't even know what I'm saying!" and mean it— they always managed to eventually pull themselves out of the fire because their timing was perfect.

Their timing was just as perfect in real life. In a sense, they *were* the 1940s. Paddy Costello put it succinctly: "They hit when the war broke, and they made America laugh. If for no other reason, that ensures them their place in the annals of comedy." Abbott & Costello were motherhood and apple pie in an era, pushed to the brink by world events, that longed for such sentiments and sentimentality. Patriotism seemed an unambiguous and universal virtue then. (It wouldn't always be so for Lou Costello.) Even Donald Duck enlisted in the war effort, torn, in one frightening 1943 Disney cartoon, between good—his Scottish conscience imploring him to save his money to pay his taxes and fuel the war effort—and evil—a carnival barker duck with Hitler's mustache above his beak, seductively luring

Donald to spend on sin. It was in that all-out, patriotic spirit that in a matter of days The Boys reportedly raised between $75 million and $89 million in war bonds.

But the 1940s had another, less philanthropic side. Hollywood was in full flower by the 1940s. Big stars commanded salaries of astounding magnitude, and southern California was their playground. If the Okies of the 1920s found the land inhospitable, those who blew west two decades later to make their fortunes found the welcome mat out. And for much of the 1940s, no stars were bigger than Lou Costello and Bud Abbott.

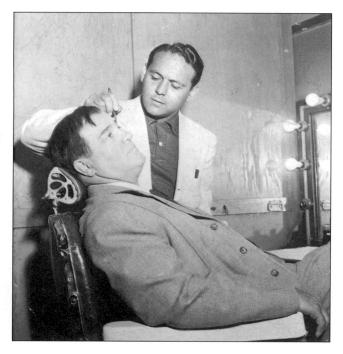

Veteran makeup man Abe Haberman works on Lou's puss. (Courtesy of Abe Haberman)

Abe Haberman in the early 1990s. (Photo by John Lofflin)

Not only were they the biggest box-office draw for much of the decade, they made an enormous number of movies to swirl those turnstiles. After the surprising success of *Buck Privates* in early 1941, Abbott & Costello made three more films for Universal before the year was out. In 1942 Universal released three more of their films, and MGM, one. That's a staggering eight films in twenty-four months.

In fact, The Boys worked the poor golden-egg-laying goose to death throughout the 1940s. They made two films that Universal released in 1943; one at Universal and one at MGM in 1944; two at Universal and one at MGM in 1945; two more at Universal in 1946; two in 1947; three in 1948, including one on their own; and two in 1949. That's twenty-three films

Stuntman Vic Parks shares a story about working as Lou Costello's double. (Photo by John Lofflin)

completed before 1950. So the duo can be forgiven if the plots and the sketches used in those films weren't all fresh and innovative.

And they had eleven more pictures to do before the goose gave out in the mid-1950s. They released one in 1950, two in 1951, three in 1952, one each in 1953 and 1954, two in 1955, and one in 1956. Lou was a solo in his last picture, *The 30 Foot Bride of Candy Rock,* at Columbia. Most critics agree he should have stayed home. His movie double, Vic Parks, thought the sheer physical demands of the movie killed him. If they hadn't, the reviews would have.

Don't let the years of Abbott & Costello's demise fool you. In their time, in the heart of the fabulous forties, they defined glamour and glitz and a chunk of the American dream.

They weren't averse to acting the part of glamour boys, either. When Lou arrived on the set at 7:00 A.M., he usually already had one of those big Carona Carona cigars cocked in the side of his mouth. He'd sit in Abe Haberman's makeup chair, and Haberman, who worked on Costello at Universal in the 1940s and for TV's *The Abbott and Costello Show* in the 1950s, would make up the "unoccupied" side. "OK, other side," Haberman would say, and Lou would just roll the cigar from one side of his mouth to the other without touching it.

Like others, Haberman remembers the poker games more than anything else from those Universal days. "Lou was really a lousy poker player," he says. "He'd bet a thousand and draw to an inside straight. Lou would sit there playing with a towel around his neck, sweating like hell. I'd have to dry him up for the next scene."

He would, that is, if the game was at a convenient stopping point. Charlie Barton directed nine of The Boys' films. "What I did find annoying," he wrote in *Closeups: The Movie Star Book,* "was the entourage of sidekicks Lou and Bud invited to the set for their big-money poker games. Whenever either of them ran out of cash, the game stopped while one of their stooges would go to the bank and withdraw $10,000 or so. In the meantime, the boys wouldn't shoot a scene until their money arrived. When I was assigned to an Abbott & Costello movie, I didn't know whether to laugh or cry."

Lou with his longtime stunt-double, Vic Parks, during the production of Abbott and Costello Meet the Keystone Kops. *(Courtesy of Vic Parks)*

Their penchant for poker was a product of their burlesque days. It started as a time killer on long train rides and during endless afternoons waiting for evening performances. In Hollywood, Bud and Lou's games became legendary. There was money enough to burn, and The Boys never did anything modestly during those early Hollywood years. Playing poker for matchsticks just wasn't their style, nor the style of their era.

"They'd sit there and play poker with one another for hours, for days," recalls Norman Abbott of the time he spent on their sets at Universal learning the trade and watching his Uncle Bud ply his. "I never saw anything like it. There were tens of thousands of dollars on the poker table. They loved their gambling. They'd play stud poker and five-card draw. Just the two of them if nobody else was available. There was an ex-hoodlum from Chicago named Mike Potson who owned the Chez Paree there—wonderful character—who was their pal.

"When Mike would go down to Universal and the crew'd say 'Okay, ready on the set,' you couldn't get them away from the table. They just stopped production. I remember the production office coming down. The poor assistant directors would pull their hair out," says Norman.

Charles Barton on Abbott & Costello

"Both Abbott and Costello had photographic memories, enabling them to look at a script only once and know it by heart. I discovered the best way to direct them was to allow them moments in the script for spontaneity—their timing is what made them so great.

"Although Lou Costello played a sweet little guy who made a lot of mistakes, and was the perfect patsy for Bud—or anyone else—in real life, Lou's was the stronger personality. Lou made the decisions for the team, including which routines would be used in a film. He was a good family man but—like Bud—a poor businessman. Once when he was unhappy with a certain studio decision, instead of trying to work it out, he took a trip to Europe and invited thirty-two guests to go with him. It was like Lou to run away from problems in his professional life.

"During almost every picture I worked [on] with the team, props would disappear from the set. Once a grandfather clock was missing. Nobody knew where it went. It turned out that Lou had a truck come to the studio, pick up the clock, and deliver it to his house. Another time, a canoe disappeared. It had become a planter in front of Lou's house. Despite these problems, Lou's childlike antics were excellent at relieving tension on the set.

"While analyzing their professional efforts and the personalities behind the performers, I noticed certain [traits]. Lou was the first to admit that

Bud was the greatest straight man ever. Bud was much less temperamental than Lou and never let his personal problems interfere with work. If he was frustrated, he would [vent those feelings] in the dressing room. In public Bud was always quiet and even-tempered.

"Bud and Lou sometimes disagreed intensely, but a half hour later they had forgotten all about [their spat]. Bud's feelings were more fragile, and he would become hurt quite easily when Lou treated him roughly, yet he always managed to overlook what Lou did or said to him. They loved

Lou and director Charlie Barton were really the best of pals, but played it up for the photographer on the set of Africa Screams. *(Courtesy of Julie Barton)*

each other, and the hard times they had together, the fights they had, unified them even more.

"There was one very bad period, however, that I believe did permanent damage to the team. Someone advised Lou that he should get more money for his pratfalls. So, characteristically, he threatened to quit. Of course Universal went after their gold mine, but he held out for an increase in salary and asked for a larger amount than Bud. To resolve the situation, their manager, Eddie Sherman, asked Bud to go along with the idea. He did, but it broke his heart that Lou wanted him to take a pay cut.

"What halted the success of Abbott & Costello, not once but twice in their career, was that the studio flooded the market with their films. At the same time a new film was released, an old one would be reissued. They became overexposed, and eventually, in the early fifties, [they] stopped being box-office giants. But they were important to the forties and essential to the art of comedy. As the owner of Universal Studios once said, 'Thank God for Abbott & Costello!'"

Charles Barton directed some of the best motion pictures Abbott & Costello made. He worked on The Time of Their Lives; Buck Privates Come Home; The Wistful Widow of Wagon Gap; The Noose Hangs High; Abbott and Costello Meet Frankenstein; Mexican Hayride; Abbott and Costello Meet the Killer, Boris Karloff; Africa Screams; *and* Dance with Me, Henry. *Charles Barton died on December 5, 1981, at the age of seventy-nine. This article, written by the director, was provided by his wife, Julie Gibson Barton. It originally appeared as a contribution to* Closeups: The Movie Star Book.

Sheldon Leonard on Abbott & Costello

Sheldon Leonard was one of Hollywood's classic motion-picture "heavies." His deep, resonant voice, tall stature, and cold, deep stare made him the classic thug. A veteran of films and television shows, Leonard was still active in Hollywood in the 1990s. Leonard died in 1996.

"I did two pictures with Abbott & Costello," he said. "Mostly I remember the practical jokes. I was the victim of a few of them."

Leonard was one actor who didn't appreciate The Boys' work habits. "They didn't take the work seriously," he said. "An awful lot of card playing and extracurricular activity went on."

Eight years after his first film with Bud and Lou [*Hit the Ice*] Leonard again worked with the team, in *Abbott and Costello Meet the Invisible Man.* In retrospect, he noticed that there was a difference in the duo since their first film.

"There was a change," he said. "They were getting into deep water—owing money and being in hock with salaries. They weren't as carefree later on, you could tell. Their attitude was more like 'Let's get this done and get the hell out of here.'"

Lou goes for the throat of Sheldon Leonard in Hit the Ice *(1943). (Personality Photos, Inc.)*

Sheldon Leonard worked with the duo in two films. One of his most recognized big-screen roles was that of Nick the bartender in the holiday classic, It's a Wonderful Life. *(Photo by John Lofflin)*

Goofing around with Bobby Barker, who is donning Bela Lugosi's Dracula cape in this behind-the-scenes photograph taken during the filming of Abbott and Costello Meet Frankenstein.

Vic Parks remembered electricians watching those poker games from the scaffolds overhead. They had a bird's-eye view, he said, of pots that would curl a workingman's hair. Parks said the pair often gambled $10,000 to $15,000 a day in their trailers or on the set. "There would be guys on top of guys, watching 'em," he said.

Parks looked less like Lou in the 1990s than he did in the 1940s, when he was fifty pounds heavier, but the jaw cut the same bold stroke, and his eyes wee uncannily familiar. (It's interesting to note that Lou was just one year, to the day, older.) "People would sometimes say to me, 'Lou, how do you feel today?'" Parks said with a mischievous chuckle. "I was standing on the set of *Abbott and Costello Meet the Mummy,* and a fella who had a small part in the movie walked up to me and said, 'Thanks, Lou, for the bit in the picture.' I said, 'Glad to have you.' Lou was standing next to me and heard the whole thing.

"So Bud says to me, 'Hey, Lou, let's finish the game.' Lou starts into the trailer and Bud says, 'Not you, I was playing with Costello,' and he points at me. So I sit down with Lou's hand in front of me and Lou looking over my shoulder.

"I couldn't do anything wrong after that," continued Vic Parks. "I had five straight winning hands, and I was up about $4,000. Bud says, 'This is where you get off, buddy. You are not Costello. Give me back my money.

"Lou says, 'No, you asked for it, and, besides, I have to go now.'"

Bobby Barber was the recipient of endless pranks from Bud and Lou. "But he loved it," says Norman Abbott. "He knew what they were doing. He had a ball going along with it all, the poor little man."

When The Boys took the long trip by rail each year to New York City to play their annual gig at the Roxy, Potson would meet the train in Chicago, his suit pockets full of cigars and poker money.

The other fixture on the set of an Abbott & Costello film was Bobby Barber, a burlesque crony hired by Lou to do little more than keep things loose and be the brunt of his endless practical jokes.

"Lou loved Bobby," Norman Abbott says. "He'd put Bobby up to all kinds of pranks. While we were doing *The Wistful Widow of Wagon Gap,* we were out on a western ranch and the planes were flying over and we couldn't get a shot. Lou said to Bobby, 'Take this red flag. See that mountaintop over there? I want you to go up there, and when you see a plane fly over, wave the flag and stop the plane so we can shoot.'

"Bobby always played it straight. Never laughed. That little man, it took him two hours to get up that mountain. Waving. We all had binoculars and we were laughing our heads off. Lou especially," says Norman.

"Bobby used to fall asleep a lot on the set," he continues. "One day, Lou tied his ankles to the director's chair. Bobby seemed to be asleep, although he may have been awake. Then they shoveled horse manure in front of him. A whole bed of horse manure. The director said, 'Bobby Barber on the set, please!' Bobby jumped up and fell right into the manure. They carried Lou out; he was crying like a baby. Sadistic humor, I must say. But I know Bobby knew what was happening. He was like a little monkey."

In the book *Nightmare of Ecstasy: The Life and Art of Edward D. Wood Jr.,* author Rudolph Grey quotes Phil Cambridge, an artist and friend of cult-movie auteur Ed Wood. Cambridge recalled:

> Ed told me that he had been on the set [at Universal] with Lou Costello on a couple of films. Lou, unlike the personable little guy he was, was really an s.o.b. in person and hated Bud along with everyone else. Ed said Lou had a chauffeur [Bobby Barber] and he would always humiliate this chauffeur whenever he was angry with someone—he would kick him or hit him, whatever he felt like doing. One day, he got the guy to come inside and he got a bar of soap and said, "Now you eat that." And the guy ate it.

In his 1975 publication, *The Abbott and Costello Book,* author Jim Mulholland described one of Bud and Lou's pranks. "One day the whole cast was assembled at the Universal commissary. Bobby Barber was having a bowl of soup and when he wasn't looking, Lou emptied an entire salt shaker into the soup. When Barber tasted the soup, he gasped. Then Bud handed him a glass of water, shouting, 'Quick! Drink this!' Barber downed the water, which, of course, Bud had also spiked with salt." (It's a wonder poor Bobby Barber didn't vomit in front of everyone in the commissary. Or maybe he did.)

Paddy Costello remembers visiting the sets for her father's movies and being delighted by the sight of Bobby Barber running around with fire-

Shemp Howard is "Gunner," a myopic sharpshooter in Africa Screams. According to Babe Howard, Shemp's widow, Costello attempted to put him under personal contract, ultimately to prevent him from working at Universal. She noted that Costello was "a bit jealous" of Shemp's comedic ability and attempted to inhibit his career, despite the fact that Bud and Lou employed Shemp in several films. Babe Howard noted that Shemp was usually disturbed that his best material in Abbott and Costello films always ended up on the cutting room floor. (Courtesy of Joe Wallison)

With Hillary Brooke and Shemp Howard in Africa Screams. Brooke noted years later, "I never got any cues," because of Bud and Lou's constant improvising.

crackers tied to his shirttail. "Bobby was a big ham," she says. "He loved that. He enjoyed doing that. It was just crazy.

"A memory I have from *Mexican Hayride* was that there was a gal in the picture who was Russian. She was a huge pain in the ass. They were out on location, and they had a big catering tent set up. They had troughs of ice for the drinks, and, eventually, somebody picked her up and just threw her into this trough of ice. I guess it calmed her down. She didn't give anybody any more trouble."

With Charles Laughton in a publicity still for Abbott and Costello Meet Captain Kidd. *Initially, Laughton was apprehensive about working with his favorite comedians. Ironically, because Lou admired Laughton's dramatic abilities so much, the comedian was edgy himself. After the first day of shooting, however, the two got along quite well.*

Joe Besser, of the Three Stooges, made only small appearances in *Abbott and Costello Meet the Keystone Kops* and *Africa Screams,* but he was a regular as Stinky, a neighborhood brat dressed in an oversized Little Lord Fauntleroy suit, on Abbott & Costello's television show. "Lou loved to play practical jokes on the set," Besser said before his death in 1988. "In one of the episodes of the TV show, I remember Stinky is in a drugstore and he's supposed to drink castor oil. Lou had put real castor oil in my glass, and I drank it during the take. The film is black and white, but if you could've seen me, you'd see I turned a nice shade of green."

Guest stars who shared the marquee with Abbott & Costello were subjected to slightly more mature pranks, but pranks nonetheless. Some such as Charles Laughton, who appeared with The Boys in their 1952 film *Abbott and Costello Meet Captain Kidd,* found the fraternity atmosphere refreshing. It prepared him to do comedy, he said. But others were not pleased. Classic film heavy Sheldon Leonard did two films with Abbott & Costello, *Hit the Ice* and *Abbott and Costello Meet the Invisible Man.*

"*Hit the Ice* was the first picture I did with them," Leonard says. "When I came on the set, I was warmly greeted by everyone. Then, as we started rehearsing, some little mustached character with a hat on his head came rushing in and said, 'No, no, Mr. Leonard. Not that way. Say it this way. Don't say it like that. Here's how you do it.'

"Here I'd been in the business for years and this guy's gonna tell me how to read my line? Charlie Lamont was directing, and we resumed rehearsal. About halfway through, again this little guy steps in and says, 'You didn't do it the way I told you.'

"I said, 'What the hell do you want? Leave me alone, will you!' He just kept harassing me until finally I said, 'Either he goes or I go. I'll kill the little son of a bitch if he does it again.'

"Everybody burst into laughter. Abbott & Costello had set him on me. All hell broke loose. And from that point on, I always looked over my shoulder when I worked with them," said Leonard.

"They didn't take the work seriously," he continued. "An awful lot of card playing and extracurricular activity went on. You have to understand this about them. I don't want to sound negative about this, either. They were basically burlesque comics. Maybe the best burlesque comics. They were not very profound or complicated. They loved to laugh, eat, drink. . . . When you say 'get to know them' . . . there really wasn't much to get to know."

Whether or not The Boys took their work seriously, they got the job done. As Norman Abbott says, "They were not irresponsible men. Their films came in on time."

And the time was short. Most of the early films were shot on a twenty-nine-day schedule and on a suitably economical budget.

Original publicity art for Hit the Ice.

Scooting around the backlot of Universal Studios.

When shooting was over, however, the set was often lighter than it was when filming began. That's because Lou and Bud had "sticky fingers," as Norman Abbott puts it. "They would just take things home," he recalls. "There would always be a terrible problem because you'd have to come back and reshoot a scene and match everything, but half the props would be gone.

"Lou would tell Bobby, 'Put that in the car. That candle—that goes in the car, Bobby.'

"One day, a white van pulls up to Lou's house with two guys in white moving outfits. They say, 'Mrs. Costello, we're here to pick up the piano. Here's the bill of lading,' and they show it to Anne. 'Mr. Costello wants the piano down on the set.'

"She lets the two movers go in and pick up this lovely grand piano. Their living room was like a showroom," says Norman Abbott. "You didn't sit in the living room, only the den. That evening, Lou comes home and says, 'Where's the piano?'

"'What piano?' Anne asks.

"'Our piano,' says Lou.

"'You sent for the piano on the set,' she replies.

"'I didn't send for it,' says Lou.

Bud demonstrates the proper way to handle a razor in Abbott and Costello in Hollywood.

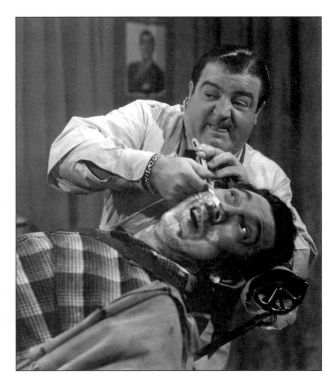

Fellow burlesque performer Rags Ragland doesn't think a shave by Costello is such a good idea in Abbott and Costello in Hollywood.

"About then, the phone rings," Norman continues. "It's Bryan Foy, who was working on one of their pictures. He says, 'Lou, when you bring back every single thing you've stolen from my set, I'll return your piano.' Lou returned the stuff."

Charles Barton told a similar story of a grandfather clock Lou had delivered from the set to his home, and a canoe that became a planter in the front yard of Lou's house on Longridge Avenue.

But Bud and Lou were also known for their generosity on the set. Abe Haberman and others recall them ordering pizza, sandwiches, and cold cuts from their neighborhood haunt, Barones, for the entire cast. Their generosity also had Vic Parks in charge of peeling off one-hundred-dollar bills for out-of-work burlesque chums who blew into town and made it out to the set.

This spirit of giving was all part of the family atmosphere at the great B-movie studio in the 1940s. In fact, many colleagues say Bud and Lou were saviors. The studio was still turning out films at Universal City, but those films weren't making much money. The stars weren't very bright, nor were the plots, and the decisions were being made by committee, which doubt-

Entertaining America during their phenomenal War Bond Tour in the early 1940s. (Courtesy of John Burger)

less accounts for the studio's lackluster performance. The presence of a box-office draw like The Boys in its stable gave Universal new life. Their films were also a place to showcase new talent and package old, such as the monsters to which the studio had rights and that it put to good use in Abbott & Costello films after 1948.

Universal might have made much more money from The Boys' work if it hadn't been so greedy and released Abbott & Costello's films at such a frantic pace and worn the audience out with them. But at least somebody at the top knew enough to admit that Abbott & Costello were the comedy experts and to leave them alone when they made a picture.

The Boys knew that to make comedy, a certain looseness of the joints was required not only from the actors but from the crew as well. They were used to working before live audiences—some critics think that's where Abbott & Costello were absolutely unrivaled—so on the set the crew had to fill the void.

Universal was also home because both comedians brought their families to the studio—both those they employed and those too young to be

Bud Abbott Jr. meets Glenn Strange as Frankenstein's monster: "When I went to see the film, I was disappointed that it was in black and white. It was so great to meet the monsters in person and in color." (Courtesy of Abbott and Costello Enterprises)

employed. Naturally, the children remember the making of *Abbott and Costello Meet Frankenstein* in 1948 most of all.

"*Frankenstein* was really great fun for us," says Paddy Costello. "The monsters were great makeup jobs. It was fun to see the monsters during the lulls in shooting do things like anybody else would do—have a cup of coffee, read the paper.

"There's a scene where my dad is backing up and he doesn't realize Frankenstein's monster is right behind him and he winds up sitting on the monster's lap. Every time Dad would sit down, Glenn Strange, who was playing the monster at that point, would crack up. He'd just laugh and laugh. And to see Frankenstein's monster laugh!

"Our being on the set never stopped Dad and Bud from playing poker," she says. "And everybody who worked on those sets was great to us. They'd organize softball games for us. If we got bored, we'd go into a projection room and some poor sucker would have to show us Johnny Mack Brown westerns all afternoon.

"Universal was like one big happy family then. It was smaller than it is now, and everybody got along well. There was always something funny going on," says Paddy Costello.

Only one thing made Lou really uncomfortable on the set. Animals. He had a truce with horses, although he much preferred them from the grand-

Charles Laughton and The Boys pose with a group of visitors to the set of Captain Kidd. *(Courtesy of Abe Haberman)*

HUNTERS HUNTED—Bud Abbott and Lou Costello shown after they had been caught by the fox after a hard chase. Use of this reverse English in a movie hunting scene won the comedians the praise of humane officials.
—International News photo.

Fox Chases Abott, Costello; Animal Kindness Honor Asked

Humane treatment of a fox-hunting episode in their current picture, "Abbott and Costello in Society," has brought recommendations that the comedy team be awarded special citations, Richard C. Craven, western regional director of the American Humane Association informed the pair yesterday.

The recommendations asked that Bud Abbott and Lou Costello be cited by the Humane Society for their insistence that the film script call for the fox to chase them instead of vice versa, thus eliminating any reference to animal beating.

"This was," Craven said, "in commendable contrast to the brutal, inhumane fox-hunting episode of Holmes County, Ohio, which shocked the national consciousness earlier this year."

The recommended citations were also intended to recognize the comedians previous promotion of animal kindness on the screen, according to Craven.

In Africa Screams, *poor Stanley Livington is petrified of any size feline: "I was fifteen years old before I ate my first animal cracker."*

stand. Paddy Costello recalls her father, on a trip to the track at Santa Anita, telling about his ill-fated first journey to Hollywood. "A director asked him if he rode a horse, and he said 'sure' although, growing up in Paterson, he had never seen a real horse," she says. "He immediately fell off." From then on, working with animals terrified Lou. The animals must have sensed it, because they did their best to make him miserable.

In a similar vein, Abe Haberman fondly remembers Bingo the chimp on *The Abbott and Costello Show.* "It loved everybody but Lou," he says. The chimp just beat the hell out of Lou. Its knuckles were like hammers. One time the crew had to tie the chimp to the bed for a scene with Lou. He didn't like Lou, and Lou didn't like him."

In an early 1940s movie-magazine interview, Lou even made fun of Bud's prized Great Danes and, coincidentally, The Boys' wives:

"Seriously," Lou said, when asked how he and Bud met their showgirl wives, "they were having a fistfight. We pulled 'em apart. Then we played meeny-miny-mo to see who got which. He got Betty, I got Anne. . . . Listen, honey, we're both married seven years. The only difference is, my wife was at the wedding—"

"Don't pay him no heed, honey," Bud said. "The only difference is, I love my wife—"

"He loves his wife and he's got three dogs," Lou said. "I don't love mine and I've got two children. You figure it out—"

Visiting relations on the set of It Ain't Hay *in 1942. Back row: Lou, Jim Muccia, Pat Costello, Norman Abbott. Front row: Babe Abbott Muccia, Olive Abbott, Betty and Bud Abbott. (Courtesy of Olive Abbott)*

At little Bud's christening in 1944. L-R: Olive Abbott, Anne Costello, Betty Abbott, Babe Abbott Muccia, Betty Abbott Griffin (partly obscured), Jim Muccia, Bud, little Bud, Reverend Mueller, Elsie Abbott, and godfather Lou. (Courtesy of Betty Abbott Griffin)

Bud and Betty Abbott's dream came true when they adopted a three-year-old child in New York City in 1942 and named him Bud Jr. (Courtesy of Tom Frederick)

"Sure, and what good are they?" Bud asked. "You sit around waitin' till they get married and walk out on you. I can get new dogs. Can you get new kids?"

"I *got* new kids," Lou said. "Patsy's four, Carole's two, so he calls them old? What good are your dogs? Can they say, 'Good luck on your broadcast, Daddy?'"

What Lou told Arthur Daley of the *New York Times,* however, was no joke. One script called for a live bear to be driving a car Lou and Bud were riding in when it came out of a tunnel. The trainer, it seems, couldn't get the bear to keep its paws on the wheel, so he wired them there. All during filming, a terrified Lou pleaded with the trainer not to aggravate the animal. The bear clouted the trainer and, in Lou's words:

> Abbott scrams, slamming the car door behind him. I want to get out, too. So does the bear. So he climbs over me. I start running as soon as I reach the floor of Stage 12, with the bear in pursuit. Everyone else is up on the catwalks. . . . "Watch out for the process screen!" hollers a technician, valuing the screen over my life, which is where we disagree slightly.

Maybe that's why Lou always seemed to be having so much fun on radio's *The Abbott and Costello Program.* The only animal he had to contend with there was Bugs Bunny.

Bud and Lou imprinted the cement at Grauman's Chinese Theatre on December 8, 1941, the day after Pearl Harbor was attacked. (Photo by Steve Cox)

CHAPTER 5

"Talk Sense, Costello": The Boys Take to the Air

WOMAN IN A
CROWDED STORE: *Just a minute, young man; you can't squeeze in
                    here.*
LOU: *Okay, babe, let's go outside.*

It's 1944, about 7:02 P.M. Pacific time on a Thursday. Lou Costello and Bud Abbott are gathered around a microphone owned by NBC Radio. About twenty million homes are tuned in. At the top of the show, a telegram arrives from "the Yankee Clipper," Joe DiMaggio. DiMaggio, it seems, is injured and hopes Lou will be kind enough to take his place in New York on opening day.

It's difficult to imagine anyone in the studio audience or at home huddled around hulking Motorolas who doesn't know Abbott & Costello are getting ready to do their most famous routine, "Who's on First?" But The Boys only toy with it in the opening dialogue. The Yankees, it turns out, will open against the Cleveland Indians, and who do you think will be on the mound for Cleveland? You guessed it. Feller.

"Feller pitching?" Bud asks his overjoyed pal.

"Sure there's a feller pitching. Who'd you think they'd use? A girl?" Lou replies.

"I said, Feller pitching?"

"What feller?"

"Feller, with the Cleveland Indians."

"Look, Abbott, there's nine guys on the Cleveland team. Now which feller are you talkin' about?"

"The Feller that pitches. There's only one Feller with Cleveland."

"You mean nine Yankees are gonna play against one feller?"

"That's right."

A Thanksgiving publicity picture for their NBC radio program, circa 1942.

"You mean there's no fellers in the outfield?

"That's right."

"And there's no fellers in the infield?

"No. Cleveland only has one Feller."

"Well this feller must be pretty good if he don't need any other players but himself."

"Waidaminute!"

Bud, of course, is referring to fireballer Bob Feller, who's built a bit like Lou, come to think of it. Well, The Boys have to get Lou something to wear, so off they go to the sporting goods store to pick out a uniform.

"I'd like to see something Lou can wear," says Bud to the clerk.

"So would I!" he replies.

Marilyn Maxwell sings a rapturous "Do You Know What It Means to Miss New Orleans?" in honor of New Orleans's Jazz Week. Before you know it, the show is down to its last five minutes, and The Boys are back at the microphone.

"You know, Bud, I don't know the guys on the team. You're gonna have to help me with their names," implores Lou.

Faster than a speeding bullet, Abbott & Costello are deep into their trademark routine—crazily batting back and forth the players whom history will never forget. Who, on first; What, on second; I Don't Know, at third; and I Don't Give a Darn, at short. Tomorrow's on the mound and Today's behind the plate. The Boys take the routine at a clip, like bop musicians playing a standard in double time. And no matter how many hundred times they've done their routine before, this time seems like the first time. Lou is getting wilder and wilder as the piece goes on. By the time they get to left field, you're certain the little man will explode if he doesn't get some straight answers to his oh-so-logical questions.

NBC may have owned the microphone, but Thursday night belonged to Abbott & Costello. Nowhere was their wild success more apparent in the 1940s than across the radio waves that carried *The Abbott and Costello Program* from coast to coast.

The show premiered on NBC on October 8, 1942, then moved to ABC after the 1946 season. When Abbott & Costello left NBC, their show was still in the top fifteen. In fact, all fifteen top-rated shows were on NBC. Abbott & Costello were thirteenth, behind Fibber McGee & Molly, Bob Hope, and Jack Benny, but ahead of Burns & Allen. Being in the top fifteen was an accomplishment in 1945, when nine out of ten families owned a radio and Americans spent more time listening to it than doing anything else except working and sleeping.

The Abbott and Costello Program featured a familiar cast: singer Connie Haines, the Freddie Rich Orchestra, announcer Ken Niles, and Lou doing his Little Sebastian character. Every week, his trademark "I'm a baaaaad boy!" squealed from Little Sebastian's lips, and when it did, the studio audience erupted in laughter.

The program's format was adapted from vaudeville, as were most radio variety shows. From the 1930s on, Bob Hope, Red Skelton, Fred Allen, and Jack Benny, among others, translated their vaudeville experiences to radio with increasing sophistication. By the 1940s the format was polished to a shine, and when translated again to television by Milton Berle in the 1950s it became institutionalized, giving way to everything from *Your Show of Shows* to *Saturday Night Live.*

In fact, the spontaneity seen in the 1970s with The Not Ready for Prime Time Players on *Saturday Night Live* could be found more than two decades earlier on radio in *The Abbott and Costello Program*—and on prime time to boot. The half-hour program had the texture of live theater, which it was. Like *Saturday Night Live,* it was full of unedited mistakes, and it featured rather wooden appearances by under-rehearsed guest stars such as Jane Wyman, Veronica Lake, Mickey Rooney, and Bela Lugosi. The Lugosi performance occurred after the show moved to ABC and included a segment based on Abbott's real-life experience as honorary sheriff of Encino, California. Lugosi was absolutely terrible on radio—although his voice was suitably demented, he couldn't read the lines correctly to save his wretched life.

On the other hand, one of the funniest episodes was broadcast on November 11, 1943, and featured Lucille Ball, then known more for her sultriness than for her now-famous dizziness. Unlike Lugosi's, her timing was perfect. The show's humor was a forerunner of Lucy's own brand of comic madness. In one sketch, Lou must procure a pair of war-scarce nylons in order to win a date with singer Connie Haines. Naturally, Lucille had bought the last pair at the department store, and Lou is in a quandary.

"I'm gonna dash right out to Lucille Ball's house, get those stockin's, and dash right back," he tells Abbott.

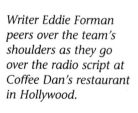

Writer Eddie Forman peers over the team's shoulders as they go over the radio script at Coffee Dan's restaurant in Hollywood.

Highlights from Abbott & Costello on Radio

During their extensive career on radio, Bud and Lou broadcast over every major network. In addition to their own shows, they guest-starred on programs hosted by other entertainers such as Eddie Cantor, the Andrews Sisters, and Paul Whiteman.

1938
2/3 Bud and Lou's radio debut on *The Kate Smith Hour* on CBS, Thursday evenings. (They remained with the show for ninety-nine weeks, through 6/28/40.)

3/24 Bud and Lou first perform "Who's on First?" for a national audience.

1940
7/3 Bud and Lou are summer replacements for Fred Allen's show on NBC, Wednesday evenings (for thirteen weeks, through 9/25).

1941
4/6 Bud and Lou become regulars on *The Edgar Bergen & Charlie McCarthy Show* on NBC, Sunday evenings (through 6/8/42).

1942
10/8 Premiere of *The Abbott and Costello Program* on NBC, Thursday evenings (for a five-year run through 6/9/47). Regulars: Iris Adrian, Elvia Allman, Artie Auerbach, Mel Blanc, Tom Brown, Joe Kirk, Sidney Fields, Cliff Novaro, Alan Reed, Connie Haines, Marilyn Maxwell. Announcer: Ken Niles. Music: Freddie Rich Orchestra; Will Osborne Orchestra; Skinnay Ennis Orchestra. Writers: Ed Cherkose, Paul Conlan, Pat Costello, Sidney Fields, Eddie Forman, Joe Kirk, Parke Levy, Don Prindle, Martin Ragaway, Leonard Stern. Guest Stars during the Program's Run Included: Veronica Lake, Marlene Dietrich, Bela Lugosi, John Garfield, Basil Rathbone, Billie Burke, Lucille Ball, Charles Laughton, Mickey Rooney, Andy Devine, Bert Lahr, Joe DiMaggio, the Andrews Sisters, Peter Lorre, Cary Grant, Lana Turner, George Raft, Henny Youngman, Rudy Vallee, Frank Sinatra, Turhan Bey, Carmen Miranda.

1943
11/4 Season Premiere. Abbott & Costello return following an eight-month sabbatical due to Lou's illness. That day, Lou's son drowns, but the comedian appears on the show in a personal tribute to "Butch." The audience remains unaware of the tragedy until Bud delivers a heartfelt speech at the show's close.

1947
10/1 *The Abbott and Costello Program* moves to ABC, Wednesday evenings.

12/6 Bud and Lou add a new program, *The Abbott and Costello Children's Show* on Saturday mornings on ABC (through 3/26/49).

Ah-ah! Three on a match is unlucky. Actress Sally Eilers visits Bud and Lou at the NBC radio studios in 1944. (Courtesy of Joe Wallison)

"But what if she's putting them on?" Abbott asks.

"Pilot to navigator," Lou says, using another of his trademark radio lines, "cancel that last dash!"

Typical of that era's radio variety shows, Lou does some adventuresome improvising, and Bud is terrific at retrieving lost lines and missed cues. And off-mike, Lucy is laughing to beat the band, her hacksaw cackle erupting just above the roar of the studio audience. From the sound of it, she was in stitches the entire half hour.

Mel Blanc was, of course, Bugs Bunny and the elevator operator in the department store where Bud and Lou had shopped for stockings. Lou had demanded Blanc's presence on the show from the outset and once referred to this Man of a Thousand Voices as "the finest radio artist I know." Before his death in 1989, Blanc said:

I did so many different radio shows that one time I remember running from one studio to the next with my script in hand, even changing cigarettes in my mouth to please the other sponsor when I ran in. On Abbott & Costello's program I did a Scottish fellow—Botsford Twink, a resident at the boardinghouse

Lucille Ball chats with Bud, Eddie Cantor, and Lou in 1957. About Lou, she later comment-ed, "He was a gentleman and a gentle man...he was childlike but not childish." Ball always remembered that Costello was one of the few who stood by her when she was accused of being a communist during the McCarthy era "red scare." (Neal Peters Collection)

where Bud and Lou lived—who used to say to Costello, "Get yer finger off the buzzer! Yer usin' up the electericitee!"

A parade of glamorous stars walked in the halls of the NBC Radio studio at the corner of Sunset Boulevard and Vine Street in Los Angeles, where Abbott & Costello's program originated. Helen Gurley Brown, then a script girl on *The Abbott and Costello Program,* fawned over those stars back then. You can still hear the giddiness in her voice as she describes those years.

"I remember it all as just utterly glamorous," she says. "Those were the war years, but I was too young for that to really sink in. Being part of Abbott & Costello in those times was very exciting.

"I want to say it was pure bliss, but I was too terrified for that. It was utterly thrilling to be near anybody so famous. I was just twenty at the time, and it was just my third job," recalls Brown.

Abbott and Costello called Mel Blanc "the finest radio artist" they knew. The voice of Bugs Bunny as well, Blanc appeared frequently on radio with the team. (Courtesy of Blanc Communications)

Imagine the woman who gave us *Having It All* and the Cosmo Girl dressed in a pinafore and seated on a folding chair at the edge of the NBC Radio stage waiting for The Boys' live performance. "I really shouldn't have been there," she says. "I should have been in the control booth. Actually, my work was done for the day, so they didn't need me anywhere. They were sweet to let me feel I was a part of things.

"The program was done absolutely live," she continues. "We did two shows, first one for the East Coast and then one for the West Coast. Of course, by the time the West Coast show came around, we had had a shakedown, and there were a lot of arguments about what should stay in and what should go. It was deadly serious stuff, those decisions.

"Martin Gosch was the producer, and he had four comedy writers, [including, probably, Hal Fimberg, Don Prindle, and Joe Kirk]. During the week, there were very heated arguments about what material to leave in and what to take out. And when Bud and Lou showed up for those script meetings, which they did once in a while, it was a bloodbath among the eight or nine of them.

"Then they'd say, 'Miss Gurley, would you step in here, please?' And I'd pick up my pad and go in, and they'd say, 'Awright, is this funny god-

Father Flanagan of Boystown was guest of Bud and Lou in Hollywood in 1944.

Actor Turhan Bey makes a guest appearance on The Abbott and Costello Radio Program. *(Personality Photos, Inc.)*

In August 1942, while out on a whirlwind War Bond tour, Bud and Lou were approached by a young boy who had sneaked up to their suite at the Fontenelle Hotel in Omaha, Nebraksa. Jerry Young—a fourteen-year-old, freckled-faced local—mustered his courage and invited Mr. Abbott and Mr. Costello to perform at his backyard benefit for the Red Cross. He offered them all he could scrape up: 70 cents. Why not? That evening, the local police roped off the streets surrounding the youngster's neighborhood as crowds quickly multiplied in his backyard. Bud and Lou arrived by motorcade and performed routines and signed autographs for the awestruck Midwest fans.

damnit, or is this not funny goddamnit!' I was too terrified to laugh. I really just wanted to cry. Here I was put in a pivotal position . . .

"The whole experience, for me, held a tinge of terror," says Brown. "I made lots of mistakes. Once I called the Great Gildersleeve [Hal Peary] for a rehearsal, and then the rehearsal was canceled, but I forgot to call his agent back and tell him. He shows up at NBC and—no rehearsal. That was a major mistake. He wasn't quite in Abbott & Costello's league, but he was pretty important—as important as, say, Danny DeVito today.

"I knew Lou better, of course. He was more approachable. Bud was more remote. Lou was absolutely adorable. I've met so many stars since then, so many people who were said to be 'sweet,' but he was just a pussycat. A sweet human being. He wasn't even on the make," says Helen Gurley Brown.

He and Bud, however, were on an incredible roll. To understand how big they were as stars during that period, says Brown, think of Tom Cruise or Robin Williams or maybe even Michael Jackson.

She remembers traveling with The Boys once when they took their show on the road to entertain troops stationed stateside. She and Carmen Miranda were the only women in the entourage.

"Carmen could handle things better than I could," she says. "She was older, and of course she had this incredible bosom. But I did OK too. All the members of the band were men, and all the writers were men. It was a total man's world, and it was filled with wonderment and unadulterated glamour."

She says Lou and Bud rarely did "Who's on First?" on the air because they didn't want to wear their ace out. But they'd often do it just for the studio audience and the crew after signing off.

"It's something I'll remember to my grave," she says.

If a dozen of *The Abbott and Costello Program* broadcasts were memorable for their laughs, the sadness of one will never be forgotten. In his 1988 autobiography, *That's Not All, Folks,* Mel Blanc tells this story:

> We were in rehearsal at NBC's Hollywood studios for the 1943-44 premiere, when around five o'clock, Lou's manager was summoned to the telephone. It was Costello's sister on the line, bearing the tragic news that his eleven-month-old son, Butch, had drowned in the swimming pool. Lou raced home, then the phone rang an hour before airtime to say he would be back for the broadcast. Evidently Butch had planned to listen to his father on the radio for the first time that evening and, heartbroken, Lou was determined not to let the child down....
>
>   The premiere went on at seven o'clock as scheduled, Costello bantering with Abbott as if nothing were the matter. You can imagine the misty eyes among the cast, which included me, Sid Fields, Frank Nelson, Artie Auerbach, and Lana Turner. As soon as we signed off, Lou broke down sobbing, and Bud had to quietly explain to the studio audience and radio audience about the tragedy.

1437-28.

Hard-Luck Lou: A Broken Heart among the Roses

The closing moments of the November 2, 1943, episode of *The Abbott and Costello Program* finally arrived. Bud Abbott returned to the NBC microphone. Normally he said good-bye to Lou, and Lou said good-bye to him. That day, however, he addressed the studio audience and the listeners at home:

> Now that our program is over and we have done our best to entertain you, I would like to pay tribute to my best friend and a man who has more courage than I have ever seen displayed in the theater. The old expression "The show must go on" was brought home to all of us. Just before our broadcast, Lou Costello was told that his baby had died. In the face of the greatest tragedy which can come to any man, Lou Costello went on tonight so that you, the radio audience, would not be disappointed. There is nothing more that I can say except that I know you all join me in expressing our deepest sympathy to a great trouper. Good night.

The next evening, the headline in the *Citizen News,* like dozens of other headlines, read "Lou Costello's Baby Drowns; Show Goes On." It's too bad the writer of the news article didn't get a byline for these touching words:

> Costello, following the trouper's tradition that the audience must not know what twists in his heart while the show goes on, insisted upon working the scheduled appearance last night.

Lou Costello's Son Christened

HERE IS SCENE as Comedian Lou Costello's son, Lou Costello Jr., was christened yesterday. Left to right: Pat Costello, Mrs. Bud Abbott (holding baby), Bud Abbott, Father Joseph S. Burbage, Mrs. Lou Costello, Lou Costello.

—Los Angeles Examiner photo.

Lou quipped and squealed as usual with partner Bud Abbott. He even carried off a scripted gag about life insurance. Comedian Mickey Rooney stood by, lest Costello falter, but the veteran of vaudeville, stage, and films took his lines unflinching and met every cue.

There were tears in his eyes when, after the half-hour broadcast, he was led to his car by his physician, Dr. Victor Kovner, who had advised him to forgo the ordeal of making the radio appearance.

It was Lou's first appearance on the show in nine months, much of which time he had spent in bed recovering from rheumatic fever. Lou had taken ill after a winter-long bond tour The Boys had financed out of pocket, a grueling schedule complicated by difficult travel conditions during the war. The team had two movies in the can, *Hit the Ice* and *It Ain't Hay,* which, Chris Costello says, were shot almost simultaneously.

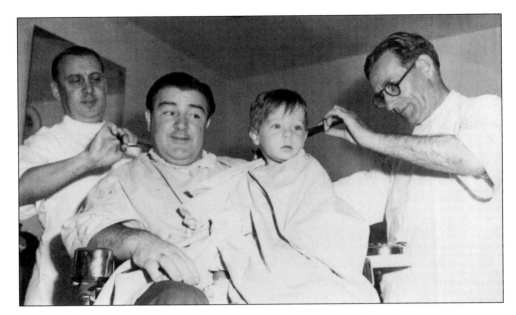

Little "Butch" gets his first haircut just days before his tragic death. (Courtesy of Chris Costello and Press Associates)

Paddy, age 5, and Carole, age 3, getting hula lessons from their father. (Courtesy of Chris Costello)

But Lou's heart had never been particularly strong. Even before Lou's bout with rheumatic fever in 1943, Vic Parks remembered Lou's doctor pointing to a chair on the set and telling him that the best way to keep Lou going would be to make sure he sat down between scenes. Vic says that's when he realized the magnitude of Lou's heart condition.

By November, Lou was finally recovering from the rheumatic fever, at least enough to do the radio show. He was, of course, happily anticipating his son's birthday, which was November 6; he had left on the bond tour just a few months after the boy was born.

Like others, Chris Costello contends her father was never really the same after the tragedy. Although she wasn't born until 1947, long after Butch's death, she says the changes in Lou were obvious to all who knew him; this knowledge was already part of the family legacy when she arrived. Her sister Paddy was eleven when Butch died.

"I can recall the day, but I was too young to pick up on the changes in Dad," Paddy says. "I was never treated any differently. All I can do is surmise he did a lot of suffering. I don't think you can lose a child and ever

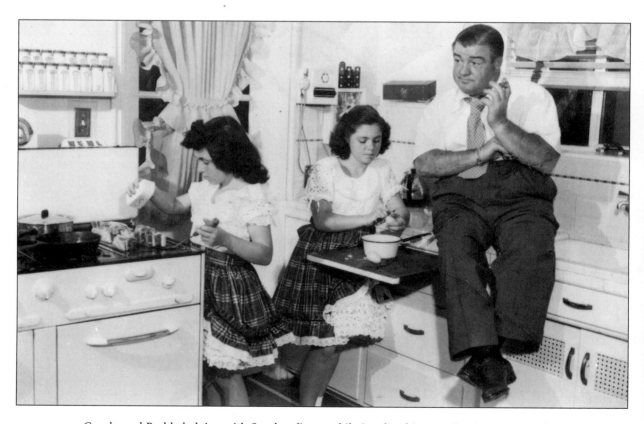

Carole and Paddy helping with Sunday dinner while Lou lets his appetite ripen. Noticeable in this family snapshot is the chain bracelet Lou had permenently welded around his right wrist after his son "Butch" died. The bracelet was a constant reminder of his beloved little boy, and Lou never removed it. (Courtesy of Chris Costello)

Lou and Anne at a party in 1949. After the couple's son, "Butch," drowned in the family pool, Anne began to drink excessively. She died in 1959, just months after Lou.

really get over it. Those are my adult observations, but as a child I didn't notice anything."

The adults around Lou *did* notice a change, Chris says. "The baby's death really zapped him. It stripped him of all meaning."

Chris says her mother's grief during the ordeal was often ignored by those close to the family. "My mom was a very down-to-earth woman who would have been happy living with my dad in a two-room shack," she says. "She was never one to be out there with stars' wives. I think my mother tried desperately. Her alcoholism came after the baby's death. She got very little support from my father's family. Their concern was all focused on my father and very little on her . . . realize, Butch was her son too . . . she was given a terribly black mark as a mother.

"And her being a bad mother was not true. There was no way this woman, who adored her kids, would ever have done anything to neglect one. I do think it was highly unfair. To be honest, as a granddaughter I never felt close to my grandmother. I felt in competition with her. It wasn't like having a grandmother you could run to and put your arms around. She was very cold to me. She thought of Dad as 'her son, the Star.' This has never been said to me by anybody, but I think she was jealous. She was jealous that Dad had a wife that he could give to. I think that deep down she probably blamed my mother for the death of that boy," says Chris.

Prizefighters Jack Dempsey (left) and Tom Gibbons are appointed sports advisors to the Lou Costello Jr. Youth Foundation in Los Angeles in 1947. Dempsey and Gibbons' first contribution was to autograph boxing gloves for the foundation. (Acme Photo courtesy of Tom Frederick Collection)

The ribbon-cutting ceremony for the Lou Costello Jr. Youth Foundation.

Sharing the Sunday comics with the kids at Lou's home. (Courtesy of John Burger)

"If anybody could have seen the grief that my mother was going through . . . There were all these people around the bar consoling Lou, and there was not one person with my mother. I think everybody, with Dad being a star, focused the attention on him, on his loss, without realizing she had a loss too. And I can tell you this, from my perspective as a kid, she was the most dependable, loving mother you could ever have had. She was not a falling-down drunk, and I've always resented that picture of her. My mom was always there for me."

Chris says her father was protective of the family and the children after Butch's death. "When you're famous, you're always under the threat of kidnapping," she says, "so of course you're going to be protective. Any major star during that period would be. Look what happens today with the fanatics. . . . I think when you become famous, you become a target.

"To me, the baby's death was probably foul play which nobody will ever know the truth about. Look at the circumstances surrounding it. I did look at the death certificate. It says 'under investigation' . . . twenty-four hours after the death, somebody closed the investigation," she says.

"Mafia? No. In the first place, the Mafia would not do that. My father was not the one in the family who had the strong Mafia connections. The Mafia does not do that. Whatever I think is completely assumption. It will

Lou in his Oldsmobile Starfire convertible, a top-of-the-line beauty in 1951. (Courtesy of Chris Costello)

always be an assumption, because no one knows what happened," says Chris.

Paddy Costello says that during that period the family received letters containing kidnapping threats. "I remember we were not allowed to go beyond a certain point out in front of our house," she says. "As bad as it was then, it's worse for famous people now. One incident is really funny, however. I don't know if I should tell you this. The one letter I remember actually came from a family member. Sure, it was a serious letter. But they got it all worked out."

Little Butch's death began to erode Lou's naive trust in people. In the year after the baby's death, Bud and Lou pumped a half-million dollars into an East Los Angeles community center that Lou had established in Butch's memory. Chris says he was particularly shaken when the movie stars who pledged money to the youth center began to renege and he was forced to turn the center over to the City of Los Angeles, which operates it today. "It was like he finally was forced to take off his rose-colored glasses," Chris says. "The world probably wasn't as beautiful as he thought it was."

Despite World War II, Lou Costello's world had been full of blue skies up to that point. He and Bud had amassed undreamed-of riches as they made their way across vaudeville stages in the mid-1930s. The year Butch died, they took home one of the country's largest paychecks, $469,170, which they split. In 1945 their gross income from movies, radio, and stage shows

In this family photo, Bud presents his sister Babe with jewelry for her birthday in 1944. Left to right: Jim Muccia, Bud, Betty, Babe Abbott Muccia, and Olive Abbott. (Courtesy of Olive Abbott)

topped $2 million. They estimated that by that same year they had earned more than $5 million in show business.

In the fifteen years Abbott & Costello were at Universal, their films alone netted them earnings in the neighborhood of $25 million on nearly $150 million gross. For ten years they were among the top ten box-office draws. To put those numbers in perspective, consider this: In 1942 Abbott & Costello appeared on the cover of the menu at Coffee Dan's Hollywood Cafe, where two eggs over easy, hash brown potatoes, coffee, and toast then cost eighty-five cents.

They simply went through a lot of money in a short period of time. Their penchant for card playing took its toll. It's impossible to determine how much they lost to each other, but many say those losses were nothing compared to the amount they lost to others. Bud Abbott Jr. recalls his father losing $40,000 in Las Vegas—his entire salary for a two-week stint there.

There were other financial problems, and The Boys' own generosity also eroded their savings.

Right after making *Buck Privates,* The Boys moved large portions of their extended families to Los Angeles. There they bought homes for their parents and new cars for other family members. They bought themselves plenty of luxuries: mansions with swimming pools, fancy cars and boats, ranches and vacation homes, and racehorses. Bud even had a gasoline pump in the backyard to keep his five-car fleet running. Lou invested in electronic paraphernalia for his house. Each had a home movie theater and rumpus-room bars that seemed to stretch for miles. (Lou's had a nautical theme.) The remodeling of Bud's Encino home in 1952 added 2,400 square feet. If that wasn't enough, each of The Boys bought an entertainment spot nearby—Lou's was called Lou Costello's Band Box; Bud's was called Abbott's Backstage.

Now, nearly fifty years later, Lou's home on Longridge Avenue in Sherman Oaks still looks like a piece of the American dream. It could have been used in the scene that opens *Leave It to Beaver*. Oranges still grow in

Horsing around on the set of Ride 'Em Cowboy. *(Courtesy of Tom Frederick)*

the corner of the front yard, the white picket fence is recently painted, and the shade is almost perfect. At home Lou and Anne worked to make family life as normal as possible despite their wealth and celebrity status. They went around the corner on Ventura Boulevard to Barones for pizza. Likenesses of Bud and Lou were painted on the wall there, among those of dozens of other stars. The girls went to church, although Lou stayed home. He told them he'd start going too, just as soon as he learned some prayers. Like any proud parent, he sat in the front row when daughter Carole won parts in school plays at Marymount.

"When we were growing up, there was a great emphasis on having as normal a childhood as possible," Paddy explains. As normal as possible, that is, when your father is Lou Costello.

"I remember the time my father was teaching me how to drive. We had this little Nash Rambler, and we were on this winding road," Paddy remembers. "I thought I had my foot on the brake, but I couldn't get the car to stop. Well, my foot was actually on the clutch. My father had his cigar clenched between his teeth, and he never took me out again. Never.

"You see, if he ran into a stumbling block or something he couldn't handle, he would turn to Mom and say, 'Anne, you do it!' 'You take her out, Anne.'"

Lou was apparently no great driver either. As Paddy explains, he'd tailgate so closely that "you couldn't read the license plate on the car in front of you. Sometimes the cops would stop him and . . . poor cops. They'd wind

After posting $250 bail for drunk driving, Lou Costello is led from the Van Nuys, California, jail on June 18, 1952. Police said Costello's automobile hit two fences, backed into a parked car, and cruised down a boulevard on the wrong side of the street. Attorney Nathan Freemen later appeared in court, pleaded guilty for his client, and paid a $150 fine in lieu of the comedian spending thirty days in jail. (Associated Press)

up so intimidated. They'd want to give him a ticket, and he'd talk them out of the ticket. The minute he would talk them out of the ticket, he'd say, 'Well, why aren't you giving me the ticket? You're supposed to give me the ticket.' And the poor cops would just be going crazy not knowing what to do. In fact, several of them became close friends of the family. They'd always stop up at the house.

"One time, when Carole was very little, she grabbed some doughnuts from the kitchen table and ate 'em; she wasn't supposed to do it," says Paddy, "but she did. So there's a knock at the front door and it's one of those cops. Carole was right behind Mother, and the minute she saw this cop she screamed, 'I didn't do it! I didn't do it!' Nobody knew what she was talking about. This three-year-old kid just came unglued."

Paddy says that even after Butch drowned, the swimming pool in back of the Longridge home wasn't off-limits to the kids. "Dad's whole thing was,

Holiday greetings sent out by The Boys.

you go on and live as normal a life as possible," she says. "You keep on goin'. We'd be in that pool from sunup till sundown, and there was always a bunch of children from the neighborhood in there. We were very family-oriented." Lou typically washed his makeup off in the pool each evening.

Never was that closeness more on display than at Christmas. Paddy remembers the holidays on Longridge this way:

The people who had the house across the street had a thing they would do every Christmas because my father's display was so incredible. They'd simply put up a sign that said "See Our Display Across the Street."

Dad was just a big kid. The outside of the house would be decorated. The inside would also be decorated, and the pool table would be piled high with gifts. One year they had a horse trucked in for me. At midnight we all went out to the sideyard, and there was a horse under the tree.

Other years, at midnight everybody would be seated in the rumpus room, and the kids would take the gifts off the table, hand them to Dad, and then he would call out the names.

Of course, during the rest of the year he'd be walking through the house and he'd see something and say, "Here, Anne. Polish this up and give it to so-and-so for Christmas." And they'd get it the following year.

Christmas was Lou's favorite time of the year. Left to right: Anne, Lou, Chris, Carole, and Paddy. (Courtesy of Abe Haberman)

Bud and Lou (with Jean Porter) strike it rich in Abbott and Costello in Hollywood.

Chris Costello remembers the holiday season traffic jams in front of their Longridge house. Throngs of people would turn off Ventura and slowly make their way south up the first half-block toward the hills to see the Costello home, which was decked with lights (strung by electricians from Universal) and featured animated figures on the roof. She remembers standing outside the white rail fence with her father, handing out Christmas candy to the parade of onlookers.

"Christmas was magic," she says. "Here was a man who came from mediocre beginnings, and suddenly he had money. Paddy and Carole recall the pool table in our theater filled to the ceiling with gifts. Not just for the family, but for coworkers and friends too. Dad used to go out, and if he saw a television, he wouldn't buy just one; he'd buy out a whole floor of television sets. And he'd have everybody at the house on Christmas Eve, and he'd have Carole and Paddy running gifts."

Christmas at the Costello's actually became a tradition for what seemed like half the residents of North Hollywood. It was not uncommon for an entire household to pack in the family car and drive to the Costellos' to gawk at the massive, glittering light display. The traffic on those brisk evenings would be jammed down Ventura Boulevard with police attempting to keep the vehicles and onlookers moving. People drove by, hanging out car windows. And to accommodate the spectators, Lou Costello hired a strolling Santa to walk down the street from car to car and hand out candy canes.

Besides the fantastic electrical display and elaborate animated animals on the front lawn and roof of his home, Costello projected cartoons onto a huge screen outside, just like a drive-in movie. Occasionally, Lou would be out on the front lawn waving with his family. Anyone who could find a place to park could go up and get an autograph or a picture of the comedian. It was a true Hollywood spectacle, and a holiday convention for countless families in southern California.

Both daughters have a bittersweet memory of those times. Many of the people gathered in their rumpus room were classic hangers-on. The conversation at the bar might be: "Oh, all you got was a gold watch? Last year he gave me this. . . ." Says Chris, "Dad and Bud were extremely generous with their friends. Dad wanted everybody to have what he had. He wasn't stingy with his money."

Butch's death may have taken the edge off Lou's innocence, but it didn't make him bitter and it didn't make him joyless. He was "momentarily irate" when Paddy eloped at age seventeen, but he soon got over it. Ironically, Paddy's marriage gave him something he needed.

"Looking back, I can see that it was all meant to be, because out of that marriage came three incredible people," Paddy says of her sons. "And my father got such joy out of those boys. He had always wanted a son, and here he had three little boys. He would take them down to Sportsman's Lodge.

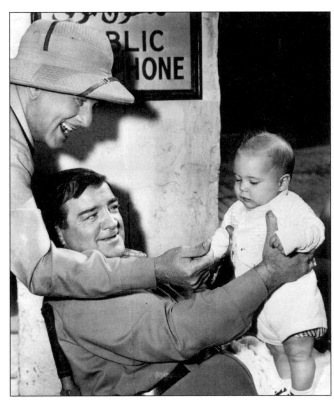

Lou holding his first grandson, who was named after him. Little Lou, Paddy's son, later changed his last name to Lou's real surname, Cristillo.

There were several man-made lakes there at that time. They'd stock the lakes with trout, and you'd rent your fishing pole. He'd take my kids, and they'd just have a ball.

"I very seldom saw my father laugh with gusto," she continues. "But one day he took the kids down there, and when he brought them back he was laughing so hard he could hardly talk. Michael, who was three years old at the time, never spoke much. He'd just go 'uhh, uhh, uhh' and point if he wanted something. Dad took them down to Sportsman's Park and bought them some popcorn. They had very large ducks down there. One of the ducks came up to Michael. It was as big as Michael was, and it wanted popcorn.

"Michael looked straight at that duck and he went, 'Uhh, uhhhh, uhhhh-hh!' My father came home and all he could talk about was this kid standing

Little Bud and Vickie Abbott enjoyed a rich lifestyle as youngsters. (Courtesy of Vickie Abbott Wheeler)

up to that duck. He was not going to give up his popcorn. Dad laughed and laughed," says Paddy.

Neither Abbott nor Costello was "on" at home. Lou's children remember him sitting quietly in his big chair, reading the newspaper and guiltily stashing the wrappers from candy bars between the cushions. They also remember him raiding the refrigerator. Paddy recalls once waking in the middle of the night, going down to the kitchen, and finding her father hiding behind the open refrigerator door, chomping on a large piece of chocolate cake. Paddy was sternly admonished to return to bed immediately.

Bud's children also remember their father as being quiet at home, routinely beginning each day with a cup of hot tea and a tall glass of milk, and smoking a cigarette from his familiar four-inch cigarette holder.

"Not very many people have had the life we've had," said Bud Abbott Jr. his father's diamond and ruby ring that spells "BUD" flashing on his hand. "We had a live-in butler [Smallwood Golf], a handyman, a maid, a cleaning girl, one full-time gardener, and a bodyguard. My dad told me that at one time it took $10,000 a month to maintain that."

Bud Jr. recalled card games at home in which the pots approached $6,000—in one-hundred-dollar bills.

Some Abbott family snap-shots with Bud Jr. and Vickie. (Courtesy of Vickie Abbott Wheeler)

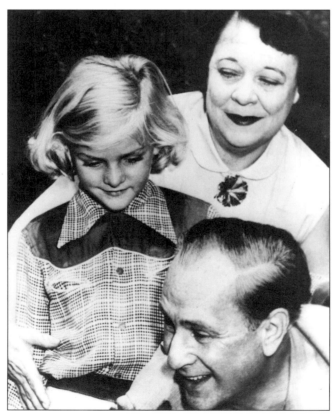

"Even our butler wouldn't take a day off, he made so much money serving drinks," Bud Jr. said. "One time he had to take his day off and he didn't like it. I was about twelve and Dad asked me if I wanted to serve drinks. They kept pulling money out of the pot for me." When he finally settled into bed that evening, Bud Jr. had $800 in tips to shove under his pillow.

Bud Abbott always invited old show-business buddies to live in the two-bedroom guest house on their property in Encino. "I'd see him put down payments on houses for people," said Bud's son.

Bud Jr. chuckled over the drunk who wandered into their rumpus room one night thinking he was at the local country club. The guy ordered a drink, and the bartender looked to Bud to straighten him out. Instead, Bud laughed and told the bartender to go ahead and serve the stranger whatever he wanted.

Bud Jr. and Vickie were both adopted as children. One news account reported that at the adoption hearing Vickie thought she was becoming a citizen, not being adopted by the family she'd already lived with for several years, and the judge in the hearing helped pull off the ruse.

Both Bud's and Lou's children remember fathers who seemed to stand the stress of their decline with grace. Neither took it out on the family members. But today they also all remember a lifestyle destined not to last.

Autographs

According to those who knew them, Abbott & Costello were always gracious to autograph seekers during their career. Being kind to their fans was important to The Boys, who enjoyed a rags-to-riches life yet always remembered exactly whose appreciation of their talents made them successful . . . their fans'. Even after Bud Abbott retired, his address circulated among fans, resulting in persistent letters and requests for his signature until the day he died. Bud and Lou signed thousands of autographs during their lifetimes and penned their names with a smile, whether they were at a restaurant, at a ball game, backstage at a theater, or at the supermarket.

Bud and Lou routinely presented inscribed photographs to relatives, friends, and coworkers as keepsakes. During the wrap parties on the sets of their movies, associates would request a signed photo as a memento of the work they shared, so Lou would promptly call the studio publicity office and have another hundred eight-by-ten glossies printed and sent over. You would think The Boys thoroughly enjoyed this seemingly burdensome yet necessary task of their employment—and probably they did.

"If it was studio mail, photographs, or fan mail, I signed all of it," says Aida "De De" Polo, Lou's personal secretary since the early 1940s. "Lou told me to practice his signature. I had it down pretty well.

"He wouldn't even sign his own personal mail," Polo added. "He would write his aunts and uncles and he'd never even read it. I didn't know what to say to his relatives and he'd tell me, 'Just improvise!' Lou signed all of his checks, though. He felt that was important enough, but he probably would have gotten out of that if he thought he could have."

Today, finding these pieces of inscribed scripts, scraps, and sentiments is like panning for gold. Collectors have scrounged for years, successfully locating a diversity of items signed by the duo, such as contracts, canceled checks, yellowed autograph-album pages, pieces of correspondence, "Who's on First?" record albums, and virtually anything bearing what is hoped to be an authentic personalization. To fans and collectors alike, these items are a means of capturing and owning a tiny piece of the era of these film idols. Although it took the stars just seconds to scribble their names, the autograph holder may pay a sore sum for those capsulized moments.

The price for a signature of Bud Abbott and Lou Costello (which is how they usually signed their names) naturally has ballooned since their deaths. The cost depends on how much was written, whether the inscription is in pen or pencil, the

condition of the article, and the year it was signed. Some autograph dealers offer the team's penned signatures on paper for more than $1,500. A matted and framed signed photograph of the duo obviously costs more.

Among themselves, collectors can purchase an article signed by the pair within a more realistic range of between $350 and $500, which is the average cost today.

Locating these signed pieces is like finding gems, which is to say that they are rare and, when found, securely guarded. Since Bud and Lou were very approachable and popular for many years, their autographs can be unearthed through a variety of dealerships and film magazine ads and at places such as TV and movie memorabilia shops and film conventions.

A baseball signed by Bud and Lou . . . Now that would be a sweet piece.

Lou signs autographs for teenagers in his hometown. Getting a signature in person was really the only way to insure an authentic Costello autograph since his secretary, Aida "De De " Polo, was authorized to sign most of his fan mail. (Courtesy of North Jersey Herald and News)

CHAPTER 7

Free Agents: The Final Inning

Almost from the time they assembled their act more than sixty years ago, Bud Abbott and Lou Costello began getting used to the press treating them like prey. As far back as the mid-1940s, rumors of their splitting up surfaced. Stories of feuds, stormy arguments, and breakups appeared in newspapers and surrounded the comedy team's whole existence. This flood of interest and speculation was a fact that Bud and Lou accepted and sometimes toyed with, giving misinformation to reporters just to confuse them or to keep them on their toes.

Years later the rumors and misconceptions persist. People have assumed that both men died paupers, left destitute after Uncle Sam squeezed them dry. Many people believe that Bud Abbott died, completely broke, in a nursing home. One recent trivia book contains a story about how Bud and Lou took out a sizable insurance policy with Lloyd's of London, stipulating payment if any of their audience died laughing. In most cases, there aren't even shreds of truth to stories such as these.

The news media of the 1940s and 1950s loved to tell stories of the team's lavish lifestyle and supposed rivalry. United Press International observed:

When Abbott bought a fancy mansion, Costello bought a fancier one. When Bud put in a swimming pool, Lou started digging too. Bud bought a super trailer and Lou bought a super-deluxe one. Lou bought a nightclub; Bud bought a restaurant.

In December 1947 the fan magazine *Movie Show* reported:

Shortly before the War, Abbott bought a small trailer for a dressing room and Costello immediately got a deluxe job which outshown Abbott's. Things were

In between filming scenes of Africa Screams, *Lou accepts a citation for efforts on behalf of under priviledged children at the Lou Costello Jr. Youth Foundation. Herman Barnett presents the declaration from members of Alpha Phi Alpha, Inc., a National Interracial College Fraternity. Ironically, when* Africa Screams *was released, it was heavily criticized as racist with an unfavorable depiction of blacks. (Courtesy of Joe Wallison)*

at a standstill during the War, but a few months ago Abbott brought forth a super-duper number that took front seat once more. [Then] while they were making *Buck Privates Come Home* at Universal one day, a truck pulled up next to the soundstage towing the biggest trailer ever seen in Hollywood—thirty feet long and fourteen feet wide. Lou gleefully ordered the stage's doors opened so the truck could pull the trailer in, but suddenly the truck stopped. The doors were twelve feet wide. Abbott howled as Lou's pride and joy was hauled off the lot, probably to be sold as a house.

The competition between the two started almost from the day they met and remained almost until the end of their partnership. It was never a vicious race, just a friendly rivalry to see who could outdo or outwit the other. *Movie Show* magazine reporter Rae Lynn wrote in 1947 of the time the two worked in the Steel Pier Minstrels. "It was then Bud proved to be a masterful orator, carefully talking himself out of doing blackface and just as carefully talking Lou into it."

Lou proudly displays mounted badges from Police Chiefs from all over the country. The team started their badge collection at the the suggestion of a U.S. Treasury Department representative who accompanied them on their exhausting 38-day War Bond sales tour in 1942. Covering 85 cities and 28 states, the team raised $78 million for the government.

There was a trick, however, to removing the burned-cork makeup used in the blackface routine, and Bud purposely neglected to instruct Lou. "The more Lou scrubbed his face after every show, the more black stayed on his skin—and the sorer his face got." Later, after finally refusing to do any more blackface, he found out you remove burned cork with cold water and a sponge. He was using hot water and a towel.

Norman Abbott, Bud's nephew, remembers when Lou purchased an enormous diamond ring for his wife, Anne. "I remember Lou saying to Bud, 'I'm gonna make your wife put her hands under the table when we go out together!'" he says. "Anne's rings were gonna be bigger than Betty's rings, you know. I remember Bud saying to Anne, 'Where do you keep the batteries for that thing?' The ring was so big."

Promotion for Foreign Legion *in New York.*

Some say the competition got downright ugly at times. There were certain demands. For instance, Bud made certain that Lou's name came after his. "The straight man is always first," he'd say. In the early years, Bud received a hefty 60 percent of the paycheck, which was common for the straight man, and Lou took the remainder. Lou always resented that fact and wanted to switch the billing.

While Lou was laid up recuperating from an attack of rheumatic fever for several months in 1943, a young woman called his manager several times to say that she had seen Lou Costello on the streets and at the Band Box nightclub. Lou was under doctor's orders that he get complete bedrest. Having caught Lou ignoring those orders, the lady threatened "that if he doesn't shell out a few thousand," she was going to go to the studio's insurance companies and tell. A columnist on a small paper also blithely reported that he "had seen Lou dancing at Charlie Foy's the night before."

However, the woman and the columnist had seen *Bud,* not Lou, at these locations. The bribery incident infuriated Lou, but the mistaken identity irked him even more.

There was another such instance, this one on the set of The Boys' motion picture *Rio Rita.* Lou was supposed to do a sequence with a "talking" dog. "Okay now," the director shouted over the loudspeaker, "the dog and

Costello on the set." Lou burned. "How do you like that?" he cracked. "Abbott & Costello. And now I'm 'the dog and Costello.' Can't I ever be first? I'm going to call myself 'And Costello.'"

In 1945, after The Boys' years of hard work and after they had made about fifteen successful motion pictures together, the press announced a split between the two comedians. An Associated Press headline read:

"Abbott, Costello Still A-Feudin' But This Is Off-Stage." The press spread rumors across the country, which aggravated the true situation, noted Costello years later. Some newspapers claimed the two were not on speaking terms, while others suggested that the performers refused to work with each other at an appearance scheduled at the Hippodrome Theatre in Baltimore.

On July 11,1945, Earl Wilson's syndicated New York column noted a "Coolness Between Abbott and Costello":

> [Costello] personally denied to me that the famous comedy team is in danger of splitting up or is battling over money. . .
>
> "But I hear you don't talk [to each other]," I said.
>
> "Oh we don't talk so much," Costello said, "but we don't pass each other up without saying hello to each other. It's not like it used to be, but then we never were like man and wife."

Lou's brother, Pat Costello, worked as the comedian's stunt double in several films. Pat was so simlar in size that many times Lou sent him in for wardrobe fittings instead of going through the task himself.

When Wilson visited Bud in his dressing room directly after the writer's interview with Lou, the comedian said:

> I live with Lou *more* than he does with his wife. I'm with him day and night. Do I have to go to him and say, "I want to go out with the boys tonight?" God forbid, if anything happened to him, I'd retire, because we came up together and we're going down together; only I hope it's a long time off. The trouble is, I might slap him in the kisser on the stage or in a nightclub kidding around, and already it's a big battle in the papers.

The Boys are clowning in a Chicago courthouse corridor prior to submitting testimony regarding a government lawsuit against their friend, Mike Potson. A restauranteur and gambler, Potson was charged with failure to report income tax on gambling winnings. Costello testified that he lost $15,000 to Potson in a poker game, while Abbott claimed he was out between $20,000 and $25,000 playing seven-card-stud.

Abbott's wishes were real. The team patched up any arguments that developed between them, and they went on to many more years of performances, friendship, troubles, family outings, and good times together. It wasn't until years later that Costello commented about the truth underlying the mid-1940s reports:

> We split for the first time—in 1945—over a really ridiculous thing. I had fired a maid. I had three maids working for me, and when I refused this one a raise, she held meetings in my home, so I fired her. She went to work for Abbott. I explained to Bud why I let her go, and asked him to fire her, but he wouldn't. So we had a fight—just as we were leaving on a personal appearance tour. We wouldn't talk to each other except when we were on stage.

Abbott & Costello Meep Hope & Crosby: This rare photo was taken backstage prior to a television appearance on the Olympic Fund Telethon, June 21, 1952, broadcast from the El Capitan Theater in Hollywood. The fourteen-hour program, aired on both NBC and CBS, raised over $1 million for the 1952 U.S. Olympic Team Fund. Other personalities on the program included Dean Martin and Jerry Lewis, Dorothy Lamour, Frank Sinatra, Eddie Cantor, and William Bendix. (Courtesy of Bob Hope)

During filmmaking in the 1940s, Norman Abbott watched his uncle and Lou grow together and then drift apart. He worked as Bud's stand-in and also as dialogue coach on several of The Boys' films, noticing the team's every move. To him, Bud and Lou's separation was a gradual process, he says, but it was noticeable.

"Over the years, it was strange to see this antipathy occur," he says. "Bud enjoyed his life and worked very hard, and so did Lou. Odd things happened. It's like a marriage. I don't know where the ugliness started to set in, but it did. They were very competitive with one another, and eventually, when they did a TV series, Bud was working for Lou. Lou would not take the deal unless it was done by *his* company and was *his* project and . . . 'me, me, me, me, me.' Eddie Sherman, their manager, very wisely advised Bud to go along with Lou or else the team would break up. Bud did."

Bud was a unique sort, according to his nephew. "He never bad-mouthed anybody," he says. "He was very passive. Extremely passive. I think it had to do with his illness. Just imagine, he couldn't get into the car and drive. That was a big problem for him. He had to hide behind someone else doing that for him."

The thin, suave comedian with the razor-sharp delivery was diagnosed with epilepsy in his early twenties, says his sister Olive. The seizures stemming from the incurable illness would come and go but got worse as Bud's life progressed.

"He'd have his epileptic fits while he was working," Norman Abbott reveals. "And many a time, Lou carried him off the stage.

"I remember, they opened at New York's Roxy Theater, which was a very important booking. Bud had an epileptic fit onstage. A vertigo. The stomach ties up in knots, and to combat it Lou had to punch him in the stomach to stop the contraction of the muscles," says Norman.

"So they're in the middle of doing the routine, and Lou can see it in Bud's face—his eyes would go. He'd actually turn Bud away from the audience and start punching him in the belly to stop the fits. I was there when that happened. It was very scary.

"You'd have to stick a pencil in his mouth so he wouldn't bite his tongue," says Norman. "He'd lose control of his bladder and other body functions. Lou had to bear that cross. The doctors at the Mayo Clinic said, 'We don't know what to do for you, but a drink now and then would help you.' So Bud started drinking."

It was no secret in Hollywood that Bud Abbott drank. In *Bud & Lou,* Bob Thomas argues that Bud became "a social dropout" as a result of the fear he felt because of his epilepsy. By all accounts, he never drank on the set. But after Bud went back out through the gates of the studio, he used alcohol to help himself put the day's events behind him. It helped him sleep without fear, he told family members.

"He wasn't an alcoholic in the sense that he drank night and day," says Norman Abbott. "He worked, but at the end of the day, he liked his blast of scotch. It would relax him. He could sit down and not worry about what was going to happen."

Bud Abbott Jr. never saw his father have an epileptic seizure, but his sister, Vickie, did. Both remember the pencils that their father kept by his nightstand. The family also discovered that certain foods—such as pickled

Even in 1950, these guys were smokin' in their success . . . from Abbott and Costello in the Foreign Legion.

herring—would set Bud off, so these were cut out of his diet. "I found out years later why Dad had a bodyguard," Bud Jr. said. "It wasn't so much because he needed protection, but to have someone around who was trained and knew what to do if he had a seizure."

As friends explain it, the team's final split was encouraged by little instances gradually building over the years—nothing extreme or sudden. Through it all, a brotherly bond and love held the act together. Nevertheless, little things gnawed at them and finally prodded and stretched their relationship until Costello called for their split.

"Bud had a tremendous love for Lou," says Norman Abbott. "But Bud would chide him. I remember Bud would always put Lou on, and he'd call him 'Little Fat Man' just to give him a little shot. Lou didn't see himself as a little fat man. Not at all. He took umbrage at that. I never knew how he took those slaps, but after a while he stopped Bud."

"Lou was a physical guy," Norman continues. "He could take great falls and never get hurt. Bud would slap him across the face to make a point. It was part of the act. They were slapstick comics. When I think of it now— that must have hurt. Bud would literally slap him. Finally one day, Lou said, 'Ouch! Don't ever touch me like that again!'

"The problems between them were private problems," says Norman Abbott. "Lou would get angry at Bud and say, 'Goddamnit, he's drinking and

Lou doesn't like what the fortune teller (Katharine Booth) predicts in Lost in a Harem.

At one point in their act, Lou decided Bud was never again to slap him across the face. Thereafter, the team's slapstick was noticeably subdued. (Personality Photos, Inc.)

Bud meets the beast in Abbott and Costello Meet Dr. Jekyll and Mr. Hyde.

Producer Robert Arthur in a discussion with Lou during production of Abbott and Costello Meet Frankenstein. *(Personality Photos, Inc.)*

Dialogue director Norman Abbott going over the script with Glenn Strange and Bela Lugosi. (Courtesy of Norman Abbott)

we can't do a gig tonight!' Bud was no good after seven o'clock. Well, Bud didn't want to have an epileptic fit after seven, so he had a couple of blasts of scotch. He felt he was entitled to them. After seven at night, forget it. He was in his *own* home with his *own* friends and his *own* family and his sixteen-millimeter projector watching a movie and minding his *own* business. Never did any harm to anyone. Never drove a car, no drunk driving. Never carousing around, making a jerk of himself on the Sunset Strip or at Cyros."

Because of Bud's illness and drinking, Lou felt that he had to carry the weight, so to speak, and do all the work for the act, says Norman Abbott in retrospect. "Lou honestly felt that.

"It was always Lou and Eddie Sherman versus Bud," notes Norman Abbott. "But in order to survive, I guess it had to be that way. Lou felt he was the business head and that Bud would just go along. So Lou took advantage of that and ran with it. But he didn't make bad decisions for them. I also think their manager, Eddie Sherman, handled them very well. He grew with them. He was cognizant of what the team was and what he had to do to keep it together . . . in order to keep this machine grinding out the money. Even beyond that there was a sense of love and camaraderie. No matter what anyone says."

By 1950 Lou had discovered the courts. First, he sued Eddie Sherman for overpayment. Even though Lou and Bud had severed their relationship with Sherman, the former manager was still collecting money on their previous

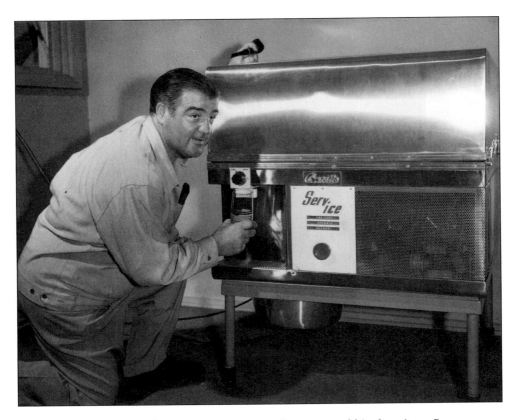

Frozen Assets: Lou Costello invented an ice-cube dispenser and hired engineer Bayer Goodman to produce a machine based on his concept, which would generate ice cubes in quantites suitable for hotels, restaurants, bars, and hospitals. Eventually, the collaboration ended in dispute. Goodman sued Costello for payment and Lou countersued—and lost. "After the machine was delivered it wasn't working," Costello coldly told a judge. "It never worked. Whenever I wanted it to work, I had to call Mr. Goodman."

contract. Lou lost the suit, and Sherman wound up with $400,000 over a period of four years. (Lou later asked Sherman to return as his personal manager. To Lou's mind, if Eddie was going to get paid $100,000 a year, he might as well work for it.)

There were other financial problems. In 1949 Lou invested $27,017 in an ice-making machine to be designed by an engineer named Bayer Goodman. One visitor recalls seeing Lou demonstrate the machine at his home on an occasion when it ran amok, spewing ice cubes every which way, Costello frantically looking for a way to turn it off as ice showered his head. He was not doing a comedy bit. Lou lost a legal battle in 1951 over the machine and was forced to pay not only the $27,017 but also a 7 percent interest accumulated since 1949, when he withheld the final payment on the contraption.

Then in 1951 Abbott & Costello sued the hand that fed them, Universal Pictures Corporation, for $5 million, claiming that the studio schemed to

One of the team's more exotic flicks, Africa Screams.

"cheat and defraud and deprive them of their rights and to destroy their interests in films." Among a laundry list of court-documented charges were two quite serious ones: first, that Universal developed a confusing accounting system that helped hide nearly $600,000 in sales on reissues of The Boys' films; and second, that Universal created shorts from pieces of Abbott & Costello's movies, garnering sales of $1.25 million, and made no accounting to the team at all.

The Boys lost the legal gamble. On October 31,1952, *Variety* reported:

Termination of suit, by a judgment in favor of Universal, was announced by the comedians in a statement which said in effect they found, after a complete examination of all the facts, that the evidence did not support the charges contained in their action. At the same time, they expressed regret over any injury that might have been caused Universal by various charges made during the litigation.

The ruling was a bitter pill, made more bitter by the financial thunderstorm that loomed on Abbott & Costello's horizon. In 1953 they were each visited by Internal Revenue Service investigators, who had a field day untangling The Boys' finances. Enormous deductions were disallowed, and the IRS found hundreds of thousands of dollars in income unaccounted for by Lou's and Bud's tax preparers. The sleigh ride was over; they had each reached the bottom of the hill.

The Boys talking with servicemen at Harry S. Truman's Inaugural Gala on January 19, 1949, in Washington D.C. (Courtesy of U.S. Marine Corps)

Said Vickie Abbott Wheeler on the A&E *Biography* of Abbott & Costello, "My father lost everything . . . almost everything that took him twenty-something years of his success to earn. Our big home, his ranch, everything he had. Lou—the same thing."

Chris Costello shakes her head a moment before forming the words to explain this story.

"What brought the IRS in was that my father's business manager failed, unbeknownst to him, to file payroll taxes on his corporation for eighteen months. He was constantly asking for extensions," she says. "It was a matter of the business manager never keeping any canceled checks, any receipts, nothing—which made my dad look as if he were, in fact, defrauding the U.S. government."

Lou's attorney hired Arthur Manella, a former Justice Department special assistant, to untangle his finances and prepare a defense. "Arthur Manella realized that what he had to do was go in and show the Internal Revenue Service that there was no way Lou Costello, who had, with Bud Abbott, funded a bond tour during World War II to raise $80 million in three days, would want to defraud the U.S. government.

"Dad was like apple pie and the American flag," says Chris Costello. "And it killed him inside to think that the government would assume he was capable of this kind of an act. I think that killed him more than what he had to pay out in back taxes."

Meeting famed member of British Parliament Patricia Hornsby Smith (second from left) with an unidentified British chap during a visit to England. (Courtesy of Olive Abbott)

Chris contends that the IRS decided to make an example of Abbott & Costello, digging back seven years into the comedians' records. "It was sad to think that here were two men who gave so much to their country, gave so much to their industry, and they were put on the chopping block," she says.

"Arthur Manella finally got the Internal Revenue Service to knock off the penalty tax, which dropped the amount owed down from $750,000 to something like $375,000 apiece. He told me, 'I called your father and asked him to come into my office because I wanted to share something with him. He was very nervous. He sat in that chair, and when I told him that the IRS was dropping the penalty tax and that all he would owe was $375,000, your dad sat in the chair and he put his hands on his face and started crying.' He said Dad's entire body was just shaking from crying."

Besides Manella, an accountant named Ralph Handley was sent over to put the pieces of Costello's jumbled finances together. Handley, who also did limited work on Bud's accounts, had been employed for several years at Business Administration, the largest accounting firm in Beverly Hills at the time.

By 1953, when Handley arrived on the scene, the damage had already been done. "It took years to straighten that mess out," he says. "During the original assessment of money owed, we were selling properties, film rights back to Universal, and everything to clear all that up during the years I was with Lou. Even after Lou died, we were still straightening out his finances.

"I had more authority than anyone had had in the past, as far as the financial end goes," says Handley, now in his mid-seventies. "During one of the first meetings I had with Lou, I told him I was going to do things my way. Everything would be aboveboard and I'd tell him the good with the bad. I'd let him know everything. Bud and Lou listened.

"Just before I got there, Bud and Lou had three productions going on down at Hal Roach Studios, and their young accountant wasn't doing anything right. I mean stealing money, not filing reports, and so forth. Lou fired him and was gonna send him to jail, but the accountant's wife and kids got into the act and pleaded that Lou not send him to jail. He finally did go to jail after working for another outfit in Fresno, California. He got seven years but was out on parole in three. Later I found out that after serving time he worked as the chief accountant for the Democratic Party in Beverly Hills. I thought to myself, *He won't be doing that for long if he pulls what he did before.*"

Handley noticed that a large problem in Abbott & Costello's finances was that both Bud and Lou lost track of what they spent. A few secret accounts of Lou's popped up, and Handley made Lou agree to surrender information about every bit of his finances. Checks would appear for $5,000 and $10,000 that "we knew went for gambling of some kind," he says. "When Bud and Lou both did that last show in

Looking unusually thin in Meet the Mummy, *Lou had just recuperated from another bout with rheumatic fever before production started.*

Vegas, we were so short of money the only way Eddie Sherman and I would let them appear was if I personally went and picked up Lou's check every week, and Lou had to agree not to charge anything against it. We backed Lou up in a corner and made him do it that way. Enough water had gone over the dam so that by the time I came on the scene they—especially Lou—were a little more willing to listen to somebody."

When Handley finally disentangled the Costello accounts, both Bud and Lou were appreciative, he says.

The team's last film together was a United Artists release titled *Dance with Me, Henry,* which hit theaters in December 1956. Although it was their motion-picture swan song, the film did not reflect the classic comedy of

Bud and Lou find themselves surrounded by gangsters in their final flick, Dance With Me, Henry, *and also surrounded by rumors in the press that a split was destined.*

Abbott & Costello. In fact, reviewers noticed a difference in their style right away. A critic for the *New York Herald Tribune* wrote:

> This time, the team is more sedate. . . . Costello doesn't take a pushing from Abbott, who has mellowed to the extent of feeling sorry for the rotund comedian. In fact, Costello is developing along the lines of a Chaplinesque character, pathetic and the victim of a conniving world.

News that Abbott & Costello were calling it quits broke on July 14, 1957. Almost every paper in the country picked up the wire-service announcement. The breakup was a mutual decision of the team. There were no harsh arguments, no fights between the families, and no bloodshed—except in the minds of some of the press. According to their families, Bud and Lou continued to speak on the phone and visit each other in their homes. There were never any hard feelings.

Eddie Sherman, The Boys' manager, commented at the time to hounding reporters:

> Every time I call Bud up about jobs, he turns them down, saying he's not ready to come back to work for a while. Bud is fixed well, and he's in good shape with the income-tax people. He just wants to take it easy after [his] many years [in] show business.

continued on page 139

(NY14-July 14) FRIENDLY PARTING--Lou Costello, left, and Bud Abbott, one of show business' most famous and successful teams, has broken up. The split without a fight or hard feelings was confirmed in Hollywood today by Costello. The reason for the break is that Abbott, now 61, and some 10 years older than Lou, doesn't want to work for a while. They are shown here on movie set in Hollywood last year where they were working on film, "Dance With Me Henry." (APWirephoto)(see wire story)(rocll737fls-stf)1 957

This Is Your Life . . . Lou Costello

November 21, 1956. While shooting a promo for the film *Dance with Me, Henry* at NBC television studios in Burbank, Calfornia, Bud and Lou were suddenly interrupted.

Ralph Edwards, with a bound scrapbook in hand, approached Lou to announce the surprise that he would be the center of a televised tribute—immediately—on the popular TV show *This Is Your Life.* Bud, the coconspirator of the event, wiped sweat from his brow in relief and laughed at Lou's astonishment. The camera swiftly moved in for a closeup of Lou's face in time to catch him utter, "Oh, God."

Taken totally unawares and obviously nervous about just being himself, Lou kept his hands buried in his pockets, and was, for the most part, serious and contained throughout the whole show. This revealing program is one of the few times Lou Costello was captured on camera as a genuine individual, an actor, one-half of a team, a son, a father, a kindhearted man. It is such a departure from the impish characters he portrayed so often in his work. Why, even in the Costello family home movies, Lou, the consummate entertainer, loved to mug—even doing retakes of his hammy overacting.

Ralph Edwards narrated the trip down memory lane, touching on the wonderful and even tragic times in the comedian's life.

The program included a variety of guests: four additional members of the Armory Five basketball team from his youth, Lou's mother, his wife and children, and manager Eddie Sherman. The program's staff even rounded up several individuals from Costello's past who had been the recipients of his financial generosity. One fellow was a young boy from Lou's hometown, who spent eleven years unable to walk—much of it paralyzed in bed. On that day, an adult Frank Borbito briskly walked across the stage toward Costello and thanked the comedian for funding his spinal operation. "God bless you," Borbito said, choking up.

Challenging Costello on the spot, Edwards led the comedian to a regulation backstop and hoop and handed him a basketball to test his free-throw skills. Lou took the ball, hardly aiming, and impressed the audience by sinking it, first try.

Later, Lou's gray-haired mother, Helen, proudly described Lou's dream of success: "Well, Ralph," she said, "Lou always wanted to be an actor. And he used to say to me, 'Mother, someday I'm going to take you to California, to Hollywood, and I'm gonna buy you a little white house.' And you know, Ralph, he did all that."

In a chilling recollection, Lou's voice seemed to crack as he spoke of the day he and Anne lost their only son, "Butch," saying, ". . . we were doing a broadcast. It was my first broadcast after my illness."

Somberly, Eddie Sherman continued the story:

Abbott and Costello's final television appearance together. On live TV, Bud and Ralph Edwards suprised Lou, an unsuspecting subject of a This is Your Life *tribute on November 21, 1956. (Courtesy of Ralph Edwards Productions; Photo by Herb Ball)*

Lou was planning to use some funny sounds that night so little Butch could hear him at home because he knew how much Butch loved them. And his wife, Mrs. Costello, was gonna have the baby awake at night to hear the show. That afternoon at the studio, I got the tragic call from Lou's home, that the little baby had drowned in the family pool. . . . While Mrs. Costello had gone out shopping, the nurse had put little Butch in the playpen, but somehow he worked one of the slats loose and climbed out by the pool and dropped in unnoticed. Lou was terribly heartbroken . . . the whole world tumbled from under him. He said to me, "Eddie, I want to go back to the studio and do the show. I promised little Butch that he would hear me tonight and wherever God has taken him, I know he will hear me and I want to keep my promise."

When it was time for Bud Abbott to appear again, his voice preceded his entrance: "I liked Lou's clean brand of comedy and believed we could make a hit of it if we got together." Lou recognized his partner's gravelly voice and gave a quick, "Hey Abbott!"

Bud said, "Our timing was perfect for each other, but it took at least three years of struggle to get our first act organized and the material together."

When Edwards reminded Bud of the first time Lou was struck down with rheumatic fever, Abbott said, "I walked into Lou's sickroom and he had tears in his eyes and was propped up over hundreds and hundreds of letters from kiddie fans who were in the same predicament as Lou—bedridden with rheumatic fever. And the months that he was in bed, he answered those letters."

Almost as if it were prewritten, Bud delivered a little speech about his personal relationship with Lou. Patting his partner on the front of his shoulder as he frequently did, Bud looked down occasionally, but sometimes right into the eye of his partner, as he said:

I only wish I had always protected our friendship. But everyone knows that Lou and I had a rift in 1945. Like a lot of people do, we magnified a difference of opinion and we let a molehill become a mountain. Lou, I thank God we came to our senses. . . . Today our friendship seems all the more precious to me because we almost lost it—forever. For foolish pride.

Today, Bud's words seem ironic, since *This Is Your Life* took its place in history as the team's final television appearance together. Even so, according to those close to both Bud and Lou, their friendship did not wane in the face of their separation.

Lou and actress Dorothy Provine, his thirty-foot bride.

continued from page 134

Bud was almost sixty-two, and Lou was a decade younger. For them, it was time to call it quits as a team. Lou wanted to plunge into more engagements as a solo performer. The Associated Press wrote:

> In the works for Costello are a movie based on the life of the late Fiorello La Guardia, one of New York's most colorful mayors; solo nightclub appearances in Las Vegas; and the job of master of ceremonies of a new comedy quiz show on television. Lou wants no other partner.

Lou tried unsuccessfully to go it alone in comedy, as did Bud Abbott. In a 1957 interview with Marie Torre of the *Philadelphia Inquirer,* Costello said:

> I feel like a baby starting to walk. I want so much to make the right move in my career that I'm afraid to say yes to what's offered.
>
> Somewhere in this world there must be a guy [in television] who has the format for me. I've been looking hard, but I haven't had any luck. I've been accused of being too cautious, but I don't think that's the case. It's just that I can't afford a flop, not at this point.
>
> What I'm looking for is something with pathos, instead of slapstick. I don't want to be the brash, pie-in-the-face clown anymore. Unfortunately, I've been associated with slapstick, and that's the sort of thing I'm offered.

It was a strange turn. Precisely three decades after his career had begun, Lou was back where he started—in Hollywood, looking for a good dramatic

Comedian Lou Costello Dies

HOLLYWOOD, March 3 (UPI). —Roly-poly comedian Lou Costello died in Doctor's Hospital today of a heart attack complicated by a blood clot.

The famed movie-radio-TV funnyman would have been 53 on Thursday. Stricken a week ago, he was considered to be recovering. He died a few minutes after his wife had visited him.

Surviving are his wife, Anne, three daughters, Patricia, 22, Carol, 20, and Christine, 11, and a brother, Pat, all of Los Angeles.

THE FAMED rotund member of the Abbott and Costello comedy team was given last rites of the Catholic Church when he entered the hospital last Wednesday night. During the week, Bud Abbott was a frequent visitor.

Abbott wept uncontrollably on hearing the news from Costello's manager, Edward Sherman.

"What can I say?" he sobbed. "It's the worst thing that ever happened. Poor little Lou. He's dead. He's dead."

Abbott, in a state of shock, was treated by his physician.

COSTELLO, a cracked-voice clown with a heart as big as his girth, had feuded frequently with Abbott during the past five years. But they continued to be friends.

Recently he had devoted much time and money to charity, including a youth foundation.

Costello was born Louis Francis Cristello in Paterson, N. J., March 6, 1906. As a youngster in Public School No. 11 in Paterson Costello originated his famous line, "I'm a ba-a-a-ad boy."

A SAD DAY FOR HALF OF COMEDY TEAM

ALONE . . . Bud Abbott, well-known comedy team partner of the late Lou Costello, reads of the death of the man with whom he had gained fame in a 22-year partnership. Said Abbott, in his Encino, Calif., home: "My heart is broken. I've lost the best pal anyone ever had." Costello, who would have been 53 tomorrow, died in a Beverly Hills, Calif., hospital of a blood clot following a heart attack. The team made more than 40 movies, earning them an estimated $30,000,000.

role. He certainly wasn't as broke as he had been in 1927, but he wasn't flush either, and he was forced to sell his prized Longridge home. Later his tax problems forced him to sell his ranch too.

Lou's dream of doing *Man of La Mancha* or playing the late mayor Fiorello La Guardia (after whose nickname Lou had nicknamed his late son, Butch) never materialized. The proposed quiz show didn't work out either, but the Las Vegas gig at the Dunes Hotel broke all attendance records. In addition, he guested on *The Steve Allen Show* eight times, performing old routines with show regulars Louis Nye and Tom Poston. After his first appearance on the

Friends of Lou Costello, including Bud Abbott, carry the casket containing the comedian's body into St. Francis de Sales Church for funeral services on March 7, 1959. Following the casket are Mrs. Anne Costello (with hand to face) and daughters Paddy (left) and Carole (behind her mother). (Courtesy of Personality Photos, Inc.)

show, Costello told the *Oakland Tribune,* "[Bud and I] will always be friends. He even sent me a telegram before the Allen show saying I'd better be awfully good without him because he'd be watching and I'd have him to answer to."

Costello was still bothered "by this little Internal Revenue guy," he said, who kept coming after him. Lou wanted—he *had*—to work and could not retire. In 1958 he made what was announced as his dramatic debut on TV's *General Electric Theater.* The episode, titled "Blaze of Glory," received mild reviews. Then he did a serious role on *Wagon Train.* His performance was so good, show business critics pondered if inside the uncomplicated little sidekick beat the heart of a fine actor—perhaps, under other circumstances, another Mickey Rooney.

Then Lou took a role in a movie with the working title *Lou Costello's Thirty Foot Bride,* which was later changed to *The 30 Foot Bride of Candy Rock.* It was a cute little film that was shot at Columbia Studios. It was also his last work. Lou fell ill just weeks after completing his scenes. Vic Parks, who atypically did *not* work as Lou's stunt double in the film, remembered attempting to reach Lou on the phone days after the shooting.

"The first I spoke with him, he said he had never been so tired in his life," Parks said. "I told him he shouldn't have done the picture. I told him *before* he started not to do it. The next time I called, his wife tried to cover up and told me he was in Montana. I knew better. He was in bed resting after having made the movie. Anne finally told me, 'He's a sick man.'"

One of the last portraits taken of Lou Costello. (Courtesy of Joe Wallison)

On February 26, 1959, Lou's youngest daughter, Chris, witnessed her father having a heart attack at his home. On A&E's *Biography*, she recalled, "He was standing between the bedposts, clutching on . . . he was dripping wet, in a sweat. His coloring seemed to be very gray, and I remember him with his head down, turning and looking at me and trying to act very normal about it, but he said, 'Christie, go get your mother.'"

Lou was rushed to Doctors Hospital in Beverly Hills. Only a few days later, he had guests in his hospital room. Anne and the kids visited him, as did Eddie Sherman and Bobby Barber. (There are conflicting reports as to whether Bud had knowledge of Lou's illness, and whether he visited him in the hospital.)

On the morning of March 3, 1959, just three days before his fifty-third birthday, Lou seemed to be improving. Eddie Sherman told a reporter for the *Los Angeles Times:* "We were kidding around all during the morning. At about 10:30 A.M., he said he felt like eating a strawberry ice-cream soda. I got him one and he really enjoyed it. He was a real happy man. . . ."

Lou's wife had visited him that afternoon, and around 3 P.M., he suggested she better go home and prepare dinner for their daughter, Christine, Sherman recalled.

At 3:55 P.M., with only a private duty nurse present, Lou said he wanted to turn over on his side. "I think I'll be more comfortable," he told the nurse. Before she could reach him, Lou slumped back on his pillow, "and was gone," the nurse said. He had died of a second heart attack.

In the editorial pages of the March 5 morning edition of the *Los Angeles Times,* a cartoon tribute appeared. It depicted a baseball player near the mound, holding his head down, with a derby in his hand rather than a cap. A wreath lay atop the base. The caption read: Lou Was on First.

Of all the obituaries, the one Bob Thomas wrote for the Associated Press was the most moving. Later Thomas would write *Bud & Lou,* a biography that was roundly criticized by Abbott & Costello's faithful fans. But nobody could criticize what went out on the AP wire March 4 under Thomas's byline:

> As far as can be judged, Lou Costello had no enemies. Even Bud Abbott, with whom he sometimes feuded, couldn't stay mad at him for long. The reason was that Lou was completely outgoing. He was generous to a fault. . . . When he worked, he worked hard. When he played, it was the same way.
>
> Last fall, he was proud that he broke the Las Vegas attendance record at the Dunes. He was as funny as ever, but strangely restrained. Few realized that Lou was then a sick man, still playing the clown because he had to.

Actor Fred Clark and Bud Abbott at an event in 1955.

Some say that Bud was crushed when Lou decided to close the curtain on their act. Not long afterward, he was even more devastated when he learned that his partner was dead. Bud and Betty were watching television at home when the news flash interrupted programming. He cried and said, "My God, what can I say? My heart is broken. I've lost the best pal anyone ever had." News of Costello's hospitalization was kept from Bud because Lou didn't want him to worry. "Nobody thought Dad was going to die," says Chris Costello. "They weren't estranged at the time. They were talking."

When the *Los Angeles Times* reporter caught Bud Abbott on the telephone, the comic was sobbing. Attempting to gather his composure, Abbott spoke before breaking down again:

> My wife and I were here. And do you know what we were watching on TV? "Who's on First?" The picture was going into our baseball routine when our agent, Eddie Sherman, called me and told me Lou had just passed away. Tell

Bud Abbott and Barbara Stanwyck were on hand at Goldwyn Studios in Hollywood when Elvis Presley presented a check for $50,000 to the Motion Picture Relief Fund, June 1965. Presley was filming Frankie and Johnny *at the time. (Neal Peters Collection)*

me, why was I watching that picture at that particular time? I never watch it. After all, I've seen it a thousand times. And yet, there were Lou and I doing that. . . . and then Eddie calls me and tells me.

Tell me, why did I happen to be watching that picture at that time? Why?

It was not just a cute parallel concocted by Eddie Sherman for the press. The coincidence was true. Los Angeles's KTTV (Channel 11) aired *The Abbott and Costello Show* weekday afternoons at 4 P.M. Bud Abbott's daughter, Vickie, said, "I never saw my father cry in all the years . . . but that day, he did break down and cry."

During the years after his partner's death, Bud attempted to stay busy. Newspapers reported that he would next team up with Eddie Foy Jr. and go on the nightclub and television circuit, but that never materialized. He was teamed up with comic Candy Candido for a revival act that played a few nightclubs, but he decided the partnership wasn't working. He appeared with Lee Marvin in a 1961 dramatic television performance of *General Electric Theater*. The episode, titled "The Joke's on Me," had Bud playing the talent agent to Marvin, who portrayed a comic. It was a successful episode, but no more television roles came Bud's way.

In the midst of these limited pursuits and while enjoying semiretirement with Betty, Bud Abbott was suddenly struck with an IRS bill for seven years of back taxes. Once again Bud was back in the headlines, and he was forced to try to repair long-buried damages.

"His accountant had said, 'Hey, don't worry. We'll pad your expenses over the years,'" says Norman Abbott, commenting on the situation. "His accountant did, and the IRS caught this deception. They took Bud's house over. God, it was terrible. The accountant was the one to blame, but of course Bud had said yes to him.

"I remember that the IRS wanted some more money from him," continues Norman Abbott. "When Bud realized the government would take his entire earnings *plus* demand he pay taxes on them, he said, 'What! I have to pay to work? Forget it. I'll retire then.'

"He had bought a small house out in Canoga Park. He tried to make a loan on the house and couldn't do it because of the lien. Governor Brown had the lien lifted so Bud could refinance the house, then put the lien back on. The governor did that for him," says Norman.

During his tax entanglement, Bud guested on a television show hosted by Paul Coates. His appearance raised quite an uproar. "I saw the show," remembered Bud Jr. "Dad was joking. What he said was 'If all my friends would send me a dollar, I'd get out of my tax jam.' It was just a joke. Boy, the next month, he had fan mail containing dollar bills stacked up all over the house. It just floored him. Of course the press played up the story, claiming that Bud was asking for help, but he really wasn't. He was actually embarrassed."

Following the IRS affair, the lifestyle to which the Abbott family had become accustomed was toned down considerably. A June 3, 1959, United Press International story by Rick Du Brow reported Bud saying the government tax audit had left him broke.

"'All my so-called pals suddenly don't know me anymore now that the booze has stopped flowing,' the sixty-three-year-old star said in an interview at his home which was up for sale to help pay taxes. 'The government took it all but peanuts. The thing that did it was when they disallowed $500,000 of deductions. Then they put a lien on practically everything.'"

Bud attempted to maintain comfortable surroundings. The press, however, persisted in publishing stories of a destitute and ailing Bud Abbott. Chris Costello says, "Listen, that man never, ever, would have cried out for money. He wasn't that type of person. I remember him . . . back in the late sixties—I mean, this poverty story was not true. I was at his home. He had a nice pool, he had a guest house, he lived comfortably. He was very much at peace with himself. He loved recalling the good times he spent with my father. And I remember at one point he kind of drifted off and said, 'I lost my best friend when your father died.'"

Bud suffered a mild stroke in 1964 and was hospitalized, but he was still able to walk a bit and to talk, although his speech was garbled and heavy. His niece, Betty Abbott, used to drive him to the Motion Picture House and Hospital for therapy and treatments.

Bud Abbott was forced to sell his home in Encino, California, in May, 1959, due to an IRS tax audit which "left him broke," newspapers reported. Said his son, Bud Abbott Jr.: "I saw a change then, in my dad...he never recovered. Simply because of all [Bud and Lou] did for the U.S. government during WW II, and then have the government come back and use them as an example...Dad felt he was stabbed in the back." (Personality Photos, Inc.)

"I remember taking Uncle Bud to the hospital and helping him fill out the forms," she says. "He didn't have as much money as he used to because of the tax situation, so he had to apply for aid. One line had the question, How much did you make in your career? I asked Uncle Bud, and he just said, 'I don't know.' I had him take a guess.

"'Ten or twenty,' he said.

"'Ten or twenty *what?*' I asked.

"'Million.'

"That was staggering. My eyes popped. I remember writing that amount on the form. The magnitude of his loss really hit me then," says Betty Abbott.

In 1965 Abbott turned to cartoons. He provided the voice for his own character in a cartoon series bearing the team's name. The series of 156 episodes, produced by Hanna-Barbera Productions and syndicated in 1967, revived interest in Abbott & Costello for a short while, and Bud began to receive fan mail once again.

One hard-core fan contacted Abbott, saved his money to purchase plane fare, and actually met his idol. It was in December of 1968 that Bill Honor, a teenager from New York, got to shake hands with Bud Abbott.

"While we chatted, the television was on in the background, but not loud," he remembers. "Then it seemed like all of a sudden *Ride 'Em Cowboy*, one of their movies, came on, and he invited me to watch it with him. If just meeting him wasn't enough for a fan, the next few hours managed to top it.

"During the movie, I would look out of the corner of my eye and watch Bud's reactions. He never laughed out loud. I did. But he was smiling and almost studying the movie as he watched it. When Lou came on, he'd grin as though he were remembering something that happened on the set or something special about that scene," says Bill Honor.

Honor was given a tour of the house by the gray-haired Abbott, who was then able to walk with a cane. When the comedian showed him a giant scrapbook of his career, Honor flipped the pages while Bud narrated a bit. "When

Liberty

10¢

MAY 23, 1942

BUY UNITED STATES DEFENSE SAVINGS BONDS

ABBOTT, COSTELLO AND HITLER

The Private Life of PRIVATE JOE LOUIS

(Joe Wallison Collection)

Above: Bud and Lou with a swan boat used in Keep 'Em Flying—one of the many props that mysteriously disappeared from the studio and wound up at the Costello home. Right: A vintage souvenir postcard, circa 1940s. Below: "Loafing."
(Personality Photos, Inc.)

Above: Rare color portraits of Anne and Lou Costello and Betty and Bud Abbott, circa 1942. Below: Bud and Betty enjoying sunny California in the backyard of their Encino estate. (Personality Photos, Inc.)

Original, hand-tinted Abbott & Costello
lobby cards have become relics for fans.
(Joe Wallison Collection)

Top: Easter at the Costello home in 1946 with Robert Mitchum and his two sons, Elizabeth Taylor, Bud Abbott Jr., and Carol, Paddy, and pappa Lou. (Joe Wallison Collection) Bottom: "Heeeyyyy Abbott!" (Personality Photos, Inc.)

Above: A current trading card from DuoCards, Inc. Top right: Harvey Korman and Buddy Hackett are Bud and Lou in this controversial TV movie (1978). Bottom right: No one quite knows what Bud and Lou were doing in gladiator get-up, circa 1950s. (Photofest)

The Abbott & Costello comic books featured unique artistic styles. Clockwise from top: October 1948, April 1953, May 1955, May 1968. (Joe Wallison Collection)

Left: When The Boys were animated by Hanna-Barbera in 1966, Bud Abbott briefly came out of retirement to provide the voice of his own character. (Courtesy of Jomar Productions and Hanna-Barbera Productions) Top right: Bud Abbott at home in 1971. (Photo by Bill Honor) Bottom right: After his IRS ordeal, Bud revealed a bitter side in 1969. (Photo by Paul Rubin)

he referred to Lou," Honor says, "it was as his 'Little Buddy.' I could tell he missed him.

"I was about to leave when Bud said, 'Go into the kitchen and pull out the right drawer. There is something I want you to have.' I went to the left drawer. He said, 'Right.' I was so nervous and stumbling, I felt as if we were doing a routine. The gift was a 78 RPM record of 'Who's on First?' in a brown sleeve, which he autographed for me. Later I had it framed," says Honor.

In the early 1970s, Abbott fell, broke his hip, and was confined to a wheelchair. Shortly after, he fell again and broke his left leg, and to complicate things further, suffered a series of strokes. Later, Bud was diagnosed with inoperable prostate cancer.

In October 1973, *The National Enquirer* ran a story (naturally accompanied by some garish photographs and startling head-lines) detailing the seriousness of Abbott's condition. "Doctors say Bud has three to six months to live, but only God can tell," said Bud's son-in-law, Don Wheeler. "His condition changes from day to day. Sometimes he seems okay and, in the next moment, he is incoherent and oblivious to those around him."

To keep him comfortable in his final days, Bud was confined to a hospital bed, which the family had moved into the area that was once their dining room. Betty Abbott sat with Bud during the day, holding his hand and comforting him. During the night, a male nurse sat at his bedside to make sure his needs were attended and that he would not die alone. On April 24, 1974, Bud Abbott died, with relatives around him. He and Betty had just celebrated their fifty-fifth wedding anniversary.

Bud's daughter, Vickie Abbott Wheeler, remembers the memorial service for her father. She says that although friends seemed to have forgotten Bud when he was in his tax jam, many people attended the funeral. "I looked up, and the church was com-pletely packed with people," she says. "I looked around, and a lot of people said how much love they had for my father. It was amazing. I was really very surprised at how many people did come."

When Bud Abbott died, he closed the chapter on the last of the era's great movie comedy teams.

Bud Abbott, 78, Comic Pal of Costello, Dies

Los Angeles, Aprl 24 (AP) — Bud Abbott, 78, who made and lost millions as straight man to

**Abbott
Bud**

Lou Costello in their routines for movies, radio and television shows, died of cancer today at his Woodland Hills home.

The slender, acebric Abbott had done little performing since the death of his rotund partner 15 years ago. In recent years he had suffered a series of strokes, and he lived with his wife, Betty, in a modest home that contrasted with the high living he enjoyed in his heyday.

Partners for 32 years, Abbott and Costello scored a sensation in their first movie, "Buck Privates," in 1941. For a decade they remained among the top 10 money-making film stars, earning a million dollars a year.

Gambled Heavily

"They were making big money, and they thought it would never stop," their long-time manager, Eddie Sherman, remarked after Abbott's death.

The two comedians also gambled heavily, and they were struck with tax bills at a time when their careers were waning. Abbott was forced to sell his $250,000 house and the rest of his property.

Born William Abbott on Oct. 2, 1895, in Atlantic City, N.J., Abbott grew up around circuses; his father was an advance man, his mother a bareback rider. Abbott worked in vaudeville and burlesque before teaming with Costello in a Brooklyn theater.

The Abbott & Candido Story
by Joe Wallison

For over two years Bud waited for his little pal Lou to rejoin him, but it never happened. Not long after the death of his ex-partner, Bud Abbott, the greatest straight man in the business, was in need of a new comic. He was anxious to perform again in front of live audiences, and in June 1959 he announced he would team with Eddie Foy, Jr., but that pairing went nowhere. Not only did Bud need the money, but he simply couldn't get show business out of his blood.

Bud had caught the act of a popular nightclub and radio comedian named Candy Candido, who was appearing at Ben Blue's club in Santa Monica, California. Bud and manager Eddie Sherman stayed after Candido's show one evening to propose a new teaming: Abbott and Candido.

"They tried Mickey Rooney with Bud," says 83-year-old Candido. "But it didn't work out. 'Cause nobody's gonna change Bud Abbott and nobody's gonna change Mickey Rooney."

Bud and Eddie Sherman's proposal was to first go on the road, possibly do some movies and TV, and Candido would stick to Abbott and Costello's tried-and-true Burlesque routines. "As for the money, I insisted on fifty-fifty," Candido recalls, "and Bud agreed without hesitation."

John Baptist Candido, nicknamed "Candy" by his mother, grew up in New Orleans and aspired to be a musician. When he was thirteen years old, he organized a neighborhood band called "Candy's Jumping Jacks" which included a few other adolescents—one by the name of Louis Prima. At nineteen, he married his childhood sweetheart, Anita Bivona, and eventually teamed with a guitar player named Coco. Candy and Coco played the various clubs in the French Quarter.

Years later, his first big break came when he and Coco became part of a newly formed trio called Gene Austin, Candy and Coco. (Austin, an immensely popular singer, had hits which included "My Blue Heaven," and "Melancholy Baby".) This led to nightclub and radio engagements where Candy was eventually spotted by Jimmy Durante and his long association with the legendary "Schnozzola" began.

Ironically, through his work on Durante's radio show in the 1940s, Candido landed an appearance on Bud and Lou's radio program. Candido had an unique talent for speaking and singing an incredible range—from ear-piercing falsetto to a gravelly, deep basso profundo. On Bud and Lou's radio show, he portrayed a vocal coach attempting to teach Costello to sing. Candido recalls that he also sang one of his bizarre, signature tunes, "One Meatball."

Another claim to fame for Candido has been his career in the voice-over field, which included everything from Disney characters to matching wits with the master, Mel Blanc, in animated beer commercials. (For Disney, he supplied vocals in many films, *Peter Pan, Sleeping Beauty,* and *The Great Mouse Detective,* among them).

A Little Taste of Candy: The short and bittersweet teaming of Bud Abbott and Candy Candido ended after just a few engagements. (Courtesy of Joe Wallison)

In February 1960, less than one year after Lou Costello's death, word hit the trade papers that Bud Abbott had officially signed with a new partner. Columnist Louella Parsons noted, "Candy [Candido] reminded him of his late partner in both appearance and manner...The comedians expect to be active in a few weeks and plan to make both motion pictures and TV."

Weeks turned into months, recalled Candido. "For six months, I drove from my house in Burbank to Bud's home in Woodland Hills to learn the Abbott and Costello routines," he says. "Bud had a smaller house in the back where we rehearsed. He had printed scripts and we watched old Abbott and Costello films. It was to make sure I knew every line and every reaction—of his too. Bud was a great perfectionist."

Abbott refused to perform until their timing was perfect. The pair practiced every look, every turn, every gag. As for "Who's On First?," Candido said, "That was the one I really had to work on." Although Candido refused to repeat any of Lou's famous catchphrases, he inserted his own popular trademark: "I'm Feelin' Mighty Low."

All the while, Bud was being hounded by the I.R.S. "They were confiscating everything," Candido says. He vividly recalls the day Bud slipped him thousands of dollars in cash and one of Betty Abbott's favorite fur coats to hold for him at his house. "They really screwed him."

Candy's own agent booked a series of personal appearances while Bud's representative, Eddie Sherman, was supposedly searching for film and tele-vision projects for the new team. In the dead of winter, in upstate New York, the new team premiered their act.

"It was thirty-one degrees outside," Candido says, "and when we got there, it was snowing like hell. We opened at the Green River Inn, a large nightclub in Syracuse." Because of horrible weather conditions, Candy says, the house was only one-quarter full. Despite the disappointing turnout, Abbott and Candido gave it everything they had and the audience loved it.

After a Christmas break, they started the new year off in Pittsburgh at the famed Holiday House—where two years earlier, The Three Stooges made a triumphant comeback and broke attendance records. *Variety* declared Abbott and Candido a hit:

There's good news from Pittsburgh. Bud Abbott is back with a new partner, Candy Candido, and it's as close as it could possibly be without the late Lou Costello. The same routines that made the old team famous are used. Candido doing a letter-perfect impression of Costello and retaining his own identity by doing a spot before this classic "Who's On First?" This is no fare for the modern hip nitery as the boys play it for the clean bellylaugh. They use the burlesque method of presenting three different scenes during the course of the show. Each scene is a block-buster with the "Lemond Drop" bit taking the longest, around 18 minutes.

When caught, the youngsters filled the room with their laughter at what was new to them and the adults were roaring at the familiar material so perfectly delivered.

Candido fondly recalls their act. "We did one show a day," he says, "that's all [Bud] would do. We did a one-hour show with me doing twenty minutes by myself.

Bud's way of exiting the stage and allowing Candido some solo time, was via the Mustard Routine. Bud would interrupt: "Ah, Candy, I want you to do some of the songs you did for Disney for the kids in the audience. In the meantime, I'll got out and get a hotdog. Do you want one? "'

"Yeah," Candy said, "without mustard."

From there, they went full blast into the mustard routine. Slaps and all. "I'd never feel Bud's slap," Candy says. "He had a knack of rappin' you and you'd never feel it. He'd cup his hand somehow."

Following each show, Bud insisted on unwinding. There were occasions when he and Candy ventured out into the town to catch other acts. Usually, however, Bud simply preferred the solitude of his hotel room, where he could relax in his robe, smoke cigarettes, and enjoy his scotch.

"He never drank while working," Candy added. "It was always after the show. He would drink a whole fifth of White Horse scotch, but I've never seen him drunk."

Next, they hit Detroit, where they performed at a private party for executives of the Cadillac car company. ("It was all men," Candy remembered. "We killed 'em. Especially me with the baby voice and the low voice.") Candy's agent booked The Boys into a series of state fair appearances. The biggest audience they played to—and their most lucrative gig—was the 1961 Canadian National Exposition in Winnipeg.

Abbott and Candido played the farm country of middle America: a fair in Monticello, Iowa. Unfortunately, the show was cut short. "Bud swallowed a bug," Candy says. "It was during the 'Change for a Ten' routine and a bug flew right into his mouth and he swallowed it. He started choking and coughing and I said, 'Gee, you're stupid. I told you not to eat meat on Friday!' And that broke up the audience."

Just as Abbott and Candido were flying high, the act took a nosedive while aboard a flight to Chicago. With Bud sitting in the window seat, and Candy next to him, disaster struck.

"While we're in the air," Candy explains, "Bud says to me, 'Hit me in the stomach! Hit me in the stomach *now!*' I said, 'You're crazy, I won't hit you.'" Candido was confused and argued with Bud for about five minutes. "I didn't have the nerve to hit him," Candy says, "'cause I'm a rugged little guy. Meantime, the captain is walking down the aisle, and I said, 'Captain, he wants me to hit him in the stomach. *You* hit him in the stomach. I don't know what's wrong. So the captain reached over and punched him. Ooooh, I could feel it from where I was sitting."

Unbeknownst to Candy, Bud was suffering an epileptic seizure, or at least in fear of one taking over. "So after that, the stewardess came over and poured him some kind of a little drink or something, and then we got into Chicago."

Then Bud dropped a bombshell. "He said, 'Candy, I've got to go home.'

Candy Candido holding the original edition of this book in 1997. (Photo by Steve Cox)

We hopped on the next flight back to Los Angeles," Candy says. "We had to cancel out the remainder of our tour. I was very worried about Bud. I had never seen anyone have an attack of epilepsy before. It's a seizure where you're about to swallow your tongue and choke.

"Bud was scared," Candido says. "The doctors scared him. The doctors told him 'No more.'" Bud Abbott would never perform in public again. Candy kept in touch Bud in the ensuing years, and brought old show business friends around to keep him company. Candy remembers: "There he sat, in the chair, wearing the robe, watching TV, with a diamond ring on his finger, smoking a cigarette with the holder, and a drink in his hand—now he's drinking during the day."

Candido resumed his career as a single, becoming an official Good Will Ambassador for countless state fairs around the country. "I happened to be working in Saratoga, New York, when I got the word Bud died," he recalled, "and I couldn't go to the funeral."

The saga of Abbott and Candido was short lived. As it turned out, the team had rehearsed longer than they actually performed. "In the time we were together, the audiences couldn't get enough," Candido says. "I enjoyed working with him. Hell, I practically slept with Bud the three months we were on the road. I never saw him angry. He had a good sense of humor. Bud didn't know what to think of me.

He liked me, though," Candido says. "In fact, he gave me a diamond-studded stick pin, in the shape of first base. It represented 'Who's On First?' I still have it to this day.

"What a beautiful man," Candy added.

CHAPTER 8

Dad and Bud: Chris Costello's Turn at Bat

Christine Costello is still fuming about the book Bob Thomas wrote about her father and Bud Abbott. It's been twenty years since *Bud & Lou* appeared in bookstores nationwide and since the *Wednesday Night at the Movies* television program that was based on the book aired. If time has softened her rage, it isn't apparent.

"It's like somebody walking into your home and pushing you aside and taking things and rearranging them the way they want. There's a real hurt about it," she says.

Chris Costello, Lou and Anne Costello's younger daughter, lives with two outrageously undisciplined cats across the Hollywood Hills from the home she grew up in on Longridge Avenue in Sherman Oaks. But her memories of Longridge are as sharp as yesterday, and she doesn't take kindly to what she sees as Thomas's distortion of her father's life. In 1977 she decided to try to set the record straight and wrote the biography *Lou's on First*.

In a sense, the book Thomas wrote seems to characterize for her all that's wrong with Tinsel Town and what it did to the two burlesque craftsmen it hired to make the nation laugh.

"When somebody is not here to defend himself, that gets me riled," she says. "I would defend anybody, not just my father. [In Hollywood] there's no respect for anyone. They love and worship and give awards to these people when they're alive, but, man, the minute they're put in the ground, it's fair-game time.

"I think Hollywood's very shallow. I really have very little respect for the industry. In fact, after the Thomas book came out, I left the industry as a singer and actress. It was my reality. Dad shielded us from that. In this town, it's 'honey, baby, sweetheart,' until the success starts to wane, and then where are the friends? It's the same with Bud Abbott, God bless 'im. When the man really needed his friends, where were they?

"When I did my book, I was getting to know my parents for the first time as an adult," says Chris. "My father was very important to me as a kid because he was very much The Father. I mean, he was an at-home guy when he wasn't working. He didn't live that total Hollywood life. He shielded us from it to a certain extent. Also, I had a mother who was born and raised in Scotland, who really kept the balance. It was like, you didn't have maids cleaning up your bedroom; you were responsible for your own bedroom. You got an allowance. My sister Carole said she was making hospital corners on her bed at the age of ten.

Three-year-old Christine visits papa Lou on the set of Abbott and Costello in the Foreign Legion, *1950.*

"People are human beings first," she continues. "When people say, 'Did Bud and Lou fight?' I say, 'Get real!' They were together twenty-three years, for God's sake. I mean, what two people are not going to fight? But, as my sister would tell you, you can't be together that long and not also be friends.

"Let me tell you something. You can take a person like Bud Abbott or Lou Costello . . . he can walk outside and trip going down the sidewalk, and that's not news. But if the journalists decide, Why don't we say he was walking on the roof and then tripped and fell? That's news. Sensationalism's why the tabloids sell," Chris Costello says.

Abbott & Costello's longtime manager, Eddie Sherman, Chris says, was the voice in Bob Thomas's ear, and not a particularly kind voice at that. She thinks Sherman was less than kind in his reaction to her father's decision to break up his lucrative partnership with Bud Abbott.

"Eddie Sherman, in my opinion, had a tremendous amount of animosity, a tremendous amount of anger, not for Bud Abbott but for my dad, which is why my dad was targeted in the book and in the movie," she says. "That's because it was my dad who was the voice of Abbott & Costello. He was the

Appearing at the world premiere of Jack and the Beanstalk *at the Fabian Theater in Costello's hometown of Paterson, New Jersey, April 5, 1952. (Courtesy of* North Jersey Herald and News)

one who said, 'Come on, Bud, let's do this. Let's go for that.' I'm not saying Bud didn't have a say, but my dad was just more gregarious. He knew what he wanted. When Abbott & Costello split up, Eddie Sherman's career went down the tubes. His only claim to fame, up to that point, was Abbott & Costello. When that era was over, he went after my dad."

Bob Thomas did once tell an interviewer that Sherman came to him with the idea for the book and provided about ten taped hours of memories. But the ill will between the Costello family and Sherman ran deep much earlier.

"Take a look at the day my father died," says Chris Costello. "My mother had specifically asked Sherman not to say a word to the press, and he assured her he wouldn't."

Despite his promise to Anne, Chris contends, Sherman immediately got busy calling the press with the news.

"As a result, my sister Carole, who was going over Coldwater Canyon to the hospital to see Dad, heard about his death on the car radio. She pulled the car off to the side of the road, and she started crying. She remembers crying and the mascara running down her face. She said she always remembered Daddy not wanting us to appear messy. So she immediately started cleaning up her face," says Chris.

Lou's daughter Carole made a cameo appearance in the film Abbott and Costello Meet the Keystone Kops, *1954. Named Carole Lou, after her dad, she also appeared briefly in* Abbott and Costello Meet the Mummy, *and* The 30 Foot Bride of Candy Rock. *Carole died suddenly of a stroke on March 30, 1987, at age 47.*

"She continued to the hospital," Chris goes on. "When she walked up to his floor, the nurses and doctors were standing around, and she tried to ask somebody if it was true that her father had died. Eddie Sherman was sitting there on the edge of the bed with the sheet pulled over Lou's head, talking to the press on the phone. And she said, 'Eddie, not now.' And he waved her away. And she said, 'Eddie, please, not now.' He waved her away again. Now, Carole is a very tall lady, and Eddie is very tiny. And she walked over to him, and she literally picked him up by the lapels and threw him across the room, screaming, 'Not now!'

"As a result of what Eddie Sherman did that day, Bud Abbott heard about Dad's death through a bulletin during a rerun of *The Abbott and Costello Show* on television. My grandmother heard the news of her son's death during the same newsbreak," says Chris Costello.

Lou's mother, Helen, was a frequent visitor to the set. She was his biggest fan. (Personality Photos, Inc.)

"My Aunt Marie said that Grandma was standing in the living room wringing her hands. She looked at Marie and said, 'You're not going to tell me that my boy is gone.'

"What he did literally disintegrated any kind of respect I had for Eddie Sherman," Chris continues. "Even when I was fourteen, after both my parents were dead, I can remember being at my aunt's house and finding his name in a phone book, and I called to see if I could get a photograph of Dad. I remember him saying to me on the phone, 'What's in it for me?'"

The Eddie Sherman Chris Costello remembers was "a typical Hollywood manager, with the cigar; a little guy, a shrimp. He was just phony. The *Bud and Lou* movie made Eddie Sherman look like Mary Poppins. It was really *The Eddie Sherman Story*. He *wasn't* in the room when my father died, either."

She adds, "I couldn't believe that this man, who was at our home following the funeral, who sat there and put on the best performance of his whole life, with the tears and the wailing and the 'I lost my best friend' and 'Good night, sweet prince,' would participate in Thomas's book when he had spent so much time at my father's bar drinking his liquor and eating his food.

"And what he did to Bud Abbott when he died. He came into Abbott's home and said to Betty Abbott, 'Betty, I would like to have a small memento of Bud.' Small memento! Those two men were *very* good to Eddie

Life with Fodder: Here, Lou's kids Carole Lou, 11, and Paddy, 13, sit on the stable door and watch their dad feed one of his yearlings, "Little Bazooka."

Sherman. So, poor Betty Abbott, she gives him a watch or something," says Chris.

Chris Costello doesn't want people to feel sorry for Bud and Lou because of their celebrated tangle with the Internal Revenue Service. As for that United Press International photograph of Bud looking forlorn next to the For Sale sign on the lawn of the Encino home he loved so much, his pockets turned inside out for the photographer, well . . .

"That's where I think Bud Abbott has gotten the bad end of the stick," she says. "Sure, these two men did not have the vast riches they could have had if they had had the proper business managers to guide them. But at the same time, these men did not die broke.

"Now one of the things that appalled me when they did the *Bud and Lou* movie was that they portrayed this auction happening on our lawn. That never happened.

"Abbott & Costello were the first major stars of their era to ever receive residuals on their films," says Chris. "Talk to any major figure today who was working in the thirties and forties, and ask how many of that era's stars are getting residuals checks on their films. Not many."

Chris is talking about what has come to be known as the Eleven Picture Participation Contract. Bud and Lou may have been forced to give up a lot to satisfy the IRS, but the Costello and Abbott families are still getting checks each time one of those eleven pictures is shown. In addition, Chris says, her father owned the rights to all fifty-two episodes of *The Abbott and Costello Show.* "It was his company, TCA, Television Corporation of America, which we still have today, that put the deal together, so we're still distributing," she says.

"And don't forget," Chris adds, "Bud and Lou copyrighted 'Who's on First?' in the early 1940s. So when people say my dad and Bud both died destitute, the answer is no, but they didn't have the type of money they could have had had they been as wise as, let's say, Bob Hope, who saw the value of real estate."

At one point The Boys turned down an offer that would have made them owners of a now-expensive chunk of Sepulveda Boulevard in Los Angeles. "Eddie told them it was a rotten deal, not to take it," Chris says behind a hoarse laugh.

The image of Bud Abbott laid low by the tax man is no more accurate, she says, than the image *Bud & Lou* left of Bud harangued by her father. "Bud looked like the whipping post to my father," she says. "You present a

Steve Allen once remarked, "Although it has rarely been noted in critiques of his work, Lou had a very winning smile, quite unlike the plastic show-biz smiles that are more common." The grin is evident in this behind-the-scenes shot taken during filming of the steambath scene for Abbott and Costello Meet the Killer, Boris Karloff.

book like that to the public, and they're gullible enough to start to believe it."

She thinks the book did equal disservice to Bobby Barber, Lou's hired companion and prankster.

"The press has always been very sympathetic, saying, How could Lou Costello do this to him?" she says. Barber was apparently hired solely for his willingness to be the butt of Lou's practical jokes. "Bobby loved it. He absolutely thrived on it. He could not wait to get out on the set with my father. He didn't feel he was being a stooge. My father got pies in the face, too. It was just part of their keeping the momentum up," says Chris Costello.

Lou acts as a comic chauffeur for Eddie Sherman and his new bride, Lillyn, at their wedding in September 1945. (Courtesy of Robert Sherman)

"People would also say my father had temper tantrums, he was unprofessional on the set, he was a tyrant, he was this or that," she continues. "You talk to anybody who worked on an Abbott & Costello film and they will tell you that it was probably one of the happiest times of their working life. For instance, in the Bob Thomas book they talk about pie-throwing, about how unprofessional it was for two grown men to hold up production by throwing pies. But those two men knew comedy. You can't keep that level up for that amount of time, with a director saying, 'Cut, let's reset up, cut, let's reset up,' and have them keep up the energy."

Chris says her father and Bud Abbott invented "wrap parties" during their years at Universal. Even after they had been ravaged by the IRS, they endeavored to keep the crew happy. Lou would routinely climb the scaffold on the set to make certain "each electrician, each gaffer, each grip man had a hundred dollars," says Chris.

Lou Costello handing out one-hundred-dollar bills is an image more in tune with the father she remembers than are some of the more unkind things said about him since his death. No one, however, says that Lou Costello didn't love children or that children didn't love him. When Chris turns to those thoughts, her voice softens, her eyes get big. It must have been just as good to be his child as millions of children in the 1940s were imagining it to be.

"One time Dad picked me up at school, and I remember that it was one of the first times I realized the kind of effect he had on other people," she says. "I walked out of the school yard, and there were just scores of kids around his white car. They were laughing and going crazy and he was doing his shtick for them. He was in his element. He loved it."

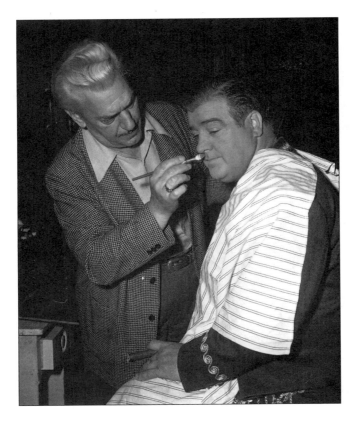

Lou getting his makeup applied by Russell Drake on the set of Mexican Hayride. *(Personality Photos, Inc.)*

Being Lou Costello's daughter wasn't always a blessing. Chris once made a new friend at school, and, like most kids, she wanted her new friend to meet her father. Her new friend, however, saw *the* Lou Costello sitting in an easy chair, with a cigar stuck in his mouth and the newspaper in his lap. And she was terrified.

"I was saying, 'I want you to meet my dad,' and she said no and started backing up. Well, Dad saw what was happening, took off his glasses, and started walking toward her. I thought she was going to faint," says Chris.

"She was pressed up against the wall. As Dad walked toward her, he did one of the best pratfalls I've ever seen. He started doing his shtick for her, and before long she was laughing hysterically and sliding down the wall," says Chris.

On Halloween, Lou liked to dress Chris up as himself, down to one uncomfortably fine detail.

"He would even put a cigar in my mouth," she says. A bubble-gum cigar? Well, no. A stage cigar? No. One of his Carona Caronas then, but surely unlit? Wrong again. "I hated it. His lit cigar burned my tongue," she says. "Every time we'd go to a relative's house and ring the bell, he'd shove that cigar back in my mouth." Finally she got tired of the joke. "I told him I didn't want to do Lou Costello anymore," she says.

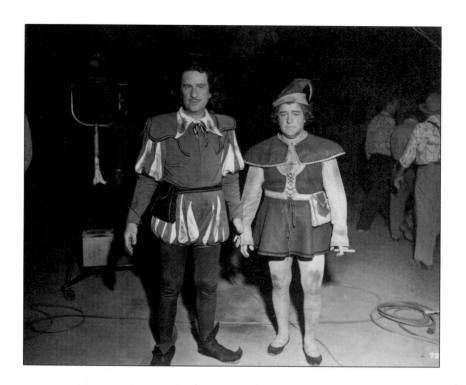

Wardrobe stills on the set of
Jack and the Beanstalk.
(Courtesy of Abe Haberman)

Playing chess on the set of Mexican Hayride *with Fritz Feld giving some pointers. Chess was one of the more subtle activities Bud and Lou participated in during their breaks.*

"I remember getting mad at him once as a kid and saying to him, 'You're not funny, you know. You may think you're funny, but you're not. I don't laugh at your jokes. You're not funny.'"

The world may remember Lou Costello as a doughy comic, perpetually off balance, both physically and mentally, as if the world beneath his feet were the deck of a ship in heavy seas. But Chris Costello remembers her father differently. She remembers the athlete in him, muscular and hard. "He shot all the baskets in *Here Come the Co-eds,"* Chris says.

It wasn't, of course, jump shots that got Lou Costello and Bud Abbott to the top rung in Hollywood in the early 1940s. They paid their dues in burlesque.

"All of the great comedy teams originated either in vaudeville, burlesque, or the British musical theatrical circuit, which is what Stan Laurel came out of," Chris explains. "That was their training ground. The Bob Hopes came out of burlesque. The George Burnses came out of burlesque.

"If you think back, each decade presented a team to boost the morale of the public," she continues. "World War I saw Wheeler & Woolsey. The depression years, Laurel & Hardy. World War II, Abbott & Costello. It's unfair to really compare any of these teams with one another because each one was unique in its style. Laurel & Hardy were brought together by Hal Roach to do films. Abbott & Costello teamed up on the burlesque stage. Laurel & Hardy worked primarily from a script format; Abbott & Costello worked from routines. You had a similarity in terms of Stan Laurel being the underdog, as was Lou Costello's character, but each comedian's approach to comedy was totally different and totally unique," says Chris.

"There was a great camaraderie between Stan Laurel and my father. They were the best of friends. Laurel's daughter, Lois, told me that she recalls many evenings of my father sitting at the dinner table, he and Stan, across from each other—they were great fans of each other—just in constant shtick. She says her cook would be laughing so hysterically he could hardly get a meal out.

"People assume Hollywood back then was like it is today, where if you use somebody's line you end up in a courtroom," says Chris. "Back then, the camaraderie was unique. I mean, how many people today would you find doing a film and, if there was a comic down on his luck, would you find them employing that comic? Back when Dad and Bud were working, they were always giving comics who were down on their luck a chance to work."

Bud Abbott wasn't as ambitious about his Hollywood career as Lou was. "I think Bud was very comfortable in burlesque," Chris says. "I think he was also very comfortable as Abbott & Costello, the team, but my father was the driving force. Dad was the type of person who wanted to become a dramatic actor, and he just happened to fall into comedy as the Dutch comic, but without using the Dutch accent or the putty nose. I think my dad was never satisfied with the level of success he achieved. He wanted to see if he could go much higher.

Chris Costello's coffee mug.

Host Bert Convy talks with guests Bud Abbott Jr. and Chris Costello on the CBS-TV gameshow 3rd Degree! *in January, 1990. Celebrity panelists had to guess the pair's relationship. (Photo by Bob Bastanchury)*

"He wanted to do Sancho Panza in *Man of La Mancha,*" she says. "He was scheduled to play Fiorello La Guardia on Broadway when he died. He did an episode of *Wagon Train.* After he split up with Bud, he did his first dramatic role, and he was brilliant. I think he knew, instinctively, that the era of Abbott & Costello was coming to an end, because of the 1950s and televisions in every home, because Universal had switched regimes and they now had the MGM group coming in. They were elevating Universal from a B-studio to one like MGM. They didn't want the Ma and Pa Kettles anymore; they didn't want Francis, the Talking Mule; and they certainly didn't want Abbott & Costello. They wanted more meat to their films. I think Dad saw what was happening. It was time to move on.

"No, I don't think Bud and my father were prepared for what happened to them when they came to Hollywood. But that was another era. People are more watchful of their pocketbooks now than they were then. Back then an actor was an actor; you simply *acted.* A business manager was a business manager. My dad, I think, had a childlike trust in people. He trusted his and Bud's business manager. The business manager *knew* that Dad didn't know what was going on," says Chris.

"They were like two kids in a candy store," she continues. "In burlesque, Dad and Bud were making a living that was comfortable, but nothing compared with what they would wind up making. And sure, for my dad it was

Abbotts and Costellos: (left to right) Chris Costello, Vickie Abbott Wheeler, Bud Abbott, Jr. (standing), and Paddy Costello Humphreys in 1990. (Courtesy of Abbott and Costello Enterprises)

like the world was a birthday party and he wanted everybody to be a part of it. Although he made many mistakes in terms of managing his money, and in trusting the wrong people, on the other hand, he was very giving.

"Take the youth center in East L.A. My dad loved the youth center. He used to send down truckloads of toys at Christmas," says Chris. "My dad and Bud made a tour of the country to raise money for that youth center."

The Abbott and the Costello children have worked hard to see that their fathers are not forgotten.

"We're feeling really good now because we're starting to get Abbott & Costello back into the spotlight," says Chris Costello. "I think for years they had been grossly ignored and overlooked by their industry. And still are, to a degree. Look at their home studio, Universal, where Abbott & Costello kept the gates open when the studio was threatened with bankruptcy. Today we finally got Abbott & Costello into the studio's souvenir stores.

"Recently they buried a time capsule over at Universal. They had Marilyn Monroe, Elvis Presley, Laurel & Hardy, and even Rin Tin Tin. Now that's a real slap in the face to Abbott & Costello," she says. "Laurel & Hardy never even filmed at Universal!"

Lou's on First helped Chris Costello to revive the memory of the father she knew for only eleven years. Writing the book brought back the man she "absolutely idolized," with whom she would eat Swiss cheese and crackers even though she hated Swiss cheese.

"As long as there's breath in me," she says, "I'll make sure the man's given a fair shake."

CHAPTER 9

Batting a Thousand

In their heyday, Abbott & Costello enjoyed more success than did most other actors and comedians of the early 1940s. Polls during that era showed the team ranking in the top ten (number one in 1942) as box-office attractions, beating such competition as Mickey Rooney and Clark Gable. Critic Leonard Maltin noted this about the team in his book *Movie Comedy Teams:*

> They lack the artistry of Laurel & Hardy; they never captured the insanity of the Marx Brothers; they did not sing or dance like the Ritz Brothers. Why, then, were Abbott & Costello so popular during the 1940s and early 1950s? This question plagues film historians today, who can find no earthly reason for the team's existence. The answer is simple: They were very, very funny.

Norman Abbott believes the team has not yet had its renaissance. "No one becomes appreciated until years later," he says.

Abbott & Costello are still often dismissed as average comedians. Even Universal Studios—the monstrous entity that was rescued from financial ruin by Abbott & Costello in the 1940s—seems to have forgotten the team.

Chris Costello recently told Abbott & Costello fans about a tour she took of Universal Studios' famous back lot. "The tour guide failed to mention Bud and Lou when she gave a brief rundown of some of the greats who came out of the studio," she said. "Posing as a tourist, I asked the guide why Abbott & Costello were not mentioned, since they saved the studio from bankruptcy. The answer from the young tour guide was, 'Universal leaves it up to each individual tour guide as to whom he or she wishes to mention. Personally, I don't feel Abbott & Costello are recognizable to the mass public."

Already, interest is growing. Universal Studios has released all of the team's motion pictures on videocassette, on their MCA Home Video label.

Metacom, Inc., a distributor of vintage radio shows on cassette, has released a complete line of Abbott & Costello programs in response to the team's currently rising popularity. Other products will be hitting the market soon: commemorative plates, posters, statues, T-shirts, baseball caps, and more.

"I think a period of time has to go by before people can step back and look objectively and see what's going on," says Paddy Costello of the imminent revival. "My son says 'Who's on First?' is the Mona Lisa of comedy, and boy, is it! That's Abbott & Costello's link to immortality, as far as I'm concerned. I was standing in line at the tennis court waiting for tennis lessons once, and the instructor yelled, 'OK, who's on first?' and I thought, *Do you really want to know?* I can't tell you the number of times that's happened to me. It's everywhere."

Commercial Appeal: From Serial to Cereal

The promotional coup of the 1980s was old stars, vintage TV shows, and classic motion pictures reworked into ads for new products. Old-timers such as W. C. Fields, the Three Stooges, Harold Lloyd, Roscoe "Fatty" Arbuckle, Charlie Chaplin, and many others were revived in TV commercials and national ad campaigns.

For Abbott & Costello, the list of possibilities was to be endless. An AT&T print ad proclaimed, "Call Your Mummy," with a photograph of Bud and

Bud Abbott Jr. and Vickie Abbott Wheeler holding up a T-shirt featuring their father in 1990. (Photo by Steve Cox)

Lou being nabbed by a mummy (from the film *Abbott and Costello Meet the Mummy)* beside it.

How about the Gillette *foamy* "for sensitive skin" TV spots that featured a clip of Bud slapping Lou? "No one knows how your skin got sensitive," the ad proclaimed, while Bud whacked Lou's face.

Another favorite of the 1980s was Hershey's *Whatchamacallit* chocolate bar and the *Go Ahead* candy bar campaigns, which used Bud and Lou look-alikes. Even Tropicana filmed a spot with Abbott & Costello impressionists promoting its orange juice. Bud and Lou also touted *Slice* soda via a clip from their television series.

Perhaps the best of the bunch used actors Ron Masak and Stan Lachow to promote Ralston Purina's *Bran News* cereal.

What the viewer witnesses in this TV ad is a startling, detailed impersonation of Bud and Lou standing in front of a curtain, duplicating the opening of TV's *The Abbott and Costello Show* in the 1950s. Masak's and Lachow's costumes and the set and props are perfect, as if they all were scrounged from the old back lot.

"I've always looked like Lou, even when I was skinny," says Ron Masak, star of the spot. "When I was a kid, I would unconsciously do Lou's faces and then sometimes purposely do a Costello 'look.'"

continued on page 174

Facts from Left Field
Did You Know . . . ?

- Technically, Abbott and Costello's first film appearance together was *not* in the feature *One Night in the Tropics*. Bud and Lou can be spotted attending the premiere of the film *The Boys from Syracuse,* captured in a Universal pictures newsreel on July 11, 1940, in Syracuse, New York.

- Bud Abbott, an avid gun collector, owned one of Adolf Hitler's shotguns and Tom Mix's pearl-handled six-shooters in his collection of firearms.

- Lou Costello was ten years younger than his partner, Bud Abbott.

- Bud Abbott wore a front-piece toupee in most of The Boys' earlier films and Lou Costello blackened his scalp to create the appearance of thicker hair. "Mom would color his head with a toothbrush," Paddy Costello says, laughing. "And then there would always be black marks all over Dad's pillow."

- For their individual home-theater collections, Bud and Lou stored 16 mm prints of every motion picture and TV show they made.

- Lou Costello's famous high-pitched squeal, "I'm a Baaaaaad Boy!" came from a grade school teacher, Mrs. Bessie Whitehead, who punished little Lou by making him write the phrase repeatedly on the blackboard. Little did she suspect that years later he would turn it into what *Liberty*

magazine called, "a veritable laugh-cry of the nation that would be easily identified by millions as Lou's signature."

- Bud Abbott owned a trick gold-colored telephone that blasted water out of the mouthpiece. "He'd have our butler ring it, and when a guest was called to

The first series of Abbott & Costello comic books was published in February 1948 by St. John Publishing. They ran until 1956, producing forty issues including one in 3-D. The cover artwork was executed by a variety of talented artists, including Mort Drucker. After the animated Hanna-Barbera cartoons aired in 1967, Charlton Comics published a series of twenty-two issues based on the cartoon characters. These comics ran until 1971.

These hand-painted stat-ues are among the popu-lar merchandising items which have been pro-duced in the last two decades. (Courtesy of Esco Products)

the phone, Dad would push the button," said Bud Abbott Jr. John Wayne hounded his pal Bud Abbott for the prank prop and finally made a deal by swapping 16 mm prints of his westerns *Hondo, Stagecoach,* and *Red River* for the gadget.

- Lou Costello was one of the first to recognize nightclub entertain-er Dean Martin's potential in motion pictures. According to comedian Buddy Hackett, Martin's manager, Lou Perry, got too demanding when Costello set up a contract for Martin at Warner Brothers—and the deal was nixed. As legend has it, Costello advanced $500 cash to

have Martin's misshapen nose fixed. Although the crooner's successful nose job was no secret, the claim that Costello funded the procedure has been denied over the years by Martin's man-ager, Mort Viner. Years later, Lou Costello's daughter Carole would marry Dean Martin's oldest boy, Craig.

- Although married in a Christian ceremony thirty-two years earli-er, Bud and Betty Abbott remar-ried on March 13, 1950, in a Jewish ceremony in Springfield, Ohio. (Betty's real name was Jenny Mae Pratt. Betty Abbott died in 1981.)

- A published report claimed that "Abbott & Costello once took out a $100,000 insurance policy with Lloyd's of London that stipulated payment if any of their audience should die of laughter." In reality, no record of such a policy exists in the files, a spokesperson for the famous agency confirmed.

- Both Bud and Lou were gadget-freaks, intrigued by innovative electronic inventions. In fact, Lou Costello was one of the first to own a color television in the 1950s. Bud Abbott owned a prototype for the big-screen television.

- Chris Costello revealed: "When my brother was born, my dad and Bud willed their routine, 'Who's on First?' to Lou Jr. and Bud Jr., hoping that one day they would continue the team and the legacy of Abbott & Costello."

- Bud Abbott was godfather to Lou Costello Jr., and Lou Costello (Sr.) was the godfather to Bud Abbott Jr.

- Studio bios and official documents have always listed Bud Abbott's birthday as October 2, 1895, and his family reports that it was always celebrated on that day. Birth records at the Bureau of Vital Statistics in Asbury Park, New Jersey, however, list this entry: William Alexander Abbott, Born October 6, 1897. Was Bud two years younger than anyone expected?

- Sufferin' Succotash! Warner Brothers animated Abbott & Costello characterizations in a few vintage cartoons. *A Tale of Two Kitties* (1942, directed by Bob Clampett) starred "Babbit and Catstello," two alley cats after a little yellow bird with a bulbous head—Tweety. This Merrie Melodie cartoon produced in Technicolor marked the debut of Tweety Bird. *A Tale of Two Mice* (1945, directed by Frank Tashlin) incorporated Bud and Lou's personas into a pair of rodents named Babbit and Catsello. Again, they were mice in *The Mouse-merized Cat* (1946, directed by Robert McKimson) with Mel Blanc supplying the vocal characterizations. In *Hollywood Canine Canteen* (1946, directed by Robert McKimson), Abbott & Costello were caricatured in a Chic Young style along with Carmen Miranda, Laurel and Hardy, and Edward G. Robinson.

- Capitalizing on the whopping success of Universal Studios' *Buck Privates*, 20th Century Fox immediately slapped army attire on Laurel and Hardy and released *Great Guns* in 1941. The original script reveals a reference to Abbott and Costello's popularity in a gag that was cut from the final release:

(Lifting a basin of water, Stan prepares to heave it out the door.)

OLLIE: Wait—

STAN: What's the matter?

OLLIE: Don't throw that water out there.

STAN: Why not?

OLLIE: The sergeant is just liable to come walking in!

STAN: What's the matter with that?

OLLIE: Don't you remember? They did that in *Buck Privates!*

Former grade-school teacher Bess Whitehead presents Lou with a tribute in 1947. In school, she presented him with chalk and the blackboard. (Courtesy of North Jersey Herald and News)

Babbit and Catstello in the Merrie Melodies cartoon, "A Tale of Two Kitties."

Ralston Purina's Bran News breakfast cereal. (Courtesy of Ralston Purina Company and Ally & Gargano; Drawing reproduced by special arrangement with Hirschfeld's exclusive representative, The Margo Feiden Galleries, New York.)

continued from page 169

Masak is taller than Costello by almost a foot, so he sat down on a bar stool during the commercial and viewers were none the wiser as the footage was shot waist up. Masak was padded to match Costello's build and he donned the checkered coat, derby, and baggy pants that almost perfectly matched those Lou wore in the old TV episodes.

This ad campaign was an interesting twist for nostalgia buffs. Some hardcore Abbott & Costello fans even bought extra boxes of the cereal to store in their souvenir collections.

"A lot of people I've worked with have called me about the commercial," says Masak, a veteran of more than two thousand TV spots. "People thought it really *was* Lou and Bud on the screen."

In 1988 moviegoers heard Abbott & Costello's most famous routine used as a recurring theme throughout the Academy Award-winning motion picture *Rain Man* costarring Dustin Hoffman and Tom Cruise. Hoffman, portraying Raymond Babbitt, an autistic savant, is obsessed with the "Who's on First?" routine. At the conclusion of this heartwarming story, Raymond's brother, Charlie, played by Cruise, gives Raymond a videocassette of the routine as a gift.

Legendary artist Al Hirschfeld frequently fits his daughter's name, Nina, into his drawings. Hidden in the Bran News ad, her name is squeezed into Bud's tie three times.

In the book *Who's on First,* comedian Carol Burnett, an Abbott & Costello aficionada, recalled a scene from the 1972 movie *Pete 'n' Tillie,* in which she and Walter Matthau costarred:

Ron Masak and Stan Lachow in the remarkable Bran News cereal commercials in the late 1980s. (Courtesy of Ron Masak)

One of the big moments in our film comes when Walter plays the "Who's on First?" routine for our son. It's a very important scene in the movie. It's not visual; it's the record. In the scene, I ask Walter what he is doing inundating this poor little child with that silliness. He says, "Abbott & Costello are not silly. This is ART." And he teaches the kid the routine.

Burnett is such a big fan of The Boys that she wrote the introduction to the 1972 book *Who's on First?,* from which the above quotation is taken. Edited by Richard J. Anobile, published by Darien House, Inc., of New York, and dedicated to Bud Abbott, the book is a collection of frame blowups from some of the most popular films the team made at Universal. Several of their best routines are illustrated throughout the picture book.

Writer Jim Mulholland took the initiative, in 1975, to publish *The Abbott and Costello Book,* which takes an in-depth look at the team's films. Mulholland went on to write successfully for motion pictures and television (episodes of *The Jack Paar Show, The Dean Martin Show, The Mary Tyler Moore Show, All in the Family,* and *The Tonight Show Starring Johnny Carson*).

"It's the first book I've written, and I still get letters about it," Mulholland says. The book has been out of print for years. "I don't necessarily want to be known as the world's foremost Abbott & Costello authority," he adds. "I've done other things. But I have to admit, I'm a big fan of the team."

Another literary endeavor about the team is the aptly titled *Lou's on First,* written by Chris Costello with Raymond Strait. This 1981 biography, published by St. Martin's Press, is still in print. "It takes an affectionate look at Lou Costello," a reviewer for the *L.A. Times* wrote. *Films in Review* called the book "a loving, deeply felt chronicle of the rotund little comedian."

There is another book, however, that enrages many Abbott & Costello relatives and fans. Chris Costello says that *Lou's on First* is her response to a book titled *Bud & Lou.*

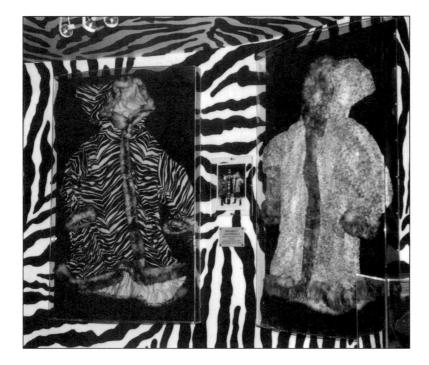

The original costumes worn by Bud and Lou in Lost in Alaska *on display at Planet Hollywood in Beverly Hills, California. (Photo by Steve Cox)*

The *Bud and Lou* Explosion

Bud and Lou, the NBC-TV movie, started out as *Bud & Lou,* a book by entertainment journalist Bob Thomas. Both the publication of the book and the release of the movie were followed by a tirade of negative publicity about these projects and also about Abbott & Costello (mainly Costello) themselves. In an interview with *Films in Review,* Thomas said:

> I had never thought much about writing a book on them until their longtime manager, Eddie Sherman, came to me with the idea of collaborating on a volume. I found, however, that Eddie's recall had a cutoff point. He could recollect about ten hours of material, but that wasn't enough for a book.

In 1978 Thomas's book was made into a television movie starring Buddy Hackett as Lou and Harvey Korman as Bud. Both comedians physically resembled the actors they portrayed.

NBC premiered the movie on November 15, 1978, as the network's *Wednesday Night at the Movies* offering. Produced by Robert C. Thompson and Clyde B. Phillips, the show was billed as a behind-the-scenes "true story of the tragic and unhappy lives of two of the funniest men in comedy history."

The plot emphasized the negative more than the positive in each comedian's life, making Costello appear to be an enraged, demanding little man who died unhappily in a hospital room. The pace of the movie is sluggish,

continued on page 180

Buddy Hackett and Harvey Korman in the 1978 NBC-TV movie of the Week, Bud and Lou.

 ## Milton Berle on Abbott & Costello

"Mr. Television," Milton Berle, hosted a compilation video of routines from *The Abbott and Costello Show* titled *Hey Abbott!* Currently available on videocassette, this documentary of sorts highlights some of the funniest moments from the show, with clips of "Who's on First?," the "Lemon" routine, "Oyster Stew," "Floogle Street," and others. Offered on tape by VidAmerica, Inc., this compilation also features live segments with Phil Silvers, Steve Allen, and Joe Besser.

Berle made this comment during his narration:

It's truly a privilege to pay homage to two of my closest friends. These guys were naturals offstage. Bud was the introvert and Lou was the extrovert—the driving spirit of the team. They had a competitive spirit and really competed against each other. I can recall when Lou built a big house, Bud built a bigger one. When Lou built a big swimming pool, Bud built a bigger one.

Bud and Lou were the highest-paid performers in the business. During [the forties], there were none more generous. . . . they remembered the days when money did not come easy.

Milton Berle (left) and Jack Haley (right) examine the programs for a tribute to Lou Costello given in his hometown of Paterson, New Jersey. (Courtesy of North Jersey Herald and News)

continued from page 177

and witnessing someone else perform Abbott & Costello's sacred routines in the movie is downright painful.

The hero of the story is the team's manager, Eddie Sherman, who fed most of the stories to writer Bob Thomas. Sherman was played by Arte Johnson, known for his "German soldier" bit on TV's *Rowan & Martin's Laugh-In.* Johnson was short and looked much like Sherman did in real life, which was the only realistic thing about the depiction of Sherman.

Buddy Hackett, who knew Costello briefly and always enjoyed his comedy, comments about the movie:

> I liked the script, and I wanted to play Lou's life. But the movie ended up making him look like a bad guy. I couldn't have known that until I saw the picture.
>
> You see, there was a scene in the movie where I'm playing Lou filming the movie *In the Navy.* He's in the hammock above a steel deck. He's trying to get comfortable, and the hammock spins over, and he falls onto the deck.
>
> Vic Parks did the stunt originally. He was wearing the funny boxer shorts that come just above the knee. He was wearing a T-shirt with short sleeves, which meant no elbow pads and no knee pads.
>
> I called Vic when I was doing the movie, and he says, "You gotta make that spin quick. You can be clear and drop to catch yourself. Hands have to be arched and toes have to come down first so you land on your toes and your fingers to catch your weight."
>
> I wanted to do the stunt myself, and I was up all night thinking how I'm gonna do it. We do the stunt.
>
> In the movie, the director wants Lou to repeat the stunt while filming *In the Navy.* Lou knew he did it right, and he got upset. Who the hell are *they* to tell him to do the stunt again? That was the point of the scene, anyway. But in the scene following it, Lou is bawling the hell outta somebody in his dressing room while playing cards. The producers left the preceding fall scene out of the picture but kept the scene where Lou curses out the director. And suddenly Lou becomes the bad guy. And that's what happened.
>
> The producers of *Bud and Lou* humored me, and we did the scene—the stunt and all that—and then they left it out! I was furious! The worst part is, the whole next scene seems out of place because they omitted the preceding one. People asked me, "What's Lou yellin' about? Was he really like that?" and I'd say no. He only appeared that way in the final cut.
>
> Unfortunately, I can't go through the whole story for everyone who asks, but that's what happened. I was unhappy with that scene.

Critics' reviews of the made-for-television movie were mixed. Viacom International, which now owns syndication rights to it, supplies these words in its press packet:

> This show business saga is better than most, and the main reason can be found in a collection of exceptionally good performances. . . . Buddy Hackett gives a

performance that is sensitive and powerful. Harvey Korman is beautifully restrained and sympathetic. Michele Lee handles the difficult role of Costello's wife with exquisite skill, and Arte Johnson is wonderfully subtle and effective as Eddie Sherman.
—*New York Times*

Earns the distinction of being that rare Hollywood biography that works. . . . Korman and Hackett not only bear a striking physical resemblance to the famed comedy team but also do their routines in high style.
—Judith Christ, *TV Guide*

Writer and critic Leonard Maltin, seen on TV's *Entertainment Tonight,* offers a different view in his best-selling book *TV Movies and Video Guide:*

[The] major intent of this hackneyed biopic on Abbott & Costello is portraying Lou as an s.o.b., but its fatal flaw is Hackett and Korman's painfully unfunny renderings of classic A&C routines. Below average.

In any biographical story brought to the big or small screen, certain elements are tampered with, omitted, and sometimes greatly distorted. Hardly anyone is ever happy with the outcome, it seems, of something so personal.

Not surprisingly, possibly the worst of the reviews came from the Abbott and the Costello families. Paddy Costello, Lou and Anne's older daughter, remarked, "I wasn't pleased about that television film that was done with [Eddie Sherman's] help. It was tough to watch because I always liked Buddy Hackett. He was a nice guy."

Chris, the younger Costello daughter, commented, "The night I saw the movie, I didn't know whether to kick the TV in or what! It was the biggest slap in the face from the industry. It certainly was not a tribute to the team or my dad. I'm glad [Lou] wasn't alive [to see it]. It would have killed him to see how fast an industry could turn its back on someone for the almighty dollar."

Norman Abbott, a filmmaker himself, remarked, "[It was] a dreadful film. [However,] I thought Harvey [Korman] did a fine job as Bud. Bob Banner did not want to pay Betty Abbott for [the use of] her likeness so they didn't have much about Bud's life in the film."

Reportedly, since Bud's widow, Betty Abbott, was still living, she was contacted regarding her character in the motion picture. Bud Abbott Jr. contends that once she read the Thomas book on which the movie is based, his mother did not want to have anything to do with the movie and refused to be portrayed in the film. None of Lou's children except Butch, who drowned, were mentioned in the made-for-TV movie. Bud Abbott appeared to be a single man, almost.

Publicity photograph for Keystone Kops with actor Fred Clark.

CHAPTER 10

The Routines

"Who's on First?" is the funniest sketch in the history of comedy teams in show business. I laugh every time I hear it. Abbott & Costello were comedic geniuses.

—Larry King

The saying *should* be "baseball, apple pie, and Abbott & Costello." The national pastime and the two comedians seem synonymous. During the vaudeville and burlesque years, a routine similar to what is now embedded in our hearts as "Who's on First?" had been repeated and reshaped by many a comedian.

But Abbott & Costello did the routine best.

No one is absolutely sure who penciled the now-famous routine. Norman Abbott claims that Lou Costello wrote it. "It was based on a piece of material called 'Cleaning and Dyeing,'" he says. "Based on this, Lou wrote the baseball sketch. That's his."

Abbott & Costello historian Jim Mulholland noted that the routine stemmed from an old burlesque chestnut titled "The Baker Scene," where the straight man and the comic discuss "loafing" with a double meaning. "The team of Bert Wheeler and Robert Woolsey performed another routine that preceded 'Who's on First?,' in which Wheeler and Woolsey, studying a map, get into an argument over two towns named 'Which' and 'What,'" Mulholland wrote in *The Abbott and Costello Book.*

The late, great comedian Phil Silvers, a veteran vaudevillian himself, once said:

Nobody knows where "Who's on First?" came from. Everybody used to do it. I did it myself with Rags Ragland. But Bud and Lou had the first crack at the big-

Doing "Who's On First?" in The Naughty Nineties, *their only film to feature the full routine. (Personality Photos., Inc.)*

time audiences with it, and nobody performed it quite like they did. It's a piece of Americana.

It is commonly understood, however, that Bud and Lou wrote the sketch together with their comedy mentor, John Grant. Whatever, whenever, and wherever its origin, the routine became the ideal Abbott & Costello vehicle. Possession is nine-tenths of the law, and Bud and Lou kept the bit for their own. They molded it, nurtured it, exposed it, claimed it, and even copyrighted it with the Library of Congress on March 13, 1944, under the title "Abbott and Costello Baseball Routine."

In the National Baseball Hall of Fame and Museum in Cooperstown, New York, the film version of "Who's on First?" (from *The Naughty Nineties*) is shown continuously on four separate monitors in the Great Moments Room.

"It's a way of presenting it to the greatest number of visitors," says Bill Guilefoil, associate director of the museum. "People laugh just as hard today. The film represents the routine better than anything else we could do in our museum."

On October 15, 1956, during *The Steve Allen Show,* Abbott & Costello presented a mounted gold record of their famed routine to Baseball Hall of Fame representatives Paul Kerr and Sid Keener. The ceremony was broadcast live on NBC-TV, and it marked the routine's twentieth anniversary. "Who's on First?" thus was officially inducted into the National Baseball Hall of Fame and Museum.

At the time, Bud and Lou estimated they had performed the routine more than fifteen thousand times. President Roosevelt requested it on occasion and The Boys gladly obliged. It was performed in almost every medium: radio, motion pictures, television, and print. Depending on what city Bud and Lou were in, they would insert the name of the appropriate ball club. Once, while in Europe, they even transformed the routine to fit soccer.

"I remember the time they did it in Las Vegas," says Paddy Costello. "They got so messed up, they got lost. My mom and I were sitting in the audience, and I thought I was gonna die. I looked at Mom and I said, 'What are they gonna do? How are they gonna get out of this?' They were just going around and around. There was a look on my father's face . . . the audience didn't notice any difference, but I could see it. I could see the look on my father's face. He was totally perplexed. He didn't know what was happening. The audience was laughing. Finally Bud and Lou just brought the routine together. They had done it so many times, and it's a tricky piece."

Performing the routine with rapid-fire speed seems to have been the secret to Abbott & Costello's success. Other comedians have attempted the routine but have struck out every time, not even hitting a foul ball. Abbott delivered a quick, sharp pounce to every question Costello posed. And when

In a scene from Keep 'Em Flying. *(Courtesy of Tom Frederick)*

Costello ran off the topic, Abbott knew when and how to quickly pull him back into the bit without missing a beat. The tempo was the secret.

"Who's on First?" remains unique, says Chris Costello, "because they never did the routine the same way twice. My dad was notorious for departing from the script, anyway."

Following is a version of the routine that features the Midwest—the home of baseball.

Who's on First?

Bud: You know, strange as it may seem, they give ballplayers peculiar names nowadays. On the St. Louis team, Who's on first. What's on second, and I Don't Know is on third.

Lou: That's what I want to find out. I want you to tell me the names of the fellows on the St. Louis team.

Bud: I'm telling you. Who's on first, What's on second, I Don't Know is on third.

Lou: You know the fellows' names?

Bud: Yes.

Lou: Well, then, who's playin' first?

Bud: Yes.

Lou: I mean the fellow's name on first base.

Bud: Who.

Lou: The fellow's name on first base for St. Louis.

Bud: Who.

Lou: The guy on first base.

Bud: Who is on first base.

Lou: Well, what are you askin' me for?

Bud: I'm not asking you, I'm telling you. Who is on first.

Lou: I'm askin' *you,* who is on first?

Bud: That's the man's name.

Lou: That's whose name?

Bud: Yes.

Lou: Well, go ahead and tell me.

Bud: Who.

Lou: The guy on first.

Bud: Who.

Lou: The first baseman.

Bud: Who is on first.

Lou (confounded): Have you got a first baseman on first?

Bud: Why, certainly.

Lou: Well, all I'm tryin' to find out is what's the guy's name on first base.

Bud: Oh, no, no. What is on *second* base.

LOU: I'm not askin' you who's on second.

BUD: Who's on first.

LOU: That's what I'm trying to find out.

BUD: Well, don't change the players around.

LOU: (tension mounting): I'm not changin' anybody.

BUD: Now take it easy.

LOU: What's the guy's name on first base?

BUD: What's the guy's name on *second* base.

LOU: I'm not askin' ya who's on second.

BUD: Who's on first.

LOU: I don't know.

BUD: He's on third. We're not talking about him.

LOU: How could I get on third base?

BUD: You mentioned the man's name.

LOU: If I mentioned the third baseman's name, who did I say is playing third?

BUD: No, Who's playing first.

LOU: Stay offa first, will ya?!

BUD: Please, now what is it you'd like to know?

LOU: What is the fellow's name on third base?

BUD: What is the fellow's name on *second* base.

LOU: I'm not askin' ya who's on second.

BUD: Who's on first.

LOU: I don't know.

Bud and Lou (in unison): Third base!

LOU: When you pay off the first baseman every month, who gets the money?

BUD: Certainly.

LOU: Who gets the money?

BUD: Every dollar of it.

LOU: When you give the guy the money, who gets it?

BUD: Yes. He's entitled to it. Sometimes his wife comes down and collects it.

LOU: Whose wife?

BUD: Yes.

LOU: Look, when ya give the guy a receipt, how does he sign it?

BUD: Who.

LOU: The guy you give the money to.

BUD: Who. That's how he signs it.

Lou (using a new approach): You got an outfield?

BUD: Certainly.

LOU: St. Louis got a *good* outfield?

BUD: Oh, absolutely.

Performing their famous baseball banter on stage in the late 1930s.

LOU: The left fielder's name?

BUD: Why.

LOU: I don't know. I just thought I'd ask.

BUD: Well, I just thought I'd tell you.

LOU: Then tell me who's playing left field.

BUD: Who's playing first.

LOU: Stay outta the infield! I wanna know what's the fellow's name in left field?

BUD: What is on second.

LOU: I'm not askin' you who's on second.

BUD: Who is on first.

LOU: I don't know!

Bud and Lou (in unison): Third base!

(Lou is exasperated at this point.)

BUD: Now take it easy, man.

LOU: And the left fielder's name?

BUD: Why.

LOU: Because.

BUD: Oh, he's in center field.

LOU: Wait a minute. You got a pitcher on the team?

BUD: Wouldn't this be a fine team without a pitcher!

LOU: I dunno. Tell me the pitcher's name.

BUD: Tomorrow.

LOU: You don't want to tell me today?

BUD: I'm telling you, man.

LOU: Then go ahead.

BUD: Tomorrow.

LOU: What time?

BUD: What time what?

LOU: What time tomorrow are you gonna tell me who's pitching?

BUD: Now listen, Who is not pitching. Who is on—

LOU: I'll break your arm if you say who is on first!

BUD: Then why did you ask me?

LOU: I want to know what's the pitcher's name!

BUD: What's on second.

LOU: I don't know.

Bud and Lou: Third base!

LOU: You gotta catcher?

BUD: Yes.

LOU: The catcher's name?

BUD: Today.

LOU: Today. And Tomorrow's pitching.

BUD: Now you've got it.

LOU: That's all. St. Louis has got a couple of days on their team. That's all.

BUD: Well, I can't help that. What do you want me to do?

LOU: I'm a good catcher, too, ya know.

BUD: I know that.

LOU: I would like to play for St. Louis someday.

BUD: Well, I might arrange that.

LOU: I would like to catch. Now Tomorrow's pitching on the team, and I'm catching.

BUD: OK.

LOU: Tomorrow throws the ball, and the guy gets up and bunts the ball.

BUD: Yes.

LOU: So when he bunts the ball, me bein' a good catcher, I want to throw the guy out at first base. So I pick up the ball and throw it to who.

BUD: Now, that's the first thing you've said right!

LOU: I don't even know what I'm talkin' about!

BUD: Well, that's all you have to do.

LOU: I throw it to first base.

BUD: Yes.

LOU: Now who's got it?

BUD: Naturally.

LOU: Who has it?

BUD: Naturally.

LOU: Naturally?

BUD: Naturally.

LOU: I throw the ball to Naturally.

BUD: No, you throw the ball to Who!

LOU: Naturally.

BUD: Naturally.

LOU: So I throw the ball to who?

BUD: Naturally.

LOU: Same as you! Same as you!

Lou joins in a high school game with coach Mort Rittenberg in his hometown. (Courtesy of North Jersey Herald and News)

Baseball hero Joe DiMaggio stops by the set of Captain Kidd to visit his buddy, Lou. DiMaggio said recently: "I visited with Lou an awful lot at his home, on the set, and on the road. I'd see him quite a bit when he and Bud used to travel and we'd have dinner…I remember the fact that Charlie Laughton did want to do a picture with them in spite of all the fame he had and the dramatic experience. He wanted to do a comedy with Lou and Bud." (Personality Photos, Inc.)

BUD: Ya throw the ball to Who. Who gets it.

LOU: He'd better get it!

BUD: That's it. All right now, don't get excited. Take it easy.

LOU (frenzied): Now I throw the ball to first base, whoever it is grabs the ball, so the guy runs to second.

BUD: Uh-huh.

LOU: Who picks up the ball and throws it to What. What throws it to I Don't Know. I Don't Know throws it back to Tomorrow. Triple play!

BUD: Yeah, could be.

LOU: Another guy gets up, and it's a long fly ball to Because. Why? I don't know, and I don't give a damn.

BUD: What was that?

LOU: I said, I don't give a damn.

BUD: Oh, that's our shortstop.

The "Mustard" Routine

After "Who's on First?" the "Mustard" routine seems to be the most popular among fans. Versions of the routine were broadcast on The Boys' radio show as well as inserted in their first motion picture, *One Night in the Tropics,* and in *The Noose Hangs High* and an episode of *The Abbott and Costello Show* titled "Police Rookies." With a shotgun delivery, at which Bud Abbott is most adept, Abbott convinces Costello he's committed all kinds of hideous acts—all because he does not prefer mustard on his hot dogs. Initially Costello is feisty, but Abbott steers the argument his way with the swift tongue of a talented con artist.

The routine begins like this: Bud and Lou are sitting at a table before a tantalizing spread of food, on which Lou is feasting. In the center is a small mustard jar, with a knife poking out of it. Costello complains about having had some hard questions asked of him while he was applying for a job. And the dialogue continues . . .

BUD: What's so hard about those questions?

LOU: I can't answer those questions. Ask me the easy questions, the little questions. I can answer those.

BUD: You can't answer *any* questions—

LOU: Yes I could.

BUD: All right. Suppose you walked over there and bore a hole in that wall.

LOU: What wall?

Sliding into the "Mustard Routine" during One Night in the Tropics.

BUD: Over there.

LOU: All right, I go over there and bore a hole in that wall.

BUD: Why? Why should you go over there and bore a hole in that wall?

LOU: I'm *not* boring a hole in the wall.

BUD: Why should you bore a hole in the wall?

LOU: You said *suppose* I go and bore a hole in the wall—

BUD: You don't know what you're talking about. Look, suppose you walked into a baseball park. What teams are playing?

LOU: I dunno.

BUD: Then what are you doing in the baseball park?

LOU: I'm *not* in any baseball park.

BUD: You see, you don't know what you're talking about.

LOU: Get me outta that baseball park!

BUD: You told me I gotta teach you these things. What is the first thing you buy in a baseball park?

LOU: Hot dogs—without mustard!

BUD: Mustard goes with the hot dog.

LOU: Not mine.

BUD: Mustard was *made* for the hot dog.

LOU: I don't care what the stuff was made for. I'm not gonna eat it.

BUD: Mustard and hot dogs go together!

LOU: Let 'em go together. I'm not gonna spoil any romance.

BUD: Who's talkin' about romance?

LOU: I mean, after all, if I don't like mustard, I don't have to eat it for you or anyone else.

BUD: Oh, well, I didn't know you disliked it.

LOU: Who do you think you are, telling me to put mustard on my hot dog? If I want to put catsup on a hot dog, there's no law sayin' I can't put catsup on a hot dog. . . . This is a free country! And if I don't want to eat mustard, I don't have to eat mustard! (pounding the table)

BUD: OK. Keep quiet. If ya don't like mustard, why didn't ya tell me that in the first place?

LOU: I don't like it because it makes me sick. I don't want to walk around the streets sick.

BUD: I don't want to see you sick.

LOU: I mean, after all, I'm a happy kid. I love life! I got three little nieces, and I help to support those three little nieces. If I walk around the street sick and don't go out there on the street to work and get money to give my sister to help support those three kids, what's gonna happen? My three little nieces are gonna starve to death. They ain't gonna eat. Somebody's gonna take those three kids and put 'em in an orphan asylum.

BUD: OK. You're taking this too seriously—

LOU: What right do you got to put my nieces in the orphan asylum? What did my nieces ever do to you?

BUD: Nothing at all.

LOU: C'mon, Abbott, get 'em outta the orphan asylum!

BUD: Now enough is enough! Do you know where mustard comes from?

LOU: I don't know—a mustard plaster?

BUD: Not a mustard plaster! They *manufacture* mustard! Do you know they spend millions of dollars every year just to put up factories to manufacture mustard? Do you know those factories employ thousands and thousands of men just to manufacture mustard? Do you know those men take care of thousands and thousands of families? All on account of mustard! And just because you don't like mustard, what do you want them to do? Close those factories down and put all those people out of work?

LOU: Are you tryin' to tell me that all those people are making one little jar of mustard like this, just for me?

BUD: No, no, you don't seem to understand—

LOU: Well if they are, Abbott, you can tell 'em not to make any more, because I'm not gonna eat it! You can lay them off!

BUD: Oh, lay them off—

LOU: Who am *I* to support thousands of people?

BUD: Who's asking you to support them?

LOU: I'm not gonna eat any mustard!

BUD: Close the mustard factories down . . . a fine argument. Put the people out of work!

LOU: I'm not puttin' anybody out of work!

BUD: . . . Fathers out of work, husbands out of work!

LOU: Fathers? Husbands?

BUD: You don't even know what a husband is.

LOU: Yes I do. A husband is what's left of a sweetheart after the nerve has been killed.

(Bud slaps Lou.)

BUD: Say you walk into a restaurant. The waiter places over here a platter of beans. And over here, a great big juicy steak. Now which one of those would you eat?

LOU: I eat the beans.

BUD: What happened to the steak?

LOU: What do I care about the steak?

BUD: Then why did you order it?

LOU: I didn't order no steak!

BUD: You see, you're starting an argument again.

LOU: You said the waiter comes in and puts the beans over here and puts the steak over here. I was nice enough not to sponge on you. I said I'd eat the beans.

BUD: Now wait a minute. Am I supporting you?

LOU: No.

BUD: Where did the steak and the beans come from? The waiter put 'em out here.

LOU: You said that some waiter—

BUD: I don't say anything. I say the waiter places 'em down here. You must have ordered them. Now you got a platter of beans here and steak over here. Which one of these two do you eat?

LOU: I said I'd eat the beans. Never mind the beans, I'll eat the steak.

BUD: Then what happened to the beans?

LOU: Throw 'em away!

BUD: Throw 'em away. People around the country starving to death, and you're throwing food away. What kind of reputation do you think you'd have?

LOU: Look, never mind, don't throw the beans away. I'll put the beans on the steak, I'll mash 'em in and eat 'em.

BUD: Do you know where that steak comes from?

LOU: A cow.

BUD: Do you know what that cow gives?

LOU: Milk.

BUD: That cow gives milk!

LOU: Give it? . . . Ya gotta take it away from it—
BUD: Never mind. That cow gives milk! Who does that milk supply? Little babies. Little innocent tots. Without that milk, they'd perish. Die! You don't care. Just to satisfy your selfish appetite, you let them go out and kill all the cows and let the little babies of the world starve to death. Are you happy?
(Lou drops his fork, embarrassed.)
BUD: How can you enjoy your meal?
LOU: Look, you got me killin' babies now. I'm killin' babies, cows, puttin' people out of work. I'm wrecking bridges . . . (exasperated) Why don't you let me alone?!
BUD: Who's bothering you?
LOU: The whole thing started with me boring a hole in the wall!
BUD: Don't mention that anymore. Now listen . . . I'm only gonna ask you one more question. This is the last. Say you're in the, ah, Grand Central Depot in New York City. Now this is simple as any little tot. You're in Grand Central Depot in New York City, and you buy a ticket. Where are you going?
LOU: I'm not going anywhere.
BUD: Then what are you buying a ticket for?
LOU: I'm not buyin' a ticket.
BUD: Then what are you doing in the depot?
LOU: You put me in there.
BUD: Yeah, you see. You argue again. Now take it easy—

The routine could go on forever, in an endless cycle of illogic that appears logical—and, naturally, always working the confounded Costello into a hilarious frenzy.

The bits that seem funniest are actually the routines that are the most illogical. Bud Abbott, a superb actor in his own right, made the audience actually *believe* what he was feeding Costello. He made every word appear perfectly sane. Abbott confused Costello with wordplay until Lou was dumbfounded.

In *Abbott and Costello Meet the Mummy,* for instance, The Boys are going to dig a ditch with the tools that Costello has assembled.

LOU: Wait a minute, I told you to take your pick.
BUD: The shovel is my pick.
(Confounded, Lou doesn't understand the wordplay.)
BUD: The shovel is my pick. My pick is the shovel.
LOU: How can a shovel be a pick?

Performing "The Lemon Bit" with Shemp Howard (left) and Joe LaCava in the team's third film released, In the Navy.

Comedienne Joan Davis (later known for her TV series I Married Joan *with Jim Backus) plays the loony radio actress Camille Brewster who specializes in blood-curdling screams of terror in* Hold That Ghost. *Here, Davis and Costello are doing the "Moving Candle" bit, one of the funniest scenes in the film.*

(Finally he attempts to make sense of the entanglement.)

LOU: The shovel is your pick, and your pick is the shovel, and the pick is my pick.

BUD: Now you've got it.

LOU: I don't even know what I'm talkin' about!

How's this for logic:

BUD: Stop smoking in here, Costello.

LOU: Who's smoking?

BUD: You are.

LOU: What makes you think I'm smoking?

BUD: You have a cigar in your mouth.

LOU: I got my shoes on, but I'm not walking.

On one of the early Abbott & Costello radio performances, Bud inquires about Lou's farm.

BUD: By the way, what kind of cow have you? A heifer cow?

LOU: No, I got a *whole* cow! Not just one, I got a whole flock of 'em!

BUD: No, no. You don't understand. Not flock. Herd!

LOU: Heard what?

BUD: Herd of cows.

LOU: Sure I heard of cows! Whaddaya think I am, a dummy?

BUD: No, I mean a cow herd.

LOU: What do I care if a cow heard?!

CHAPTER 11

The Films of Abbott & Costello

One Night in the Tropics (1940)
Produced by Leonard Spigelgass
Directed by A. Edward Sutherland
Screenplay by Gertrude Purcell and Charles Grayson
From the novel *Love Insurance* by Earl Derr Biggers
Songs by Jerome Kern, Oscar Hammerstein, and Dorothy Fields
Universal-International Studios
83 minutes

Cast: Allan Jones, Robert Cummings, Nancy Kelly, Mary Boland, Bud Abbott, Lou Costello, Peggy Moran, William Frawley, Leo Carillo, Nina Orla, Don Alvarado, Theodore Rand, Mina Farragut, Richard Carle, Edgar Dearing, Barnett Parker, Francis McDonald, Jerry Mandy, Eddie Dunn, Vivian Fay, Eddie Acuff, Frank Penny, William Alston, Charles B. Murphy, and Charlie Hall

Brief: Abbott & Costello are assigned to protect a nightclub operator's interests when the man underwrites half of a policy that will pay Steve (Robert Cummings) $1 million if he fails to marry Cynthia (Nancy Kelly). Cynthia becomes angry at Steve, her now-former fiancé, and Jim (Allan Jones), the club's owner and Cynthia's present love interest, when she learns of the bet. The ending includes a romantic double wedding on a Caribbean island.

SIDELIGHTS
• *The movie was originally titled* Caribbean Holiday.
• *Abbott & Costello were not the top-billed stars of the movie.*
• *This film and* Abbott and Costello Meet the Mummy *are the only movies in which Bud and Lou use their own full names for their characters. (Two other films have characters with The Boys' first names only:* Dance with Me, Henry *and* Abbott and Costello Meet the Invisible Man.)
• *An early studio memo suggests that George Burns and Gracie Allen were considered for the comedy relief in this film prior to the choice of Abbott and Costello.*
• *Bud and Lou rarely mentioned this film in interviews and preferred to consider* Buck Privates *as their first film.*
• *The film was released November 15, 1940.*
• *Routine Checklist: This film includes performances of "The Baseball Routine," "Jonah and the Whale," "Mustard," "Two Tens for a Five," "Smoking," and "365 Days—Firing Routine."*

SIDELIGHTS

- *This motion-picture blockbuster established the team as the third-ranking attraction of 1941, grossing $4.7 million on a modest $200,000 investment. Quite a sum for the period!*
- *The film was shot at Universal Studios in twenty-four days.*
- *After seeing* Buck Privates, *Charlie Chaplin commented that Lou Costello was "the best comic working in the business today."*
- *The Andrews Sisters had appeared in only one film prior to* Buck Privates: *The harmonizing honeys costarred in* Argentine Nights *with the Ritz Brothers, Constance Moore, and George Reeves in 1940.*
- *"Boogie Woogie Bugle Boy of Company B" was nominated for an Academy Award for best song and Charles Previn's score for* Buck Privates *was nominated for best score.*
- Buck Privates *was released January 31, 1941, just five months after the draft bill was passed . . . great timing for a film about the service.*
- *Routine Checklist: "Drill Routine," "The Dice Game," "You're Forty, She's Ten."*

Buck Privates (1941)

Produced by Alex Gottlieb
Directed by Arthur Lubin
Original screenplay by Arthur T. Horman
Special material for Abbott & Costello by John Grant
Universal-International Studios
82 minutes

Cast: Bud Abbott, Lou Costello, the Andrews Sisters, Lee Bowman, Alan Curtis, Jane Frazee, Nat Pendleton, Don Raye, Dora Clemant, J. Anthony Hughes, Hughie Prince, Leonard Elliott, Harry Strang, Frank Cook, Samuel S. Hinds, Shemp Howard, James Flavin, Mike Frankovitch, Jack Mulhall, Nella Walker, Douglas Wood, Charles Coleman, Selmer Jackson, Tom Tyler, Herold Goodwin, Bud Harris, Al Billings, Frank Penny, Frank Grandetta, Bob Wayne, Jeanne Kelly, Elaine Morey, Kay Leslie, and Nina Orla

Brief: Slicker (Bud) and Herbie (Lou) attempt to elude the police and hide in an enlistment center, where they find they are in the army. The plot also involves a playboy named Randolph (Lee Bowman) who catches the eye of a hostess. Herbie and Slicker find out their sergeant used to be the policeman who chased them.

Bud and Lou with their longtime publicity man, Joe Glaston, on the set of Buck Privates. *(Courtesy of Joe Glaston)*

In the Navy (1941)
Produced by Alex Gottlieb
Directed by Arthur Lubin
Screenplay by Arthur T. Horman and John Grant
Songs by Gene de Paul and Don Raye
Universal-International Studios
85 minutes

Cast: Bud Abbott, Lou Costello, Dick Powell, Claire Dodd, the Andrews Sisters, Dick Foran, Shemp Howard, Billy Lenhart, Kenneth Brown, the Condos Brothers, William Davidson, Thurston Hall, Robert Emmet Keane, Edward Fielding, Don Terry, Sunnie O'Dea, Eddie Dunn, Ralph Dunn, Dick Alexander, Lorin Raker, Frank Penny, Pat Gleason, Jack Mulhall, Mickey Simpson, Lyle Latell, Chuck Morrison, Lee Kass, James Sullivan, Edna Hall, Claire Whitney, Joe Bautista, Doris Herbert, Charles Sullivan, and Douglas Wood

Brief: Smokey Adams (Bud) and Pomeroy Watson (Lou) get involved with popular crooner Russ Raymond, aka Tommy Halstead (Dick Powell), and all join the navy. Assigned duty on a battleship, The Boys adjust to life at sea.

SIDELIGHTS
- *This was actually the team's third film for Universal. Hold That Ghost was their second, but it was shelved while In the Navy was produced to capitalize on the success of Buck Privates.*
- *Carole, Lou Costello's daughter, can be spotted in the film as the baby in a carriage.*
- In the Navy *outgrossed The Boys' previous hit,* Buck Privates.
- *The film was released May 27, 1941.*
- *Routine Checklist: "The Lemon Bit" (variation of "The Shell Game"), "Sons of the Neptune" (variation of "Buzzing the Bee"), and "7 x 13 = 28."*

In a stationary boat, Bud, Lou, Shemp Howard, and extras shoot a scene in front of a dark process screen for In the Navy.

SIDELIGHTS
- *The Andrews Sisters were brought in after filming wrapped (marking their third movie appearance), and the final nightclub footage was edited in after the film's completion.*
- *The film's original title was* Oh Charlie!
- *The movie includes the memorable "Moving Candle" gag that petrifies Lou in a haunted house. The routine was used again in* Abbott and Costello Meet Frankenstein.
- *Abbott and Costello re-created* Hold That Ghost *for a radio audience in August 1941 on Louella Parson's show,* Hollywood Premiere.
- *The film was released August 6, 1941.*
- *Routine Checklist: "Moving Candle," "The Changing Room."*

Hold That Ghost (1941)
Produced by Alex Gottlieb
Directed by Arthur Lubin
Screenplay by Robert Lees, Frederic I. Rinaldo, and John Grant
Original story by Robert Lees and Frederic I. Rinaldo
Universal-International Studios
85 minutes

Cast: Bud Abbott, Lou Costello, Richard Carlson, Evelyn Ankers, Joan Davis, the Andrews Sisters, Ted Lewis, Mischa Auer, Marc Lawrence, Shemp Howard, Milton Parsons, Frank Penny, Edgar Dearing, Don Terry, Edward Pawley, Nestor Paiva, Russell Hicks, William Davidson, Paul Fix, Howard Hickman, Harry Hayden, William Forrest, Paul Newlan, Joe LaCava, and Bobby Barber

Brief: Chuck Murray (Bud) and Ferdinand "Ferdie" Jones (Lou) inherit an abandoned roadhouse after witnessing the death of a gangster. While searching for hidden money, The Boys inhabit the creepy tavern with an assortment of people, such as Camille Brewster (Joan Davis), a professional radio "screamer." After battling ghosts and gangsters, Chuck and Ferdie convert the house into a resort.

Gangster Moose Matson hid his fortune "in his head," in the team's fourth film released, Hold That Ghost *(1941).*

Keep 'Em Flying (1941)
Produced by Glenn Tryon
Directed by Arthur Lubin
Screenplay by True Boardman, Nat Perrin, and John Grant
Original story by Edmund L. Hartmann
Songs by Don Raye, Gene de Paul, Ned Washington, and George Bassman
Universal-International Studios
86 minutes

Cast: Bud Abbott, Lou Costello, Martha Raye, Carol Bruce, William Gargan, Dick Foran, Truman Bradley, Charles Lang, William Davidson, Frank Penny, Loring Smith, Doris Lloyd, Emil Van Horn, James Seay, William Forrest, Earle Hodgins, Harry Strang, Carleton Young, Harold Daniels, Dick Crane, Paul Scott, Virginia Engels, Dorothy L. Jones, Stanley Smith, James Horne Jr., Charlie King Jr., Regis Parton, Dorothy Darrell, Marcia Ralston, Scotty Groves, and Elaine Morey.

Brief: Blackie (Bud) and Heathcliffe (Lou) are fired from their jobs at an aerial carnival show. They then join an air academy as mechanics. Jinx Roberts (Dick Foran), a friend of The Boys', saves a student and becomes the hero of the academy. Blackie and Heathcliffe pair off with a couple of aggressive twins, Barbara and Gloria (both played by Martha Raye).

SIDELIGHTS

- *A review in* Variety *stated, "Keep 'Em Flying is the fourth release starring Abbott and Costello within a ten-month stretch. It indicates the boys are appearing too often with their burlesque type of roustabout comedy to remain in the public popularity for any length of time, unless new material is provided for their screen appearances."*
- *Lou Costello's brother, Pat, doubled the comedian during the runaway torpedo scenes. Pat Costello recalled getting thrown from the motor-driven contraption when it got to top speed.*
- *The film was released November 28, 1941.*
- *Routine Checklist: "Go Ahead, Order Something."*

Foreign publicity for Keep 'Em Flying.

SIDELIGHTS

- *Ride 'Em Cowboy was actually filmed before* Keep 'Em Flying.
- *Ella Fitzgerald makes her screen debut and sings a song she cowrote, "A-Tisket, A-Tasket," which became a huge hit for the legendary jazz singer.*
- *The film was released February 20, 1942.*
- *Routine Checklist: "Crazy House," "Heard of Cows."*

Ride 'Em Cowboy (1942)
Produced by Alex Gottlieb
Directed by Arthur Lubin
Screenplay by True Boardman and John Grant
Adaptation by Harold Shumate
Original story by Edmund L. Hartmann
Songs by Don Raye and Gene de Paul
Universal-International Studios
86 minutes

Cast: Bud Abbott, Lou Costello, Anne Gwynne, Samuel S. Hinds, Dick Foran, Richard Lane, The Merry Macs (Judd McMichael, Ted McMichael, Joe McMichael), Mary Lou Cook, Johnny Mack Brown, Ella Fitzgerald, Douglas Dumbrille, Jody Gilbert, Morris Ankrum, Charles Lane, Russell Hicks, Wade Boteler, James Flavin, Boyd Davis, Eddie Dunn, Isabel Randolph, Tom Hanlon, James Seay, Harold Daniels, Ralph Peters, Linda Brent, Lee Sunrise, Chief Yowlachie, Harry Monty, Sherman E. Sanders, Carmela Cansino, and the Hi-Hatters

Brief: Duke (Bud) and Willoughby (Lou) are two rodeo hot-dog vendors who accompany western author Bronco Bob Mitchell (Dick Foran) out West, even though he's never ridden a horse. Willoughby leads Indians into a gambler's hideaway, thus saving a ranch from one of the crooked gamblers. Willoughby has to marry a chubby Indian squaw because he shot an arrow through her tent.

Ethel Carpenter and Diane Dorsey joking around with Costello during filming of Ride 'Em Cowboy. *(Courtesy of Joe Wallison)*

Rio Rita (1942)
Produced by Pandro S. Berman
Directed by S. Sylvan Simon
Screenplay by Richard Connell and Gladys Lehman
Special material for Abbott & Costello by John Grant
Songs by Harold Arlen, E. Y. Harburg, Harry Tierney, and Joseph McCarthy
Music directed by Herbert Stothart
Metro-Goldwyn-Mayer Studios
91 minutes

Cast: Bud Abbott, Lou Costello, Kathryn Grayson, John Carroll, Patricia Dane, Tom Conway, Peter Whitney, Arthur Space, Joan Valerie, Dick Rich, Barry Nelson, Eva Puig, Mitchell Lewis, Eros Volusia, Julian Rivero, Douglas Newland, Lee Murray, Inez Cooper, Frank Penny, David Oliver, Jenny Mac, Vangie Beilby, and Ruth Cherrington

Brief: Doc (Bud) and Wishy (Lou), who are employed in a Texas pet shop, stow away to New York City. During the trip, they are sidetracked at a hotel and are hired as house detectives by Rita Winslow (Kathryn Grayson) to get rid of Nazi spies.

SIDELIGHTS
- *This is a remake of the Ziegfeld operetta and the 1929 RKO film (starring Wheeler and Woolsey) of the same name.*
- *The songs were written and composed by most of the same folks who assembled the tunes for MGM's The Wizard of Oz (Arlen, Harburg, and Stothart). Coincidentally, character actor Mitchell Lewis, who plays Julio in this film, also played the Wicked Witch's lead soldier in Oz just three years before.*
- *The hotel laundry boy (who dumps Lou into a chute) is played by Norman Abbott, nephew of Bud Abbott.*
- *The film was released March 11, 1942.*

A rare photograph taken during production of a deleted scene from Rio Rita. The routine had Costello blindfolded, attempting to guess which one of the pretty ladies kissed him. Bud unsuccessfully tried to provide clues by patting him on the back. The bit was later reprised in an episode of Bud and Lou's television show. (Courtesy of Joe Wallison)

SIDELIGHTS
- *A New York Daily News review commented: "Most of the material in the new Universal comedy has been used by The Boys before, but Lou Costello has the knack of making every little trick of business and expression seem spontaneous."*
- *Veteran comedy writer Nat Perrin (who gave us the Marx Brothers films* Duck Soup *and* The Big Store*) was part of the team producing this screenplay. Perrin's original title for this film was* Road to Montezuma.
- *The film was released August 7, 1942.*
- *Routine Checklist: "Go Ahead and Back Up," "Tree of Truth."*

Pardon My Sarong (1942)

Produced by Alex Gottlieb
Directed by Erle C. Kenton
Screenplay by True Boardman, Nat Perrin, and John Grant
Songs by Don Raye, Gene de Paul, Milton Drake, Ben Oakland, Stanley Cowan, and Bobby North
Universal-International Studios
84 minutes

Cast: Bud Abbott, Lou Costello, Virginia Bruce, Robert Paige, Lionel Atwill, Leif Erickson, William Demarest, Samuel S. Hinds, Irving Bacon, Nan Wynn, Marie McDonald, Elaine Morey, Susan Levine, Jack La Rue, Hans Schumm, Joe Kirk, Frank Penny, Charles Lane, Chester Clute, Tom Fadden, George Chandler, Eddie Acuff, Sig Arno, Jane Patten, Florine McKinney, Marjorie Reardon, Audrey Long, Teddy Infur, the Four Ink Spots (Orville Jones, Charles Fuqua, Bill Kenney, and Deek Watson), "Tip, Tap, Toe" (Raymond Winfield, Sammy Green, and Teddie Fraser), and "Sharkey the Seal"

Brief: Chicago bus drivers Algernon "Algy" Shaw (Bud) and Wellington Phlug (Lou) drive playboy Tommy Layton (Robert Paige) and his girlfriends to California. While on a pleasure cruise on Layton's boat, The Boys are blown off course to an uncharted island. Algy exposes a phony who gets jewels from the natives by playing on their superstitions, and he becomes the hero of the island.

Publicity photo for one of Bub and Lou's more lavish productions, Pardon My Sarong. *(Courtesy of Joe Wallison)*

Who Done It? (1942)
Produced by Alex Gottlieb
Directed by Erle C. Kenton
Screenplay by Stanley Roberts, Edmund Joseph, and John Grant
Original story by Stanley Roberts
Universal-International Studios
76 minutes

Cast: Bud Abbott, Lou Costello, William Gargan, Louise Allbritton, Patric Knowles, Don Porter, Jerome Cowan, William Bendix, Mary Wickes, Thomas Gomez, Ludwig Stossel, Edmund MacDonald, Joe Kirk, Walter Tetley, Crane Whitley, Margaret Brayton, Milton Parsons, Paul Dubov, Gene O'Donnell, Edward Keane, Ed Emerson, Buddy Twiss, Gladys Blake, Eddie Bruce, Harry Strang, Frank Penny, Jerry Frank, Bobby Barber, and The Pinas

Brief: When Chick Larkin (Bud) and Mervyn Milgrim (Lou) are attending the broadcast of a mystery show, the head of the radio network is mysteriously murdered. The Boys, who are aspiring radio writers, pretend to be detectives until real investigators have them running. Chick and Mervyn discover that the murderer is a Nazi spy using the radio station to send information to his homeland.

SIDELIGHTS
- *After the release of* Who Done It? *Abbott & Costello ranked as top box-office attractions of the year.*
- *When Mervyn (Lou) claims his Wheel of Fortune prize, the radio microphone used is the actual mike from Bud and Lou's debut on* The Kate Smith Hour. *The two comedians had requested to keep the piece of equipment as a memento and saved it.*
- *The film was released November 6, 1942.*
- *Routine Checklist: "Alexander 2222."*

Character actress Mary Wickes appeared in two films with the team: Who Done It? *(1942), and* Dance with Me, Henry *(1956). Wickes later revealed that she was not too fond of the two comedians—even to the extent of commonly refusing to autograph pictures of herself from those films. "I worked with them when they were in top form at Universal," she said in 1995. "I didn't know them that well . . . nobody knew them very well. I didn't care for them. But that's alright. They just had no taste. They were coarse."*

SIDELIGHTS
- *The working title for this film was* Hold Your Horses.
- *It Ain't Hay is loosely based on the Damon Runyon short story "Princess O'Hara." Some scholars suggest that Damon Runyon's characters were prototypes for the comic/straightman motif that worked so well for Abbott & Costello and for dozens of other comedy teams.*
- *Near the end of this production (November 6, 1942), Lou Costello's wife, Anne, gave birth to their baby boy, Lou Costello Jr. The TV movie* Bud and Lou *erroneously depicts the birth taking place during the production of* Pardon My Sarong.
- *The film was released March 19, 1943.*
- *Routine Checklist: "Mudder/Fodder."*

Lou gets stuck with everybody's meal check, and he has no dough, in It Ain't Hay. *(Courtesy of Joe Wallison)*

It Ain't Hay (1943)

Produced by Alex Gottlieb
Directed by Erle C. Kenton
Screenplay by Allen Boretz and John Grant
Based on a story by Damon Runyon
Songs by Harry Revel and Paul Francis Webster
Universal-International Studios
81 minutes

Cast: Bud Abbott, Lou Costello, Grace McDonald, Eugene Pallette, Leighton Noble, Cecil Kellaway, Patsy O'Connor, Shemp Howard, Eddie Quillan, Dave Hacker, Richard Lane, Samuel S. Hinds, Harold De Garro, Andrew Tombes, Pierre Watkin, William Forrest, Ralph Peters, Wade Boteler, Bobby Watson, James Flavin, Jack Norton, Tom Hanlon, Harry Harvey, Herbert Vigran, Ed Foster, Harry Strang, Sammy Stein, Mike Mazurki, Herbert Heyes, Barry Macollum, Eddie Bruce, Paul Dubov, Charles Bennett, Rod Rogers, Janet Ann Gallow, Kate Lawson, Frank Penny, Fred Cordova, Spec O'Donnell, Stephen Gottlieb, The Four Step Brothers, and The Vagabonds

Brief: Grover Mockridge (Bud) and Wilbur Hoolihan (Lou) attempt to replace a cabdriver's dead horse by buying a new horse with money won from a bookie. They mistakenly pick up the champion horse, Teabiscuit. Wilbur enters the race and loses; but because of the switched horses, Teabiscuit ends up being the winner after all.

Hit the Ice (1943)
Produced by Alex Gottlieb
Directed by Charles Lamont
Screenplay by Robert Lees, Frederic I. Rinaldo, and John Grant
Original story by True Boardman
Songs by Harry Revel and Paul Francis Webster
Universal-International Studios
82 minutes

Cast: Bud Abbott, Lou Costello, Ginny Simms, Patric Knowles, Elyse Knox, Joseph Sawyer, Marc Lawrence, Sheldon Leonard, Johnny Long, Joseph Crehan, Edward Gargan, Pat Flaherty, Eddie Dunn, Dorothy Vaughn, Minerva Urecal, Mantan Moreland, Bobby Barber, Wade Boteler, Billy Wayne, Ken Christy, Rebel Randall, Eddie Parker, and Cordelia Campbell

Brief: Sidewalk photographers Flash Fulton (Bud) and Tubby McCoy (Lou) are hired by a crook who mistakenly thinks they are fierce gunmen. After being involved in a robbery, The Boys hide out in Sun Valley to escape the thugs. Then, following a chase scene in an ice-skating rink, the real thieves are caught.

SIDELIGHTS
- *The film was originally titled* Oh Doctor.
- *Following filming of* Hit the Ice, *Lou Costello was stricken with rheumatic heart disease.*
- *The film was released July 2, 1943.*
- *Routine Checklist: "Pack, Unpack," "The Piano Bit" (sometimes called "Alright!").*

As usual, The Boys are treading on thin . . . in Hit the Ice, *a frosty flick for a summer release in July 1943.*

SIDELIGHTS

- *The movie's climactic chase scene is actually film footage used first in W. C. Fields's* Never Give a Sucker an Even Break *(1941).*
- *This was the most expensive Abbott & Costello film to date. Universal spent nearly $700,000 on the flick, and it was shot in thirty-four days. Bud and Lou's salary was $80,000 plus a percentage of the net.*
- *Two popular songs in this film ("No Bout Adoubt It" and "My Dreams Are Getting Better All the Time") were written by the team of Mann Curtis and Vic Mizzy. In the l960s, Mizzy gained prominence for writing (and scoring) themes for some of TV's most popular shows such as* The Addams Family, Green Acres, *and most of Don Knotts's Universal pictures.*
- *The film was released August 18, 1944.*
- *Routine Checklist: "Fleugel Street" (aka "The Susquehanna Hat Company").*

In Society (1944)

Produced by Edmund L. Hartmann
Directed by Jean Yarbrough
Screenplay by John Grant, Edmund L. Hartmann, and Hal Fimberg
Additional comedy material for Abbott & Costello by Sidney Fields
Original story by Hugh Wedlock Jr., and Howard Snyder
Songs by Mann Curtis and Vic Mizzy, Bobby Worth, Stanley Cowan, Kim Gannon, and Walter Kent.
Universal—International Studios
74 minutes

Cast: Bud Abbott, Lou Costello, Marion Hutton, Kirby Grant, Ann Gillis, Arthur Treacher, Thomas Gomez, George Dolenz, Steven Geray, Margaret Irving, Murray Leonard, Thurston Hall, Nella Walker, William B. Davidson, Elvia Allman, Milt Bronson, Don Barclay, Edgar Dearing, Ann Roberts, Ian Wolfe, Charles Sherlock, Al Thompson, Luis Alberni, Tom Fadden, Dorothy Granger, Leon DeVoe, and Ralph Dunn

Brief: Plumbers Eddie Harrington (Bud) and Albert Mansfield (Lou) are summoned to the Van Cleve mansion. They make a shambles of the mansion but, by error, are invited to return. Their crooked creditor, Drexel (Thomas Gomez), tries to persuade them to steal a valuable painting. Instead Drexel steals the painting, and The Boys and Elsie Hammerdingle (Marion Hutton) are blamed—until they clear their names.

Foreign publicity for In Society. *(Courtesy of Joe Wallison)*

Sheet music for one of Vic Mizzy's biggest hits during the WW II, "My Dreams Are Getting Better All The Time." The song was featured in Abbott and Costello's In Society. *(Courtesy of Joe Wallison)*

Lost in a Harem (1944)
Produced by George Haight
Directed by Charles Riesner
Screenplay by John Grant, Harry Crane, and Harry Ruskin
Songs by Don Raye, Gene de Paul, Sammy Fain, Ralph Freed, Toots Camarata, and Maria Terese Lara
Metro-Goldwyn-Mayer Studios
89 minutes

Cast: Bud Abbott, Lou Costello, Marilyn Maxwell, John Conte, Douglas Dumbrille, Jimmy Dorsey, Lottie Harrison, J. Lockard Martin, Murray Leonard, Adia Kuznetzoff, Milton Parsons, Ralph Sanford, Harry Cording, Eddie Abdo, Sammy Stein, Duke York, Katharine Booth, Frank Penny, Frank Scannell, Nick Thompson, Tor Johnson, Jody Gilbert, Tiny Newland, Eddie Dunn, Sondra Rogers, Dick Alexander, Tom Herbert, Heinie Conklin, Ernest Brenck, Bud Wolfe, Carey Loftin, Toni LaRue, Frances Ramsden, Margaret Savage, Jan Bryant, Margaret Kelly, Elinor Troy, Symona Boniface, and The Pinas

Brief: Vaudevillians Peter Johnson (Bud) and Harvey Garvey (Lou) are stranded in a mythical city. They try to overthrow a ruler of a kingdom and repeatedly end up in a dungeon with a crazed lunatic.

SIDELIGHTS
- *Historian Jim Mulholland wrote, "*Lost in a Harem *has such a great spirit of comic insanity that one can easily overlook its flaws."*
- *Two suggested titles for this film were* Harem, Scare 'Em *and* Two Nights in a Harem.
- *The film was released August 31, 1944.*
- *Routine Checklist: "Slowly I Turned" (aka "Niagra Falls")*

Director Charles Riesner hoists a huge pumpkin over Costello's head while rehearsing Lost in a Harem.

An MGM press release for Lost in a Harem *described Bud and Lou in this photograph as "a pair of old necromancers trying to conjure up ghosts from the nether-world. And what's that on the table? Why spirits, of course!"*

The bumbling duo find themselves in prison along with a desert derelict (Murray Leonard) in Lost in a Harem.

Here Come the Co-eds (1945)
Produced by John Grant
Directed by Jean Yarbrough
Screenplay by Arthur T. Horman and John Grant
Based on a story by Edmund L. Hartmann
Songs by Jack Brooks and Edgar Fairchild
Universal-International Studios
88 minutes

Cast: Bud Abbott, Lou Costello, Peggy Ryan, Martha O'Driscoll, June Vincent, Lon Chaney Jr., Donald Cook, Charles Dingle, Richard Lane, Joe Kirk, Bill Stern, Anthony Warde, Dorothy Ford, Sammy Stein, Carl Knowles, Ruth Lee, Don Costello, Rebel Randall, Maxine Gates, Dorothy Granger, Marie Osborn, Milt Bronson, Phil Spitalny and His Band, Martha Garotto, Naomi Stout, June Cuendet, Muriel Stetson, Marilyn Hoeck, Margaret Eversole, Lorna Peterson, Ed Dunn, and Pierre Watkin

Brief: Slats McCarthy (Bud) and Oliver Quackenbush (Lou) arrive at an exclusive school for young women to work as maintenance men and watch over Slats's sister, who has been awarded a scholarship to attend. A conservative chairman decides to let the school go bankrupt because an attractive young professor decides to flaunt tradition. Oliver wins a wrestling match, which provides money to keep the school operating.

SIDELIGHTS
- *Lou Costello, in his youth a basketball player who specialized in deadeye free-throw shooting, pumped in many of the shots himself during the film's basketball game.*
- *The school's main building (the stately Shelby home) on Universal's back lot is also seen in* The Time of Their Lives *as the manor house.*
- *The film was released February 2, 1945.*
- *Routine Checklist: "Jonah and the Whale," "The Oyster Routine," "The Dice Game."*

Martha O'Driscoll plays Bud's sister in Here Come the Co-Eds.

SIDELIGHTS
- *This film is the only Abbott & Costello film to feature a complete "Who's on First?" rendition (except for compilations).*
- *During the "Who's on First?" routine, backstage hands, cameramen, and others watching the filming can be heard laughing in the background.*
- *Lou recycles the "Lifesavers Candy" routine Groucho Marx used in the Marx Brothers' 1932 hit* Horse Feathers.
- *The River Queen was actually a partial riverboat set left over from the 1936 Universal musical,* Show Boat. *Models were used for scenes involving the riverboat in motion.*
- *The film was released July 6, 1945.*

Sam McDaniel and Lou in a publicity shot for The Naughty Nineties. *McDaniel was the brother of Oscar-winning actress Hattie McDaniel, most known for her portrayal of "Mammy" in* Gone with the Wind. *(Courtesy of Joe Wallison)*

The Naughty Nineties (1945)

Produced by Edmund L. Hartmann and John Grant
Directed by Jean Yarbrough
Screenplay by Edmund L. Hartmann, John Grant, Edmund Joseph, and Hal Fimberg
Additional comedy sequences by Felix Adler
Songs by Edgar Fairchild and Jack Brooks
Universal-International Studios
76 minutes

Cast: Bud Abbott, Lou Costello, Alan Curtis, Rita Johnson, Henry Travers, Lois Collier, Joe Sawyer, Joe Kirk, Jack Norton, Sam McDaniel, Billy Green, Lillian Yarbo, Emmet Vogan, Milt Bronson, John Hamilton, Ed Gargan, Jack Chefe, Bud Wolfe, Henry Russell, Ralph Jones, Bing Conley, Tony Dell, John Indrisano, Charles Phillips, Torchy Rand, Ronnie Stanton, William W. Larsen, Donald Kerr, Bud O'Connor, Jack Worth, Delores Evers, Rex Lease, and Sid Fields

Brief: Dexter Broadhurst (Bud) and Sebastian Dinwiddie (Lou) attempt to rescue kindhearted Captain Sam (Henry Travers) from card sharks when *The River Queen* boat is docked in St. Louis. The gamblers take over the showboat and run a crooked gambling operation aboard, while Dexter and Sebastian try to get rid of the villains.

Abbott and Costello in Hollywood (1945)
Produced by Martin A. Gosch
Directed by S. Sylvan Simon
Screenplay by Nat Perrin and Lou Breslow
Original story by Nat Perrin and Martin A. Gosch
Songs by Ralph Blane and Hugh Martin
Metro-Goldwyn-Mayer Studios
83 minutes

Cast: Bud Abbott, Lou Costello, Frances Rafferty, Robert Stanton, Jean Porter, Warner Anderson, Rags Ragland, Lucille Ball, Preston Foster, Robert Z. Leonard, Butch Jenkins, Mike Mazurki, Carleton G. Young, Robert Emmet O'Connor, Donald MacBride, Arthur Space, Katherine Booth, Edgar Dearing, Marion Martin, Dean Stockwell, Bill Phillips, Chester Clute, Marie Blake, Harry Tyler, Skeets Noyes, Dick Alexander, Dick Winslow, Jane Hale, Frank Scannell, the Lyttle Sisters, William Tannen, Milton Kibbee, and Sharon McManus

Brief: Buzz Kurtis (Bud) and his pal Abercrombie (Lou) work in a Hollywood barbershop. They quit their jobs to become big Hollywood agents. To get their first client a job in a picture, the two wreak havoc around a film-studio back lot, finding the means to trick the producers into hiring singer Jeff Parker (Robert Stanton).

SIDELIGHTS
- *MGM was not especially pleased with this film's mediocre reception and box-office receipts and subsequently dropped its option to produce more Abbott & Costello films.*
- *Ralph Blane and Hugh Martin wrote the songs for this film. The year prior, their score for* Meet Me in St. Louis *won great acclaim, with such hits as "Have Yourself a Merry Little Christmas" and "The Trolley Song."*
- *A segment of "The Insomia Scene" was used in the MGM compilation film* That's Entertainment, Part 2 *(1976).*
- *The film was released August 22, 1945.*
- *Routine Checklist: "The Insomnia Scene," "Little Red Riding Hood" (a variation of "Jonah and the Whale").*

Bud poses with his costars, Robert Stanton and Frances Rafferty, on the set of their MGM film Abbott and Costello in Hollywood. *(Courtesy of Joe Wallison)*

SIDELIGHTS
- *The film was originally titled,* On the Carpet.
- *Historian Jim Mulholland wrote* "Little Giant *pretty much falls flat in every department.*"
- *Watch Bud's toupee shift during the scene where he and Lou go into the "7 x 13" routine.*
- *Professor Watkins's voice is that of actor Milburn Stone of* Gunsmoke *fame.*
- *The film was released February 22, 1946.*
- *Routine Checklist: "7 x 13 = 28."*

Little Giant (1946)
Produced by Joe Gershenson
Directed by William A. Seiter
Screenplay by Walter DeLeon
Original story by Paul Jarrico and Richard Collins
Universal-International Studios
91 minutes

Cast: Bud Abbott, Lou Costello, Brenda Joyce, Jacqueline De Wit, George Cleveland, Elena Verdugo, Mary Gordon, Pierre Watkins, Donald MacBride, Victor Kilian, Margaret Dumont, George Chandler, Beatrice Gray, Ed Gargan, Ralph Peters, Bert Roach, George Holmes, Eddie Waller, Ralph Dunn, Dorothy Christy, Chester Conklin, William "Red" Donahue, and Mary Field

Brief: Benny Miller (Lou) gets a job as a vacuum-cleaner salesman through his uncle's influence. John Morrison (Bud) has been juggling the Hercules Vacuum Company's books and is afraid that Benny will find out, so he has him transferred out of town, where Benny outsells the rest of the representatives—all due to a hoax.

Longtime Marx Brothers' foil, Margaret Dumont, gets blasted by a backed-up vacuum cleaner in Little Giant. *(Personality Photos, Inc.)*

The Time of Their Lives (1946)
Produced by Val Burton
Directed by Charles Barton
Original screenplay by Val Burton, Walter DeLeon, and Bradford Ropes
Additional dialogue for Abbott & Costello by John Grant
Universal-International Studios
82 minutes

Cast: Bud Abbott, Lou Costello, Marjorie Reynolds, Binnie Barnes, John Shelton, Jess Barker, Gale Sondergaard, Robert Barrat, Donald MacBride, Anne Gillis, Lynne Baggett, William Hall, Rex Lease, Selmer Jackson, Vernon Downing, Marjorie Eaton, Wheaton Chambers, John Crawford, Myron Healy, Harry Woolman, Harry Brown, Walter Baldwin, George Carleton, Boyd Irwin, and Kirk Alyn

Brief: When Melody Allen (Marjorie Reynolds) discovers that her fiancé is plotting with Benedict Arnold to betray the forces of George Washington, she rushes from stately Danbury Manor to warn the Colonials, but the Patriots think that she and the tinker, Horatio Prim (Lou), are traitors. They are cursed as traitors, shot, dumped in a well, and left to haunt the manor forever. A century and a half later, the house is restored to its original state. Dr. Ralph Greenway (Bud), a descendant of Cuthbert Greenway, the original butler, stays at the house with its new owners. Melody and Horatio decide to haunt the house until they find the secret that will free them from the curse.

SIDELIGHTS
- *As in their previous film, Little Giant, Abbott & Costello do not play partners or even acquaintances in this movie—an unusual twist. In fact, they barely speak to each other in the film.*
- *Bud Abbott had to learn how to drive a car for this film. To assist, the studio built a special electric car, which resembled a two-seated go-cart, and sent him home in it to practice.*
- *The film was released August 16, 1946.*

The secret of freedom for the two earth-bound spirits lay in the antique clock in The Time of Their Lives. *(Personality Photos, Inc.)*

Contacting the other side in the seance scene from The Time of Their Lives.

SIDELIGHTS
- *Actress Joan Fulton, aka Joan Shawlee, later made guest appearances on the team's 1950s TV show.*
- *A deleted scene involving Costello playing Romeo to actress Betty Alexander's Juliet is foreshadowed by the existing scene of Costello's car smashing through the rear of a theater. If you look closely, you will notice the sign for a fictitious motion picture,* Abbott and Costello in 'Romeo Junior.'
- *The film was released April 4, 1947.*

Buck Privates Come Home (1947)
Produced by Robert Arthur
Directed by Charles Barton
Screenplay by John Grant, Frederic I. Rinaldo, and Robert Lees
Based on a story by Richard MacCauley and Bradford Ropes
Music by Walter Schumann
Universal-International Studios
77 minutes

Cast: Bud Abbott, Lou Costello, Tom Brown, Joan Fulton, Nat Pendleton, Beverly Simmons, Don Beddoe, Don Porter, Donald MacBride, Lane Watson, William Ching, Peter Thompson, George Beban Jr., Jimmie Dodd, Lennie Bremen, Al Murphy, Bob Wilke, William Haade, Janna deLoos, Buddy Roosevelt, Chuck Hamilton, Patricia Alphin, Joe Kirk, Charles Trowbridge, Russell Hicks, Ralph Dunn, John Sheenan, Cliff Clark, Jean Del Val, Frank Marlowe, Ottola Nesmith, Eddie Dunn, James Farley, Rex Lease, Ernie Adams, Milburn Stone, Knox Manning, Harlan Warde, Lyle Lattel, Myron Healy, and Charles Sullivan

Brief: Slicker Smith (Bud) and Herbie Brown (Lou) return from the service, and as civilians they restart their old occupations—selling neckties. They smuggle a six-year-old orphan girl into the United States and attempt to find her a good family. The Boys get involved in the midget race-car business in order to make money to find the girl a home.

In a deleted scene from Buck Privates Come Home, *Lou is Romeo and Betty Alexander is his Juliet.*

SIDELIGHTS

- *Lou Costello's father, a western-film buff, died during the production of this movie, and as a tribute Lou listed him in the credits as Associate Producer Sebastian Cristillo.*
- *Norman Abbott, nephew of Bud Abbott, worked as dialogue director on this film.*
- *The film was originally intended as a vehicle for actor Jimmy Stewart.*
- *The story is based on a law that existed in Montana during the 1800s, whereby the survivor of a gunfight is responsible for the dependents and debts of the victim.*
- *The premiere issue of the St. John's comic book series on Abbott and Costello was an adaptation of* The Wistful Widow of Wagon Gap, *circa 1948.*
- *The film was released October 8, 1947.*
- *Routine Checklist: "Frog in the Soup" (variation of the "Oyster" routine).*

The Wistful Widow of Wagon Gap (1947)
Produced by Robert Arthur
Directed by Charles Barton
Screenplay by Robert Lees, Frederic I. Rinaldo, and John Grant
Based on a story by D. D. Beauchamp and William Bowers
Music by Walter Schumann
Universal-International Studios
78 minutes

Cast: Bud Abbott, Lou Costello, Marjorie Main, Audrey Young, George Cleveland, Gordon Jones, William Ching, Peter Thompson, Olin Howlin, Bill Clauson, Billy O'Leary, Pamela Wells, Jimmie Bates, Paul Dunn, Diane Florentine, Rex Lease, Glenn Strange, Dewey Robinson, Edmund Cobb, Wade Crosby, Murray Leonard, Emmett Lynn, Iris Adrian, Lee Lasses White, George Lewis, Charles King, Jack Shutta, Harry Evans, Mickey Simpson, Ethan Laidlaw, Frank Marlo, Emmett Lynn, and Gilda Feldrais

Brief: When Duke Egan (Bud) and Chester Wooley (Lou) arrive in the western town of Wagon Gap, Chester is accused of shooting the town drunk. Because he is now responsible for the debts and dependents of the victim, Chester is not hanged. He thus goes to work on the Widow Hawkins's (Marjorie Main) ranch, where she resides with her six wild children. Chester uses a crafty scheme to subdue a gang and is free to go when a judge proposes to the widow.

The Noose Hangs High (1948)
Produced by Charles Barton
Directed by Charles Barton
Screenplay by John Grant and Howard Harris
Based on a story by Daniel Tradash, Julian Blaustein, and Bernard Fins
Eagle-Lion Studios
77 minutes

Cast: Bud Abbott, Lou Costello, Cathy Downs, Joseph Calleia, Leon Errol, Mike Mazurki, Jack Overman, Fritz Feld, Vera Martin, Joe Kirk, Matt Willis, Ben Weldon, Ben Hall, Jimmy Dodd, Ellen Corby, Isabel Randolph, Frank O'Connor, Bess Flowers, Murray Leonard, Pat Flaherty, Elvia Allman, Lois Austin, Herb Vigran, James Flavin, Minerva Urecal, Russell Hicks, Arno Frey, Paul Maxey, Lyle Latell, Harry Brown, Sandra Spence, and Oscar Otis (announcer)

Brief: Ted Higgins (Bud) and Tommy Hinchcliffe (Lou) are window washers hired by a gangster to collect a sizable debt. After The Boys deliver it to the wrong party, they have twenty-four hours to retrieve the money.

SIDELIGHTS
• *Lou Costello's daughter Christine was born just two days before production.*
• *This is a remake of the 1939 Universal film,* For Love of Money.
• *The film was released April 5, 1948.*
• *Routine Checklist: "Mustard," "Mudder/Fodder," "You're 40, She's 10," "What Are You Doing at the Depot?" and a variation of "Pack, Unpack."*

The Noose Hangs High remains one of the rarely televised Abbott and Costello features. Several of the team's familiar routines—including "The Mustard Routine"—are performed in the film with freshness.

SIDELIGHTS

- *Vincent Price supplies the voice of the Invisible Man at the end of the movie, a somewhat unnecessary prelude to* Abbott and Costello Meet the Invisible Man, *which, by the way, did not feature Price and was not a horror movie.*
- *The film was originally titled* The Brain of Frankenstein.
- *Initially, Costello detested the script and did not want to make this film, but after the premiere his mother said that it was the best she had seen of her son's work. He was content.*
- *Many critics consider this movie to be Bela Lugosi's last piece of competent, legitimate film acting. In 1956, at the age of seventy-two, he died after suffering from a lengthy morphine addiction.*
- *Filming began February 5, 1948, and ended March 20, 1948, within a budget of $759,524.*
- *Director Charles Barton recalls that the expense of having pies on the set for Bud and Lou's off-camera antics was between $3,800 and $4,800.*
- *Reportedly, the actor who originally played Frankenstein's monster, Boris Karloff, refused to see* Abbott and Costello Meet Frankenstein, *claiming he did not want to see a parody of the monster on film. Nonetheless, he enjoyed The Boys' comedy in other films and costarred with them in two movies. (Note: Universal Studios did convince Karloff to pose for photographs outside a New York theater premiering the film—for a fee, of course.)*
- *Listen closely for Costello to accidentally yell "Abbott" instead of "Chick," the name of Bud's character.*

Abbott and Costello Meet Frankenstein (1948)

Produced by Robert Arthur
Directed by Charles Barton
Original screenplay by Frederic I. Rinaldo, Robert Lees, and John Grant
Music by Frank Skinner
Universal-International Studios
83 minutes

Cast: Bud Abbott, Lou Costello, Lon Chaney Jr., Bela Lugosi, Glenn Strange, Lenore Aubert, Jane Randolph, Frank Ferguson, Charles Bradstreet, Howard Negley, Joe Kirk, Clarence Straight, Harry Brown, Helen Spring, George Barton, Carl Sklover, Paul Stader, Joe Walls, and Bobby Barber

Brief: Baggage clerks Chick Young (Bud) and Wilbur Grey (Lou) receive an urgent call from Larry Talbot (Lon Chaney Jr.), who is really a wolf man. He tells them not to deliver the crates containing the remains of Count Dracula (Bela Lugosi) and Frankenstein's monster (Glenn Strange) to a House of Horrors. The monsters escape after the crates are delivered, and Count Dracula and his assistant attempt to transplant Wilbur's brain into the monster.

Bela Lugosi dons the cape once again in Abbott and Costello Meet Frankenstein. *(Courtesy of Tbm Frederick)*

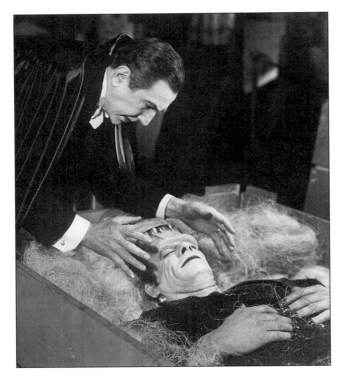

Bela Lugosi, as Count Dracula, revitalizes Frankenstein's monster, played by Glenn Strange, in Abbott and Costello's most popular film.

- *In the scene where Frankenstein's monster tosses a woman out the window, Lon Chaney, rather than Glenn Strange, plays the monster. Chaney gladly applied the makeup and subbed one day for Strange, who injured his foot on studio cables. Strange later resumed filming, with his foot unobtrusively protected by a cast.*
- *Costello accidentally suffered a blow to the nose when the Monster (Glenn Strange) beat in a door and Costello was not on his proper mark.*
- *Actor Glenn Strange also appeared with The Boys in* The Wistful Widow of Wagon Gap *and* Comin' Round the Mountain. *Strange, popularly known as the Lone Ranger's nemesis, Butch Cavendish, and Sam the bartender on TV's* Gunsmoke, *died in 1973 at the age of seventy-four.*
- *Lon Chaney Jr. (the Wolf Man), who also died in 1973, reportedly once blamed Abbott & Costello for the demise of classic horror films.*
- *This was the biggest hit for The Boys since* Buck Privates *and one of the film industry's top moneymakers of 1948.*
- *This film is one of the most popular with Abbott & Costello aficionados.*
- *The film was released August 20, 1948.*
- *Routine Checklist: "The Moving Candle."*

Two of Universal Studio's most popular entities. (Courtesy of Tom Frederick)

SIDELIGHTS
- *Pat Costello, Lou's brother, plays Tim Williams in this film. Pat's resemblance to Lou is obvious.*
- *The movie is based on the 1944 Cole Porter musical that starred vaudevillian Bobby Clark.*
- *The film was released December 27, 1948.*
- *Routine Checklist: "Silver Ore."*

Mexican Hayride (1948)

Produced by Robert Arthur
Directed by Charles Barton
Screenplay by Oscar Brodney and John Grant
Based on the musical play by Herbert and Dorothy Fields,
with Cole Porter
Music arranged and conducted by Walter Scharf
Universal-International Studios
77 minutes

Cast: Bud Abbott, Lou Costello, Virginia Grey, Luba Malina, John Hubbard, Pedro de Cordoba, Fritz Feld, Tom Powers, Pat Costello, Frank Fenton, Sidney Fields, Chris Pin Martin, the Flores Brothers Trio, Argentina Brunetti, Eddie Kane, Ben Chavez, Pedro Regas, Charles Miller, Harry Brown, Joe Kirk, Julian Rivero, Tony Roux, Roque Ybarra, Joe Dominguez, Felipe Turich, Alex Montoya, George Mendoza, Robert Elias, Rose Marie Lopez, Earl Spainard, Suzanne Ridgway, Cosmo Sardo, Mary Brewer, Marjorie L. Carver, Lucille Casey, Toni Castle, and Lorraine Crawford

Brief: Harry Lambert (Bud) sells phony oil stock, and Joe Bascom (Lou) is accused of the scheme. Joe pursues Harry to Mexico, where Harry has become the manager of a female matador named Montana (Virginia Grey). Joe ends up helping Harry sell another phony oil well.

SIDELIGHTS
- *This is one of the few films that Shemp Howard appeared in with Joe Besser, who later succeeded Howard as one of the Three Stooges.*
- *Filming was delayed because Shemp Howard became seasick while floating on a raft in the studio tank—which was only a few feet deep!*
- *Norman Abbott, Bud's nephew, worked as dialogue coach on this film.*
- *This is the least seen of all Abbott & Costello films. In the 1970s, however, the copyright lapsed for the film, and independent video dealers have released duped versions on videocassette. A newly restored*

Africa Screams (1949)

Produced by Edward Nassour
Directed by Charles Barton
Original screenplay by Earl Baldwin
United Artists
79 minutes

Cast: Bud Abbott, Lou Costello, Hillary Brooke, Max Baer Sr., Buddy Baer, Shemp Howard, Joe Besser, Clyde Beatty, Frank Buck, Bobby Barber, Burton Wenland, Charles Gemorra (gorilla).

Brief: Buzz Johnson (Bud) and Stanley Livington (Lou) work in a book section of a New York department store. They travel to Africa after convincing their client that Stanley is a big-game hunter. Diana Emerson (Hillary Brooke), not knowing they are phonies, secretly uses The Boys to find diamonds in the possession of an African tribe.

version has been released on laser disc.

• Africa Screams *is a takeoff of a 1930 documentary,* Africa Speaks.

• *This film was shot in sixteen days, on a budget of less than $500,000.*

• *This film was later colorized by computer and released on video.*

• *The film was released May 4, 1949.*

Hillary Brooke and The Boys shoot a little pool while on a break in filming Africa Screams. *(Courtesy of Joe Wallison)*

SIDELIGHTS
- *Actually, Boris Karloff is not the killer in the film, as the title suggests.*
- *The film was originally titled* Easy Does It, *and was to star Bob Hope.*
- *Another working title that was eventually scrapped was* Abbott and Costello Meet the Killers.
- *The film was released August 22, 1949.*

Abbott and Costello Meet the Killer, Boris Karloff (1949)
Produced by Robert Arthur
Directed by Charles Barton
Screenplay by Hugh Wedlock Jr., Howard Snyder, and John Grant
Original story by Hugh Wedlock Jr., and Howard Snyder
Music by Milton Schwarzwald
Universal-International Studios
82 minutes

Cast: Bud Abbott, Lou Costello, Boris Karloff, Lenore Aubert, Gar Moore, Donna Martell, Alan Mowbray, James Flavin, Roland Winters, Nicholas Joy, Mikel Conrad, Morgan Farley, Victoria Horne, Percy Helton, Claire Du Brey, Harry Hayden, Vincent Renno, Patricia Hall, Murray Alper, Marjorie Bennett, Harry Brown, Beatrice Gray, Billy Snyder, Eddie Coke, Frankie Van, Jack Chefe, Arthur Hecht, Ed Randolph, Phil Shepard, Gail Bonney, Henrietta Taylor, and Billy Gray

Brief: An attorney is murdered at the Lost Caverns Hotel, and bellboy Freddie Phillips (Lou) is accused of the crime. House detective Casey Edwards (Bud) helps Freddie rid himself of charges, while a police inspector uses Freddie as a decoy to catch the real killer.

Abbott and Costello in the Foreign Legion (1950)
Produced by Robert Arthur
Directed by Charles Lamont
Screenplay by John Grant, Martin Ragaway, and Leonard Stern
From a story by D. D. Beauchamp
Musical direction by Joseph Gershenson
Universal-International Studios
80 minutes

Cast: Bud Abbott, Lou Costello, Patricia Medina, Walter Slezak, Douglas Dumbrille, Leon Belasco, Marc Lawrence, Tor Johnson, Wee Willie Davis, Sam Menacker, Fred Nurney, Paul Fierro, Henry Corden, Jack Raymond, Dan Seymour, Alberto Morin, Guy Beach, Ted Hecht, Mahmud Shaikaly, Buddy Roosevelt, Charmienne Harker, David Gorcey, Bobby Barber, Jack Shutta, Ernesto Morelli, Chuck Hamilton, Jack Davidson, Harry Wilson, and John Cliff

Brief: Wrestling promoters Jonesy (Bud) and Lou Hotchkiss (Lou) travel to Algeria in search of a wrestler. When they are tricked into joining the foreign legion, their entire troop is wiped out by the Arabs, leaving only The Boys and a cruel sergeant alive.

SIDELIGHTS

- *Comedy writers Martin Ragaway and Leonard Stern, part of the team who produced this screenplay, worked with Bud and Lou on their radio program. Stern began his television career writing on Jackie Gleason's* The Honeymooners, *and Phil Silvers's* You'll Never Get Rich, *and later worked extensively on* The Steve Allen Show. *He later became a successful television producer with such hits as* Get Smart *and* McMillan and Wife *on his résumé.*
- *The voice of the skeleton is that of comic Candy Candido, who later teamed briefly with Bud Abbott after Lou Costello's death.*
- *The film was released July 24, 1950.*

Confronting Abou Ben (Tor Johnson) and Abdullah (Wee Willie Davis) in Foreign Legion. *(Courtesy of Joe Wallison)*

SIDELIGHTS
- *In one scene, the characters talk about the origin of the invisibility formula and the doctor who invented it. Notice actor Claude Rains's picture on the wall. Rains was the original Invisible Man in Universal's motion pictures.*
- *The film was released March 19, 1951.*

Abbott and Costello Meet the Invisible Man (1951)

Produced by Howard Christie
Directed by Charles Lamont
Screenplay by Robert Lees, Frederic I. Rinaldo, and John Grant
From a story by Hugh Wedlock Jr., and Howard Snyder
Suggested by H. G. Wells's *The Invisible Man*
Music direction by Joseph Gershenson
Universal-International Studios
82 minutes

Cast: Bud Abbott, Lou Costello, Nancy Guild, Adele Jergens, Sheldon Leonard, William Frawley, Gavin Muir, Arthur Franz, Sam Balter, Sid Saylor, Bobby Barber, Billy Wayne, John Day, George J. Lewis, Frankie Van, Carl Sklover, Charles Perry, Paul Maxey, Ed Gargan, Herb Vigran, Ralph Dunn, Herold Goodwin, Richard Bartell, Perc Launders, Edith Sheets, Milt Bronson (announcer), and Donald Kerr

Brief: Bud Alexander (Bud) and Lou Francis (Lou) are private detectives who try to prove that their client, a fighter who can become invisible, is innocent of murdering his manager. Lou fights a bout in the ring with the aid of the invisible fighter. The invisible fighter also helps Bud and Lou solve the case.

Comin' Round the Mountain (1951)
Produced by Howard Christie
Directed by Charles Lamont
Screenplay by Robert Lees and Frederic I. Rinaldo
Additional dialogue by John Grant
Universal-International Studios
77 minutes

Cast: Bud Abbott, Lou Costello, Dorothy Shay, Kirby Grant, Joe
  Sawyer, Margaret Hamilton, Ida Moore, Glenn Strange, Russell
  Simpson, Shaye Cogan, Robert Easton, Guy Wilkerson, Virgil
  "Slats" Taylor, O. Z. Whitehead, Norman Leavitt, Joe Kirk, William
  Fawcett, Herold Goodwin, Jack Kruschen, Peter Mamakos, Barry
  Brooks, Robert R. Stephenson, Sherman Sanders, Shirlee Allard,
  and James Clay

Brief: Al Stewart (Bud) is an agent for hillbilly singer Dorothy
  McCoy (Dorothy Shay) and inept escape artist Wilbert (Lou).
  Dorothy discovers that she and Wilbert are cousins and heirs to a
  hidden fortune. She takes him and Al to Kentucky to help find
  the money. There they all get involved in the Winfield and
  McCoy feud, and the treasure they discover ends up being inside
  the Fort Knox vaults.

SIDELIGHTS
• *The film was released June 18, 1951.*
• *Routine Checklist: "You're 40, She's 10."*

*Margaret Hamilton—best known as the Wicked Witch of the
West in* The Wizard of Oz—*was an equally evil Aunt Huddy in*
Comin' Round the Mountain.

SIDELIGHTS

- *This is the first of only two color motion pictures that Abbott & Costello made.*
- *Bud and Lou made an independent, two-picture deal in which they agreed that this was to be "Lou's film" and the next, "Bud's." Lou and Bud retained individual ownership of the respective films.*
- *Beanstalk was shot in twenty-two days on a budget of almost $420,000.*
- *Some scenes were shot on the existing sets from* Joan of Arc *(1948) at the Hal Roach Studios in Culver City, California.*
- *This feature spawned a record album titled* Jack and the Beanstalk *(on the Decca label), which included songs and dialogue. It was released in June 1952.*
- *The film was released April 9, 1952.*

Jack and the Beanstalk (1952)
Produced by Alex Gottlieb
Directed by Jean Yarbrough
Screenplay by Nat Curtis
Additional comedy by Felix Adler
Music score composed and conducted by Heinz Roemheld
Words and music by Bob Russell and Lester Lee
From a story by Pat Costello
Warner Brothers (Reissued by RKO)
78 minutes

Cast: Bud Abbott, Lou Costello, Buddy Baer, Dorothy Ford, Barbara Brown, David Stollery, William Farnum, Shaye Cogan, James Alexander, Joe Kirk, Johnny Conrad and Dancers.

Brief: Dinklepuss (Bud) and Jack (Lou) baby-sit and fall asleep. Jack dreams that he is the giant-killer in the famous fairy tale. Magic beans are planted, and a giant captures The Boys. Finally they and fellow captives, a prince and princess, escape down the beanstalk.

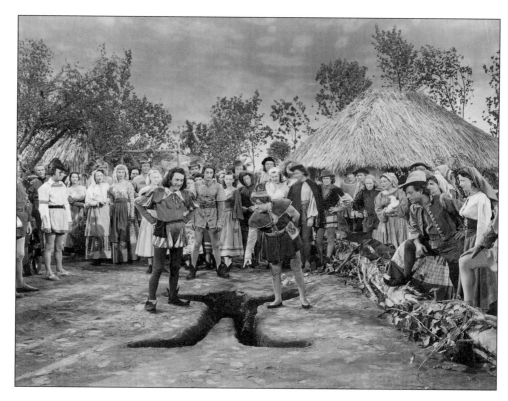

Lou Costello got the idea to produce Jack and the Beanstalk *while reading the storybook to his four-year-old daughter, Christine. He said, "I was only part way through the book when I started to look at the pretty pictures and thought what a wonderful movie this would make. Then I remembered that some of the biggest box-office smashes have been fantasies—*The Wizard of Oz *and the Disney films." (Courtesy of Joe Wallison)*

Bud, Buddy Baer, Dorothy Ford, and "Patrick the Harp" in a scene from Jack and the Beanstalk. *After the production Costello took the harp home and placed it in the family's upstairs sitting room. "I remember being terrified of it when I was a child," says Chris Costello.*

Lost in Alaska (1952)
Produced by Howard Christie
Directed by Jean Yarbrough
Screenplay by Martin Ragaway and Leonard Stern
From a story by Elwood Ullman
Music by Joseph Gershenson
Universal-International Studios
76 minutes

Cast: Bud Abbott, Lou Costello, Mitzi Green, Tom Ewell, Bruce Cabot, Emory Parnell, Jack Ingram, Rex Lease, Joe Kirk, Minerva Urecal, Howard Negley, Maudie Prickett, Billy Wayne, Paul Newlan, Michael Ross, Julia Montoya, Iron Eyes Cody, Fred Aldrich, Donald Kerr, George Barton, Bobby Barber, William Gould, Sherry Moreland, Jean Hartelle, Bert LeBaron.

Brief: George Bell (Lou) and Tom Watson (Bud) are firemen in the 1800s. George rescues Nugget Joe McDermott (Tom Ewell) from jumping into the river, and together with Joe, The Boys head to Alaska to retrieve $2 million in gold, with interferences along the way. Unfortunately, the gold is lost in the end.

SIDELIGHTS
- *This film was originally titled* The Sourdoughs.
- *The idea for this film's story line came from the late writer Elwood Ullman, who was also the head writer for the Three Stooges at Columbia Pictures for many years.*
- Lost in Alaska *was panned by most critics.* Variety *called it "a slipshod 76 minutes of footage marked by more tedious stretches than humor." The* Hollywood Reporter *labeled it, "a feeble bit of film fare."*
- *Believe it or not,* Lost in Alaska *includes the first film score efforts of legendary composer Henry Mancini. (Mancini only worked on portions of the score. Later, he worked on* Abbott and Costello Meet the Mummy.)
- *The film was released July 28, 1952.*

Makeup man Abe Haberman frosted Bud and Lou with a mixture of egg-sealer and Epsom salts. (Courtesy of Abe Haberman)

SIDELIGHTS

- *According to the independent deal struck between Bud and Lou, this film was owned by Bud. It was more successful at the box office than Lou's film, Jack and the Beanstalk—which Bud reminded his partner of often, friends say.*
- *This was the team's second and last color motion picture.*
- *Oscar winner Charles Laughton insisted on doing his own pratfalls in this picture.*
- *The film was released December 27, 1952.*

Abbott and Costello Meet Captain Kidd (1952)
Produced by Alex Gottlieb
Directed by Charles Lamont
Screenplay by Howard Dimsdale and John Grant
Songs by Bob Russell and Lester Lee
Warner Brothers
70 minutes

Cast: Bud Abbott, Lou Costello, Charles Laughton, Hillary Brooke, Fran Warren, Bill Shirley, Leif Erickson, Sid Saylor, Frank Yaconelli, Rex Lease, Bobby Barber.

Brief: Stranded on a pirate island, Rocky Stonebridge (Bud) and Oliver "Puddin' Head" Johnson (Lou) work as waiters in order to earn funds for a long-awaited voyage to America. Through a mix-up with a treasure map, The Boys are kidnapped and forced to go on Captain Kidd's (Charles Laughton) voyage to Skull Island in search of buried treasure.

"Puddin' Head" and Rocky are in constant danger aboard Captain' Kidd's vessel. (Courtesy of Joe Wallison)

Abbott and Costello Go to Mars (1953)
Produced by Howard Christie
Directed by Charles Lamont
Screenplay by D. D. Beauchamp and John Grant
Universal-International Studios
77 minutes

Cast: Bud Abbott, Lou Costello, Robert Paige, Mari Blanchard, Martha Hyer, Horace McMahon, Jack Kruschen, Anita Ekberg, Jackie Loughery, Jean Willes, Joe Kirk, Harold Goodwin, Hal Forrest, Jack Tesler, James Flavin, Sid Saylor, Russ Conway, Paul Newlan, Tim Graham, Ken Christy, Grace Lenard, Billy Newell, Harry Lang, Milt Bronson, Robert Forrest, Dudley Dickerson, Rex Lease, Frank Marlowe, Bobby Barber, Cora Shannon, and Miss Universe contestants.

Brief: Lester (Bud) and Orville (Lou) touch the starter button of a rocket ship, and they jet off, landing near New Orleans—just in time for Mardi Gras celebrations. Two convicts force them to take off again, this time landing on Venus, where they encounter a queen and her all-girl court. When The Boys return to earth, they are heroes.

SIDELIGHTS
- *Most of the Venusians were played by contestants in the 1953 Miss Universe pageant, including Miss Sweden, Anita Ekberg.*
- *Actually, the team heads for Mars but lands on Venus.*
- *The film was released April 6, 1953.*
- *Routine Checklist: A variation of the "Tree of Truth" is included.*

Probably one of the unfunniest films Bud and Lou made. (Courtesy of Joe Wallison)

Julie Dorsey, daughter of bandleader Jimmy Dorsey, makes her screen debut in Abbott and Costello Go to Mars.

Mari Blanchard gets star billing in Abbott and Costello Go to Mars. *She plays Allura, Queen of the planet Venus, which the team visits—not Mars.*

Abbott and Costello Meet Dr. Jekyll and Mr. Hyde (1953)
Produced by Howard Christie
Directed by Charles Lamont
Screenplay by Lee Loeb and John Grant
Original story by Sidney Fields and Grant Garrett
Universal-International Studios
76 minutes

Cast: Bud Abbott, Lou Costello, Boris Karloff, Craig Stevens, Helen Westcott, Reginald Denny, John Dierkes, Patti McKaye, Lucille Lamarr, Carmen de Lavallade, Henry Corden, Marjorie Bennett, Harry Cording, Arthur Gould-Porter, Herbert Deans, Judith Brian, Gil Perkins, Hilda Plowright, Keith Hitchcock, Donald Kerr, Clive Morgan, Tony Marshe, Michael Hadlow, Clyde Cook, John Rogers, Isabelle Dwan, James Fairfax, Betty Fairfax.

Brief: American police officers Slim (Bud) and Tubby (Lou) are in London and end up investigating a monster who is terrorizing the city. Dr. Jekyll (Boris Karloff) is in love with his young ward, Vicky Edwards (Helen Westcott), and attempts to sabotage—via his monster, Hyde—any other love interest she may have.

SIDELIGHTS
- *In the scene where the actors jump from a rooftop over an alley, Boris Karloff's stuntman broke his foot.*
- *The film was released August 10, 1953.*

Abbott and Costello Meet the Keystone Kops (1955)
Produced by Howard Christie
Directed by Charles Lamont
Screenplay by John Grant
From a story by Lee Loeb
Universal-International Studios
78 minutes

Cast: Bud Abbott, Lou Costello, Fred Clark, Lynn Bari, Maxie Rosenbloom, Frank Wilcox, Herold Goodwin, Mack Sennett, Roscoe Ates, Paul Dubov, Joe Besser, Harry Tyler, Henry Kulky, Joe Devlin, William Haade, Jack Daly, Byron Keith, Houseley Stevens, Murray Leonard, Marjorie Bennett, Charles Dorety, Donald Kerr, Heinie Conklin, Forrest Burns, Don House, Jack Stoney, Carole Costello, Hank Mann.

Brief: Harry Pierce (Bud) and Willie Piper (Lou) are swindled into buying the deed to an old movie studio. They head for Hollywood to track down con man Joseph Gorman (Fred Clark) and become stuntmen at Amalgamated Pictures. Now a movie director, Gorman is caught stealing from the studio and flees. The Keystone Kops join The Boys in a wild chase to catch him.

SIDELIGHTS
- *Lou Costello's daughter Carole makes a cameo appearance as the cashier in the theater window.*
- *Three members of the original Keystone Kops of silent films worked on the picture: Hank Mann, Herold Goodwin, and Heinie Conklin. There is also a brief appearance by silent-picture director Mack Sennett.*
- *After filming had completed, Lou suffered yet another bout of rheumatic fever and his weight dropped drastically.*
- *The film was released January 31, 1955.*
- *Routine Checklist: a variation of the "Oyster" routine, this time utilizing a squirrel—in a loaf of bread!*

Original publicity artwork for Abbott and Costello
Meet the Keystone Kops. *(Personality Photos, Inc.)*

Abbott and Costello Meet the Mummy (1955)
Produced by Howard Christie
Directed by Charles Lamont
Screenplay by John Grant
Story by Lee Loeb
Music supervision by Joseph Gershenson
Universal-International Studios
79 minutes

Cast: Bud Abbott, Lou Costello, Marie Windsor, Michael Ansara, Dan Seymour, Kurt Katch, Richard Karlan, Richard Deacon, Mel Welles, Veola Vonn, Harry Medozza, Jean Hartelle, Kam Tong, Robin Morse, Carole Costello, John Powell, Peggy King, the Mazzone-Abbott Dancers, George Khoury, Eddie Parker, Jan Arvan, Ted Hecht, Michael Vallon, Lee Sharon, Hank Mann, Donald Kerr, Kem Dibbs, Mitchell Kowall, Ken Alton, The Chandra-Kaly Dancers.

Brief: Peter Patterson (Bud) and Freddie Franklin (Lou) are Americans stranded in Egypt who catch wind of a mummy being transported to the States. They hope to accompany the archaeologist who found the mummy of Klaris back to the States, but he has been murdered. Lou then comes into possession of a medallion that reveals the secret of a jewel-laden tomb. Madame Rontru (Marie Windsor), as well as other fortune hunters, pursue Lou in a chase for the medallion—and the jewels.

SIDELIGHTS
- *Famous stuntman Eddie Parker played the Mummy.*
- *Mummy was shot in under a month, on a budget of $738,250.*
- *Lou's daughter Carole appears in the film as a café flower girl who unintentionally returns the cursed medallion to Lou.*
- *The great Henry Mancini scored portions of the music in this film, including the opening title.*
- *Crazy, but although their characters' names are Pete and Freddie (in the script and in the final credits), Bud and Lou use their real names throughout the film. Costello even yells "Heeeeyyy Abbott!" in the film.*
- *Just a few months after Mummy was released, Bud and Lou's longtime writer and collaborator, John Grant, died (November 19, 1955).*
- *The film was released May 23, 1955.*
- *Routine Checklist: "Take Your Pick."*

Bud and Lou pose with actress Marie Windsor, a former Miss Utah, during the Mummy movie.

SIDELIGHTS
- *This is the last film Bud Abbott and Lou Costello made together.*
- *Lou was getting quite anxious and upset about his work and wished to drastically change the image of the team with this film. He told the Associated Press: "Slapstick is outdated for us. No matter what we do, it looks like something we've done before. We tried to be different with our last picture. But it was still slapstick. The critics murdered us."*
- *The film was shot in twenty-three days on a measly $450,000 budget.*
- *This film is a pathetic swan song for Bud and Lou, with almost no laughs in the film.*
- *The film was released December 14, 1956.*

Dance with Me, Henry (1956)
Produced by Bob Goldstein
Directed by Charles Barton
Screenplay by Devery Freeman
Original story by William Kozlenko and Leslie Kardos
Music direction by Paul Dunlap
United Artists
80 minutes

Cast: Bud Abbott, Lou Costello, Gigi Perreau, Rusty Hamer, Mary Wickes, Ted de Corsia, Ron Hargrave, Sherry Alberoni, Frank Wilcox, Richard Reeves, Paul Sorenson, Robert Shayne, John Cliff, Phil Garris, Walter Reed, Eddie Marr, David McMahon, Gil Rankin, Rod Williams.

Brief: Lou Henry (Lou) is the owner of an amusement park, and Bud Flick (Bud) is his buddy. Together they share a home with two orphan children. Welfare worker Miss Mayberry (Mary Wickes) attempts to remove the children. Bud and Lou get involved in a robbery and a kidnapping, and Lou is assisted by neighborhood children in nabbing mobsters. His efforts enable him to take back custody of the orphans.

Midget acress Hazel Resmondo, who got her start in The Wizard of Oz, *worked as a stand-in for the children in* Dance With Me, Henry. *Resmondo snapped these cadids on her polaroid in May 1956. Above: Lou rehearsing with Gigi Perreau. Above right: Lou walking through a scene with director Charles Barton. Right: Hazel posing with Rusty Hamer and Gigi Perreau. (Courtesy of Tod Machin)*

Lou Costello's Solo Film Appearance

The 30 Foot Bride of Candy Rock (1959)
Produced by Lewis J. Rachmil
Directed by Sidney Miller
Screenplay by Rowland Barber and Arthur Ross
Story by Lawrence L. Goldman
Columbia Pictures
75 minutes

Cast: Lou Costello, Dorothy Provine, Gale Gordon, Jimmy Conlin, Charles Lane, Robert Burton, Will Wright, Lenny Kent, Ruth Perrott, Peter Leeds, Robert Nichols, Veola Vonn, Bobby Barber, Joey Faye, Doodles Weaver, Jack Rice, Russell Trent, Joe Greene, Arthur Walsh, Michael Hagen, Mark Scott, James Bryce.

Brief: Artie Pinsetter (Lou) is a junk collector/amateur inventor who lives in Candy Rock. His love interest, Emmy Lou (Dorothy Provine), happens upon magical springwaters that change her into a thirty-foot giant. Artie tries to restore her to normal size.

SIDELIGHTS
- *The film, Lou's last, was an utter flop at the box office.*
- *According to Vic Parks, Liberace was slated to costar with Lou in the movie but didn't.*
- *Lou's daughter Carole has a brief speaking part in the beginning. (Lou addresses her, "Hello, Carole.")*
- *Two months after completing the film, Lou Costello suffered a heart attack.*
- *The film was released August 6, 1959, five months after Lou Costello's death.*

Right: Lou with his daughter Carole on the set of The 30 Foot Bride of Candy Rock. *(Courtesy of Joe Wallison)*

Left: Lou Costello braces himself against Candy Rock for the biggest flop of his career. Costello did not live to see the completed picture. ". . . it would have killed him," said his wife, Anne, at the premiere. (Courtesy of Joe Wallison)

Compilation Works on Abbott & Costello

The World of Abbott and Costello (1965)
Produced by Max J. Rosenberg and Milton Subotsky
Editorial direction by Sidney Meyer
Narration written by Gene Wood
Narrated by Jack E. Leonard
Universal-International Studios
75 minutes

Brief: This compilation contains highlights from eighteen Abbott & Costello films, including the "Who's on First?" and "Tie-Salesman" routines and scenes from *Abbott and Costello Meet Frankenstein.*

Hey Abbott! (1978)
Executive Producers: I. Holender and M. J. Ruderian
Produced and directed by Jim Gates
Written by Stan Oliver
Creative Consultant: Eddie Sherman
Telepictures Corp. Production with ZIV International
76 minutes

Brief: This made-for-television compilation is narrated by Milton Berle and features live segments by Steve Allen, Phil Silvers, and Joe Besser. The tribute is composed of clips from the 1950s' *The Abbott and Costello Show.*

The Best of Abbott and Costello Live (1988)
Producers John Del Gatto and Paul Surratt
Video directed by Bill D'Cicco
Video Tape Editor Robert Minshall
Warner Home Video
58 minutes, b/w

Brief: Compilation video of memorable moments (not seen on television in thirty-five years) from *The Colgate Comedy Hour.* Contains many familiar routines (including the "Drill Routine" with guest George Raft) and hilarious bloopers within the live shows.

Abbott and Costello in the Movies (1990)
Produced by Film Shows, Inc.
Compiled by Sandy Oliveri
GoodTimes Home Video
92 minutes, color and b/w

Brief: A collection of movie trailers, scenes, newsreel appearances, rare bloopers and outtake footage from The Boys' films.

Biographical Depiction of The Boys

Bud and Lou (1978)
Produced by Robert C. Thompson and Clyde B. Phillips
Directed by Robert C. Thompson
Story by Bob Thomas
Written by George Lefferts
Music by Fred Karlin
Bob Banner Production for NBC-TV
98 minutes

Cast: Harvey Korman, Buddy Hackett, Michele Lee, Arte Johnson, Robert Reed.

Brief: This network television docudrama was, theoretically, a biography of the duo, focusing on the lives and careers of Bud Abbott and Lou Costello, with an emphasis on Lou. It is based on the book *Bud & Lou* by Bob Thomas.

Abbott & Costello Clips
(contain excerpts of The Boys' work)

MGM's Big Parade of Comedy (1964)
Written by Robert Youngson
Narrated by Les Tremayne
100 minutes

Brief: This compendium of moments from MGM features and short subjects produced before 1947 includes appearances by Abbott & Costello, the Marx Brothers, W. C. Fields, Laurel & Hardy, Jimmy Durante, Buster Keaton, Red Skelton, and many more.

Bud and Lou's Guest Appearances

News of the Day (Universal, 1940)

Brief: Abbott & Costello are seen attending the premiere for the film *The Boys from Syracuse* in July 1940. This is now considered the team's first filmed "appearance" together.

Picture People (RKO, 1941)

Brief: Hollywood celebrities, including Ray Bolger, Rita Hayworth, Bud, and Lou, are featured in this eight-minute short.

Screen Snapshots (Columbia, 1941)

Brief: Various Hollywood celebrities, including George Burns, Gracie Allen, Rita Hayworth, Bud, and Lou, entertain the troops at U.S. bases during World War II.

Meet the People (Republic, 1941)

Brief: Footage of a benefit thrown by a Los Angeles newspaper. Stars in attendance include Judy Garland, Mickey Rooney, Milton Berle, Bud, and Lou.

News of the Day: "It's Christmas Time" (MGM, 1952)

Brief: The Boys, with Charles Laughton, promote the sale of Christmas Seals.

The 1954 Soapbox Derby Championships (color, 1954)

Brief: This very rare short film, sponsored by Boys Club of America, was shot in Akron, Ohio, on August 15, 1954. Lou participates in a soapbox race with stars Jack Carson and Robert Cummings. Bud appears briefly in the film but does not participate in the race.

Army-Navy Screen Magazine #28 (date unknown)

Brief: Also titled *Mail Call,* this government-produced short film includes footage of Abbott & Costello performing "Who's on First?" in front of a live audience of armed forces personnel. The footage was later used in a documentary-style television series titled *Hollywood and the Stars* (NBC, 1963-64). This is the only filmed version of the famous routine in which Costello exclaims, ". . . And I don't give a *damn!*" Bud replies, "Oh, that's our short-stop."

Bud and Lou were cochairmen of a special Motion Picture Christmas Seal Committee to help in the fight for those afflicted with tuberculosis. Charles Laughton joined them in a 1952 trailer shown in theatres throughout the country.

Filming the Christmas Seals commercial with Charles Laughton. (Courtesy of Joe Glaston)

Joe Besser on Abbott & Costello

His best work in television, perhaps, was "Stinky," the effeminate forty-year-old in a Little Lord Fauntleroy getup on *The Abbott and Costello Show.* It was a hilarious, energetic role that has since been swept under the critics' carpets. Undoubtedly, it is a shame that rotund comedian Joe Besser will forever be remembered almost exclusively for his two-year stint as one of The

Before he became one of the Three Stooges, Joe Besser was "Stinky," the malevolent brat on The Abbott and Costello Show.

Three Stooges—and the least popular one at that.

The handful of two-reeler Columbia Pictures shorts Besser made as a Stooge (replacing Shemp Howard) in the late 1950s should, by no means, be the measure of his tal-

ents. It was obvious why he entitled his 1985 autobiography, "Not Just a Stooge" (with later editions titled "Once a Stooge, Always a Stooge").

"Lou was one of my best friends," remembered Joe Besser. "My wife and I were some of the only people Lou invited over to the house on Christmas morning. I'd make toys to give to the kids."

The two comics went way back, according to Besser, whose showbiz roots were in vaudeville. Born in St. Louis, Besser had a thirst to be an entertainer and at an early age he literally hopped a train and ran away with magician Howard Thurston and his troupe. In the late 1920s, Joe met Lou at the Lyric Theater in Paterson, New Jersey. "Lou would come back to my dressing room to talk about comedy," Besser related in his book.

Eventually, the two crossed paths many times and became close pals. About the same height and weight as Lou, Besser used to dress up as Santa for his visits to the Costello household—even though Besser was Jewish. Ironically, after Costello's death, Bud Abbott phoned Joe and inquired about a possible teaming. Joe held on to his belief: "No one could replace Lou," he said.

Besser appeared only a few times on radio with Abbott and Costello and made two guest-shots in the team's films. In *Abbott and Costello Meet the Keystone Kops,* Besser can be spotted in a brief appearance as a hunter, and in *Africa Screams,* he carried a more substantial role as Harry, the bitchy butler.

Joe Besser plays "Harry," the whining butler who accompanies Bud and Lou on an expedition to Africa.

Still, it was his character of "Stinky" that put Lou Costello away. Joe was one of the few comics who could do that to Lou, absolutely convulse him in laughter with a simple pinch on the arm and his trademark whine, "Ooooooooohhh, ya crazy you!" There are shots left in the television episodes where Lou clearly cracks up at Besser's crazed ranting and pinching.

Besser's famous character of the little brat with the saucer hat originated on *The Alan Young Show* on television, where he and Young both donned Buster Brown outfits and portrayed little boys. "We did these two little kids together . . . we did that twice on his show," Besser said. "That was my idea." The sketch was performed on an oversize set with gargantuan furniture—a setup highly reminiscent of the 1930 Laurel and Hardy two-reeler, *Brats.* Lou Costello saw the Alan Young sketch on TV, fell down laughing, and asked Besser to re-create it on his and Bud's new program.

The most fascinating aspect of Besser's talent was how he built a career on this perfect characterization, and how it fit him so well, without peer. On *The Abbott and Costello Show,* watch how he prances, nervously jumping around Lou like a kid who urgently needs to go to the bathroom—but ignores it because he might miss something. Besser could beautifully capture childlike mannerisms, and better yet, no one has ever been able to adequately copy his unique vocal intonation and phrasings ("I'll *harm* you!" or "Not so haaaaaarrrd!"). Immitators are usually embarrassing to watch.

Besser was a friend to Bud and Lou, which meant he was the recipient of pranks on the set of *The Abbott and Costello Show.* It came with the territory. Besser recalled an episode ("The Wrestling Match") in which Stinky and his mother (Elvia Allman) visit a drugstore where Lou is working as a soda jerk. Stinky is supposed to down a glass of straight castor oil.

During the filming, Lou handed Joe a glass of syrupy liquid, which Besser

Joe Besser and his wife, "Ernie," at home in North Hollwood, 1986. (Photo by Steve Cox)

gulped down, just as the script called for. It was the real, putrid stuff. In a matter of minutes, Besser turned a nice shade of green.

In later years, Besser did not hesitate providing his opinion of the TV movie *Bud and Lou,* in which comedian Buddy Hackett portrayed his pal Lou Costello. "How could they do that?" he said the day after it aired. "I thought it was lousy. The worst thing I've ever seen. That was not Lou at all, not the Lou Costello I knew. They got a lot of things wrong. Ernie and I couldn't believe it when we watched it. Lou was one of the kindest men I've ever known."

Despite the fact that he harbored more than a hint of resentment for the unceasing references to his Stooging, Besser was obviously proud to unveil a star on Hollywood's Walk of Fame for The Three Stooges in 1983. It was one of his last public appearances, and he didn't disappoint the record crowds who lined the streets to witness this overdue event. Swiping at Milton Berle's arm, he gave the audience some of his little-boy schtick just like the old days. By that time, he was in retirement, and like Bud Abbott, Besser's final paychecks came from voice-over work he did in Hanna-Barbera cartoons.

Joe Besser died suddenly in his North Hollywood home on March 1, 1988, of heart failure. The headlines read: Surviving Stooge, Joe Besser, Dies at 80.

CHAPTER 12

The Television Years

Bud Abbott: He's not a Republican. He's not a Democrat. He's a
cross between a Republican and a Democrat.
Heckler: He sure is. He eats like an elephant and thinks like a
jackass.

—The Abbott and Costello Show

Fortunately for us, Abbott and Costello contributed greatly to nearly every aspect of the entertainment industry: radio, motion pictures, Broadway, nightclub, television—even animated cartoons. They tagged every base while sliding their act from burlesque into movies and onto television, seemingly without hesitation. During the 1950s, about halfway through their game, The Boys were still indefatigable, merely getting a second wind.

On January 7, 1951, NBC welcomed Abbott & Costello to *The Colgate Comedy Hour* as guest hosts of the live, hour-long variety program. Other personalities to take on the alternating chores as host included Bob Hope, Eddie Cantor, Jimmy Durante, Spike Jones, Tony Martin, Phil Silvers, Fred Allen, Donald O'Connor, and Martin & Lewis. The program debuted in 1950, as a lavish, big-budget, comedy "spectacular," as such shows were referred to. Telecast primarily from the El Capitan Theater in Hollywood, *The Colgate Comedy Hour* was the first commercial series to originate in Hollywood and boasted the network's first color telecast on November 22, 1953, (as an experimental test of RCA's new color system, under special authorization from the FCC).

It was situated in a time slot with the purpose of attacking the highly rated *The Ed Sullivan Show* on CBS. *The Colgate Comedy Hour* not only gar-

nered high ratings, but it pushed Sullivan's program down from number two to number fourteen the first year *Colgate* aired.

Years before the *Colgate* era, Bud and Lou made an appearance in New York on experimental television. On July 19, 1939, The Boys were interviewed on a fifteen-minute NBC show called *This Is New York*, which was broadcast to an extremely limited audience. This appearance occurred while they performed nightly in their Broadway show, *The Streets of Paris*, at the Broadhurst Theater. In addition, Lou made two cameo appearances on Milton Berle's popular *Texaco Star Theater* television show on NBC during the fall of 1948. Especially for Lou, who was so adept at comical expressions, "the tube," became an apt and intimate vehicle.

Costello effortlessly developed a smooth style on-camera that involved looking and even talking to the camera, while deviating from the routine. Much like George Burns on his popular television program with his wife, Gracie, the delicate trick of timing a glance dead into the camera's eye was something that Costello handled with ease. It is a tradition that comedian Garry Shandling mastered and continues today.

On *The Colgate Comedy Hour*, Bud and Lou relied—as always—on their old, standby routines, which they felt were certain to win over live audiences. After all, the bits always swept the live audiences they played to in theaters and in front of live radio audiences—why not on television? The

Caricatures seen prominently on The Colgate Comedy Hour *on NBC-TV, sponsored by the Colgate Palmolive-Peet Company.*

laughter and instantaneous reaction from the live audience was sweet music to them and it fed them. The Boys proved their theory correct. Viewers howled at their routines on television and went wild at sudden ad-libs or mistakes within the routines.

It was live, anything-can-happen television. The *Colgate* shows were raucous and manic, sometimes actually causing bodily injury to Bud and Lou while executing the slapstick on live television.

"It's murder," Bud Abbott recounted in an interview. "Every sketch seemed to end with Lou being pushed through a wall, a piano . . . anything." Lou Costello agreed, describing himself as "bloodied and bruised" following most of the *Colgate* appearances. "Once I did a routine with a steel helmet that slipped and cut my face," the comedian said.

Short Order Cook: The Boys pose with "Little Oscar" (Jerry Maren) during an appearance on the City of Hope Telethon *in Los Angeles. (Maren, a veteran midget actor, was the Lollipop Munchkin in* The Wizard of Oz.*)*

Mishaps occurred frequently. Bud Abbott recalled a live television sketch that involved a lady taking Lou to court for busting her umbrella. The prop umbrella was to have bent when she cracked it over Lou's head, but the prop man had accidentally used an actual, sturdy umbrella. "It had to be bent because that was the payoff for the next scene," Abbott recalled. So Bud quickly grabbed it and manually bent the prop around his knee. One of the umbrella's prongs punctured his leg. "It was bleeding like a stuck pig," Abbott said.

That era has been labeled "The Golden Age of Television," although it was not always considered so sparkly at the moment—it was hard work that burned like fuel. Bud and Lou took advantage of this new electronic medium by guest-hosting on the *Colgate* show many times during the next few years, still rehashing so many of their old routines.

Wisely, Costello wanted to establish an independent television show for Bud and himself, so their manager pitched the concept to NBC President Pat Weaver while the iron was hot. Weaver financed the filming of the first twenty-six episodes of *The Abbott and Costello Show*, with an option to air them on NBC first. The program was actually owned outright by Lou Costello and his newly formed corporation, TCA.

Under this arrangement, Bud now worked for Lou. Like Lucille Ball and Desi Arnaz, Costello was way ahead of his time with the ownership he built and the practice of filming the episodes versus live broadcasts. Jackie Gleason took the hint as well with one—now classic——filmed season of *The Honeymooners*. Costello understood the powerful growth potential within the television industry and made sure he retained this piece of "property," which he handed down to his children years later. Moreover, he fulfilled his wish to film so many of the burlesque routines he and his partner performed, in order to claim them as the established comedy of Abbott & Costello.

In all, two seasons (fifty-two half-hour episodes) of *The Abbott and Costello Show* were shot in black and white at the old Hal Roach Studios in Culver City, Calfornia, between May 1951 and June 1953. Initial airing was delayed, but finally *The Abbott and Costello Show* debuted as a syndicated offering on December 5, 1952, broadcast on CBS (*not* NBC as originally intended).

During production of the TV show, The Boys continued to slip in additional appearances on NBC's *The Colgate Comedy Hour*. Astoundingly, Bud and Lou also continued making films at this time, churning out *Jack and the Beanstalk, Abbott and Costello Meet Captain Kidd, Lost in Alaska,* and *Abbott and Costello Go to Mars.* They took advantage of the network's television airtime to plug their current films, occasionally broadcasting clips on their *Colgate* hour.

Imagine: So prolific were the two that much of their work overlapped. In some weeks audiences could see them hosting the Sunday night *Colgate* program on NBC, then tune in a rival network on Friday night at l0:30 to catch their CBS half-hour situation comedy, and also experience their latest motion picture at the local theater.

The Abbott and Costello Show—still in syndication today—was a loosely constructed half-hour revolving around the team's residence at a boardinghouse. Many of the shows barely made sense or even contained a thread of plot, but were nonetheless fun to watch. Sponsored by Chevrolet, the show was filmed on a studio soundstage or outside on what looked like a New York street set—although they were supposed to be playing themselves, actors, residing in Hollywood. A loud and boisterous laugh track with lots of children's giggles and shrieks was added during postproduction. One critic said it "sounded as if it was recorded in the audience at the Roller Derby."

In every opening sequence, Bud and Lou emerged from behind a curtain to introduce the episode or just banter. Then, after a blink, Bud and Lou were in the middle of an African jungle, or possibly out searching for employment—a typical blueprint. Most of the sequences within the shows are completely disjointed, but seeing the team perform many of their old routines kept the viewers watching. Critics, however, winced at the show, complaining about the rehash of their worn material.

Abbott and Costello historian Jim Mulholland observed: "The earlier shows didn't bother with plots. If there was a plot, it was usually abandoned in midstream. The boys would simply walk down the street and things would begin to happen . . . . If Lou strayed from the script in the movies, he ran amok on TV."

The entire series was directed by the late Jean Yarbrough, who directed five of Bud and Lou's films (*In Society, The Naughty Nineties,* and *Jack and the Beanstalk* included). Although it's been reported that *The Abbott and Costello Show* employed the same three-camera technique used on *I Love Lucy* at the time, surviving cast member Hillary Brooke recently discounted the rumor. "We never used three cameras," she said. "Oh no. Just one, maybe two cameras at times."

Director Jean Yarbrough occasionally allowed one camera to remain focused on just Lou's face to capture his childlike expressions and another camera, a wider shot, covering the pair or the scope of the action.

Most of Bud and Lou's supporting cast and guest stars on the TV series were old cronies who had worked with them previously in burlesque, radio, or their films.

Veteran burlesque straight man Sidney Fields played the testy landlord (among other incidental characters); Hillary Brooke was the beautiful, statuesque neighbor and "girlfriend" to Louis—as she called him; Joe Besser was Stinky, the prancing neighborhood brat dressed in a Little Lord Fauntleroy getup. Stinky's only purpose was to tease Lou unmercifully, constantly pinching him, threatening him, and smacking his arm. Joe Kirk, Lou's real-life brother-in-law, played the floating character of Mr. Bacciagalupe (prononuced Botcha-galoop). Gordon Jones was Mike the Cop, who forever lost his patience with Lou, and simply got in his face for any little thing. And naturally, Bobby Barber, Lou's favorite little balding sidekick, made walk-on appearances throughout nearly all fifty-two episodes.

Sid Fields, makeup man Abe Haberman, and Bud Abbott pose for a snapshot while shooting The Abbott and Costello Show *on the Hal Roach Studios lot in 1953. (Courtesy of Abe Haberman)*

The first season, with a format created by their longtime writer, Eddie Forman, was the most popular by far. These episodes are earmarked by the opening, which includes a split screen of scenes from Abbott & Costello films, as well as the preferred, bouncy theme song. The first season's episodes move with a stride and contain great energy from Costello as well as the rest of the cast.

The second season simply opens with Costello's signature scream, "Heeeyyy Abbbbott!" and the team's names plainly scrawled across the screen. These shows, more restrained and structured in the script, lacked the spontaneity. They lag in comparison. But most obvious is the absence of some of the popular stock players like Joe Besser, Joe Kirk, and Hillary Brooke. Years later, Besser explained his departure: "I left the series after the first season when Lou decided to revamp the show's format—including the cast. I was replaced by, of all things, a chimpanzee. . . . I never lost out to a chimp before, but I never resented Lou for making this move. He had done plenty for me just by being my friend."

Brooke, who suspiciously pops up in one episode of the second season, said of her absence: "I'm really not sure what the reason was. I think I had a picture I was working on. But it was nothing bad. I wasn't fired. It just worked out that way and they didn't mind."

Of the second season's episodes, writer Jim Mulholland noted, "These lacked the genial lunacy of the early ones. Obviously, they needed to try something new since the comedians had nearly exhausted their old routines. The idea of doing stories was certainly a welcomed one . . . but the plots were trite and hampered Bud and Lou, who were better off left to their own devices."

More than once, standup comic Jerry Seinfeld—a self-professed fan of Bud and Lou's brand of absurd television—has made reference to the fact that his own highly rated network sitcom is a descendant of Abbott & Costello's.

"When *Seinfeld* first came on, people said, 'You play yourself, you're a comedian, it's kind of like *It's Garry Shandling's Show*,' and I said, 'No, it's Abbott and Costello,'" he pointed out. "This was really the genesis of the style, to be in real life as they were, then come out onstage as entertainers . . . I sometimes feel that George [Jason Alexander] and I can get into a rhythm like that. That goes back a little to [Abbott and Costello]."

Cohosting a ten-hour marathon of *The Abbott and Costello Show* on cable TV's Comedy Central in 1993, Seinfeld observed: "Truly the most bizarre addition to this entire series was the idea of Bingo the Chimp. That these two guys, who literally did not have a quarter for a sandwich, would adopt—not as a pet, but as a son—this chimp." Commentary by Seinfeld, Larry Miller, and Larry Charles, was videotaped at the backyard patio area of Bud Abbott's former home in Encino, Califoria.

The rigorous schedule during these Television Years took its toll on Lou. In 1953 he was confined to bed after collapsing from exhaustion. To complicate things further, Lou suffered from relapses of rheumatic fever and this time, a new obstacle—a gangrenous gallbladder. At one point, he almost drowned in his own body fluids. Under strict care for several months, Lou recuperated and eagerly returned to work, but his energy level never peaked again.

The team's twentieth and final appearance on *The Colgate Comedy Hour* was broadcast on May 15, 1955. Luckily, Bud and Lou ordered kinescopes of all of their live appearances and these films of the TV shows survive in their family archives today. Several selections from the *Colgate* broadcasts have been released on home video *(The Best of Abbott & Costello Live)* with surprisingly good transfer quality from the kinescopes. Reviewing the old *Colgate* shows, *People* magazine noted: "On live TV, with limited rehearsal time and frequent gaffes, the pair's verbal and physical dexterity got a real workout, and Costello, particularly, got an opportunity to flaunt his skills . . . he was

deceptively acrobatic at slapstick—he was in many ways the comedic performer John Belushi might have become."

This was productive for the team, to say the least. For five years, the dynamic duo had unleashed an unbelievable volume of work. Take a look at these impressive stats: During the period between 1951 and 1955, Bud and Lou made seven motion pictures (with personal appearance tours to promote them), appeared twenty times as guest hosts of *The Colgate Comedy Hour,* shot two seasons (fifty-two episodes) of *The Abbott and Costello Show* and toured Europe with their act.

Although income taxes were burdensome, the pair made quite a large sum during their years of active employment in television. The money later became a matter of contention between them. They received a straight salary of $15,000 per *Colgate* broadcast, and Costello alone reaped the benefits in perpetuity from ownership of *The Abbott and Costello Show.*

Under the terms of an agreement with Lou, Bud was to receive half of the net gross (but his weekly salary was not to exceed $7,500 for a total of $390,000) as payment for his participation in *The Abbott and Costello Show.* Years later, after receiving just a little over half of his fee, Abbott sued his former partner in March 1958 for the remainder, also demanding a full accounting—"Every dollar of it."

More Facts from Left Field
"The Abbott and Costello Show"

- Bud and Lou are down-and-out actors who live at the Fields Rooming House located at 214 Brookline Avenue in Hollywood, California, and pay seven dollars a week rent. Their phone number is Alexander 4444 (also Alexander 2222).

- Hillary Brooke, a neighbor to Bud and Lou, does not maintain a consistent occupation. Depending on what the episode calls for, she is a dental assistant, a registered nurse, or a secretary.

- Rarely mentioned are the last names of some of the crazy tenants in the Fields Rooming House: Mike the Cop's full name is Mike Kelly; Lou's bratty pal is Stinky Davis (Mike the Cop's nephew).

- Bingo the chimp eats watermelon for breakfast and fifty pounds of bananas a week.

- Mr. Bacciagalupe is the successful enterpreneur of the bunch: He owns a vegatable stand, an ice-cream wagon, a music store, and runs a café as well as a bakery.

The Abbott and Costello Show
EPISODE GUIDE

Premiered: December 5, 1952, on CBS; syndicated
Producers: Alex Gottlieb, Pat Costello, and Jean Yarbrough
Director: Jean Yarbrough
Writers: Eddie Forman, Sidney Fields, Clyde Bruckman, Felix Adler; and Jack Townley
Production Company: Television Corporation of America (TCA)

Cast:
Bud Abbott . . . .(himself)
Lou Costello . . . .(himself)
Sidney Fields . . . . .Mr. Fields, the landlord
Gordon Jones . . . . .Mike (Kelly) the Cop
Hillary Brooke . . . .(herself)
Joe Besser (semiregular) . . . .Stinky (Davis)
Joe Kirk (semiregular) . . . . .Mr. Bacciagalupe

FIRST SEASON

1. "The Drugstore"
With: Hillary Brooke, Gordon Jones, Sidney Fields, Joe Kirk, Joe Besser, Iris Adrian, and Elvia Allman

Bud and Lou find a job in Fields's drugstore and nearly wreck the place. (Note: An unusually lengthy opening sequence with the "Jonah and the Whale" routine.)

2. "The Dentist's Office"
With: Hillary Brooke, Gordon Jones, Sidney Fields, Joe Kirk, Virginia Christine, Ray Walker, Vera Marsh, and Bobby Barber

Lou's toothache lands him in the office of Dr. Ralph Prentiss, where Hillary is a nurse. Eventually, Lou attempts to get arrested in order to receive free treatment while incarcerated.

3. "Jail"
With: Hillary Brooke, Gordon Jones, Sidney Fields, Joe Kirk, Elvia Allman, Stanley Andrews, Iris Adrian, and Robin Raymond

Lou has perforated Mrs. Crumbcake's water pail and she drags him into court claiming 79 cents in damages. In jail, Lou's crazed cellmate becomes enraged at the mere mention of "Niagara Falls."

4. "The Vacation"

With: Hillary Brooke, Gordon Jones, Sidney Fields, Joe Kirk, and Bobby Barber

The Boys are off to the Biltmore Hotel near Phoenix for a vacation. (Note: Includes both the "Hertz U-Drive" and the "Pack-Unpack" routines.)

5. "The Birthday Party"

With: Hillary Brooke, Gordon Jones, Sidney Fields, Joe Kirk, Joe Besser, Elvia Allman, and Sara Padden

Lou throws a party for himself, but nearly poisons his guests when he tops the hors d'oeuvres with ant paste instead of antipasto. Harshly, Bud evicts his pal and Lou consoles himself by ordering a giant decorated birthday cake at Mr. Bacciagalupe's bakery.

Bingo and Lou never got along. Bingo bit Lou and that was the end of Bingo's career on The Abbott and Costello Show. *(Courtesy of Abbott and Costello Enterprises)*

6. "Alaska"

With: Hillary Brooke, Gordon Jones, Sidney Fields, Joe Kirk, and Murray Leonard

The Boys are off to Alaska to visit Costello's uncle who has struck gold. They are detained when Lou accidentally adds quick-drying cement to the water in which Bud is soaking his feet. Eventually, they stumble onto a bank holdup.

7. "The Vacuum Cleaner Salesman"

With: Hillary Brooke, Gordon Jones, Sidney Fields, Joe Kirk, Joe Besser, Robin Raymond, Vera Marsh, Dorothy Ford, and Bobby Barber

The boys visit the employment agency run by Mr. Fields's brother. Lou is hired to hawk vacuum cleaners door-to-door.

8. "The Army Story"

With: Hillary Brooke, Gordon Jones, Sidney Fields, Joe Kirk, James Alexander, Joe Besser, Robert Cherry, and Milt Bronson

Bud and Lou have joined the reserves. (Note: Includes the "Dice Game" and the "Drill Routine.")

9. **"Pots and Pans"**
　　With: Hillary Brooke, Gordon Jones, Sidney Fields, Joe Kirk, and
　　　　Anthony Caruso

Costello sells cookware door-to-door and
later prepares a duck dinner for friends with
the usual disastrous results.

10. **"The Charity Bazaar"**
　　With: Hillary Brooke, Gordon Jones,
　　　　Sidney Fields, Joe Kirk, Joe Besser,
　　　　Nicla Di Bruno, and Bobby Barber

The boys participate in Hillary's charity
bazaar raising money with the "Shell Game."
Lou blows his money at the kissing booth.
(Note: Bud delivers a salutation at the end:
"And friends, this is a toast from my partner
and myself—May you all live as long as you
want and never want as long as you live.")

11. **"The Western Story"**
　　With: Hillary Brooke, Gordon Jones,
　　　　Sidney Fields, Joe Kirk, James
　　　　Alexander, Anthony Caruso,
　　　　Minerva Urecal, Anthony Hughes,
　　　　and Bobby Barber

*Time for a trip in the
fourth episode of* The
Abbott and Costello
Show, *titled "The
Vacation."*

The Boys accept Hillary's invitation to visit
her uncle's "B-Bar-Bop Ranch," and they
become involved with a posse and cattle rustlers. (Hillary: "Oh, you'd love it. I
can see you, Louis, with all those western horses. I can see you bustin' your
bronco right now.")

12. **"The Haunted House"**
　　With: Hillary Brooke, Gordon Jones, Sidney Fields, Joe Kirk, Joan
　　　　Shawlee, Joe Besser, and Bobby Barber

According to her uncle's will, Hillary will inherit a castle if she agrees to spend
one night in the spooky manor. Bud and Lou accompany Hillary to protect
her.

13. **"Peace and Quiet"**
　　With: Hillary Brooke, Gordon Jones, Sidney Fields, Joe Kirk, Joe Besser,
　　　　Marjorie Reynolds, Murray Leonard, Veda Ann Borg, Eddie Parks,
　　　　Lillian Bronson, Milt Bronson, and Bobby Barber

Lou sleeps all day but can't doze nocturnally, so Bud takes him to see Dr. Mildew, a psychiatrist. Eventually, Bud checks Lou into a sanatarium for a night's rest. (Note: Includes the "Crazy House" routine.)

14. "Hungry"

With: Hillary Brooke, Gordon Jones, Sidney Fields, Joe Kirk, Joan Shawlee, Joe Besser, Milt Bronson, Bobby Barber, and Murray Leonard

Hillary Brooke played Bud and Lou's neighbor on The Abbott and Costello Show.

Bud and Lou visit a couple of restaurants. One café involves twin waitresses and in the other, Lou battles an oyster in his stew. (Note: Includes the "Alexander 4444" routine.)

15. "The Music Lovers"

With: Hillary Brooke, Gordon Jones, Sidney Fields, Joe Kirk, Joe Besser, Raymond Hatton, Minerva Urecal, Renie Riano, and Frank Yaconelli

Costello attempts to impress Hillary and her derelict father with his musical abilities. While pretending to perform, Bud falls asleep behind the piano, ruining the scheme.

16. "The Politician"

With: Hillary Brooke, Gordon Jones, Sidney Fields, Joe Kirk, Joan Shawlee, Selena Walters, Charles Cane, Bobby Barber, and Bingo the Chimp

Bud coaches Lou on running for public office, and Lou delivers a speech in the neighborhood park that causes a disruption.

17. "The Wrestling Match"

With: Hillary Brooke, Gordon Jones, Sidney Fields, Joe Kirk, Joe Besser, Dorothy Granger, Emory Parnell, Ben Weldon, Milt Bronson, William Newell, Bobby Barber, and Bingo the Chimp

Lou and Stinky agree to settle their differences by wrestling in a match for the policemen's benefit. The prize: $25. Stinky's kid brother, Ivan the Terrible, substitutes and Lou gets slaughtered in the ring—yet somehow manages to win the bout. (Note: This was the first episode to be aired on network television.)

18. "Getting a Job"

With: Hillary Brooke, Gordon Jones, Sidney Fields, Joe Kirk, Joe Besser, Vera Marshe, Veda Ann Borg, Milt Bronson, Anthony Hughes, Lucien Littlefield, Sid Saylor, and Bingo the Chimp

The Boys are hired to deliver a box of straw hats to the Susquehanna Hat Company on Floogle Street and encounter several lunatics along the way. Stinky attempts to kill Lou by backing him into traffic on the street. (Note: Includes the "Loafing" routine.)

19. "Bingo"

With: Hillary Brooke, Gordon Jones, Sidney Fields, Joe Kirk, Joan Shawlee, Isabel Randolph, Dorothy Granger, Bob Hopkins, and Bingo the Chimp

Mike the Cop informs Lou that he must obtain a license for his pet chimp, and Lou accidentally applies for a marriage license.

20. "Hillary's Birthday"

With: Hillary Brooke, Gordon Jones, Sidney Fields, Joe Kirk, Joan Shawlee, Chick Chandler, Lee Patrick, Anthony Hughes, and Bingo the Chimp

While shopping for Hillary's suprise birthday party, Bud flirts with the checkout lady and Lou nearly destroys the grocery store. ("Get a load of the ol' bag.") During the party, Mr. Fields is disturbed by the racket coming from Bud and Lou's apartment.

21. "Television"

With: Hillary Brooke, Gordon Jones, Sidney Fields, Joe Kirk, Joan Shawlee, Bob Hopkins, Veda Ann Borg, James Alexander, Ben Weldon, Bobby Barber, Milt Bronson, and Bingo the Chimp

Bud sported a pencil-thin mustache for most of the TV show episodes. (Courtesy of Betty Abbott Griffin)

Lou is a contestant on the TV quiz show "Hold That Cuckoo," where he wins a pack of bubble gum. Their neighbor, John Rednose, slips on a piece of the gum and hauls Bud and Lou into court.

22. "Las Vegas"

With: Hillary Brooke, Gordon Jones, Sidney Fields, Joe Kirk, Lucien Littlefield, Renie Riano, Joyce Compton, Virginia Christine, Joe Devlin, Harry Tyler, Milt Bronson, and Bobby Barber

Bud and Lou pay $90 to Friendly Fields for an automobile and head for Las Vegas, where Lou gets involved in a violent game of billiards. (Note: Includes the "Mudder/Fodder" routine.)

23. "Little Old Lady"

With: Hillary Brooke, Gordon Jones, Sidney Fields, Joe Kirk, George Chandler, Dorothy Granger, Burt Mustin, Benny Rubin, Murray Leonard, Judy Clark, Sid Saylor, Herold Goodwin, Isabel Randolph, Hallene Hill, and Bobby Barber

The Boys attempt to help an old Mrs. McGillicuddy, who has been evicted. They raise $300 from Mr. Fields's amusement park sideshow, and the old lady, in turn, calls her bookie and bets on a racehorse. (Note: The voice of the parrot is that of famed vocal characterizationist Mel Blanc.)

24. "The Actor's Home"

With: Hillary Brooke, Gordon Jones, Sidney Fields, Joe Kirk, Joe Besser, Thurston Hall, Allen Jenkins, Joan Shawlee, Lucien Littlefield, Ray Walker, Jarma Lewis, Jo Carol Dennison, and Milt Bronson

A wealthy philanthropist gives Bud and Lou some big bucks. Later, Bud assumes the money is counterfeit, having been given to them by a lunatic. Bud shreds the cash, but later realizes it was real. After Bud goes berserk, he is hauled off to the Retired Actors Home, where Lou visits him and they perform "Who's on First?" for the residents.

25. "Police Rookies"

With: Hillary Brooke, Gordon Jones, Sidney Fields, Joe Kirk, Robert Sherry, Emory Parnell, Bobby Barber, and Bingo the Chimp

Mike the Cop helps The Boys enroll in the "Police Rookie School" where Professor Melonhead, the judo expert, is a coach. Lou blows up the gym playing with a live hand grenade.

26. "Safari"

With: Hillary Brooke, Gordon Jones, Sidney Fields, Joe Kirk, Bobby Barber, and Bingo the Chimp

Hillary is caring for Bingo, who is ill with a temperature of 172, sedate, and relaxed in bed. ("He has a fever. He's raving. He's out of his head!") The whole gang travels to Africa's Belgian Congo to locate Bingo's parents and Costello tangles with a gorilla.

Second Season

27. "The Paperhangers"
With: Sidney Fields, Gordon Jones, Billy Varga, Bob Wilke, Henry Kulky, Jane Frazee, Sarah Haden, and Rex Lease

To pay off back rent, Mr. Fields has The Boys wallpaper Mrs. Bronson's apartment. Later, as waiters in a restaurant, they become involved in a brawl with hoodlums. (Note: This is one of the rare episodes where Bud takes quite a beating.)

28. "Uncle Bozzo's Visit"
With: Sidney Fields, Gordon Jones, Fortunio Bonanova, G. Pat Collins, Milt Bronson, Pat Flaherty, Max Wagner, and Anthony Hughes

Lou's eccentric Uncle Bozzo visits him from Italy, intending to stay for a couple of months. Uncle Bozzo, an opera singer, ends up annoying Mr. Fields with his booming voice.

29. "In Society"
With: Sidney Fields, Gordon Jones, Hillary Brooke, Isabel Randolph, Sheila Bromley, Alix Talton, Jack Rice, and Tristram Coffin

Mrs. Olga Van Goo, a wealthy society matron, pays Bud to attend her formal reception and impersonate the Duke of Gluten. Lou plays his cousin, the Earl of Waldo. (Note: This is the only episode in the second season with an appearance by Hillary Brooke.)

Possibly the most bizarre character on The Abbott and Costello Show *was Bingo. (Courtesy of Joe Glaston)*

30. "Life Insurance"
With: Sidney Fields, Gordon Jones, Murray Leonard, Dorothy Granger, Milt Bronson, Anthony Hughes, Joe La Cava, and Bobby Barber

Mr. Fields takes out an insurance policy on Lou, who is forced to undergo a physical examination. The doctor says Lou is too nervous and needs rest and vitamins, so Bud takes Lou on a hunting trip in the country. Lou begins to believe Bud and Mr. Fields are out to kill him for the insurance payoff.

31. "Pest Exterminators"
With: Sidney Fields, Creighton Hale, Dorothy Vaughn, Florence Auer, Helene Millard, Joan Shawlee, Robert Foulk, Jack Rice, and Bobby Barber

Bud and Lou are pest exterminators who are mistaken for psychiatrists when they attend to Mrs. Featherton's "aunts." Eventually, Mrs. Featherton assumes they have rid her of two maiden aunts.

32. "Killer's Wife"
With: Sidney Fields, Gordon Jones, Max Baer (senior), Mary Beth Hughes, Lou Nova, Lyle Talbot, and Tom Kennedy

A heavyweight prizefighter known as "Killer" has moved into the apartment across the hall. "Killer" suspects Lou of having an affair with his wife, Dixie, so Bud attempts to get Lou trained and fit in a gym.

33. "Cheapskates"
With: Sidney Fields, Gordon Jones, Paul Fix, Phyllis Coates, Tony Ward, Ralph Gamble, Bobby Barber, Milt Bronson, Teddy Infuhr, and Bingo the Chimp

Bud and Lou accidentally purchase a crate containing roller skates. Unknowingly, the skates have stolen diamonds hidden inside them and the smugglers are on the trail to retrieve the goods.

34. "South of Dixie"
With: Sidney Fields, Gordon Jones, Gene Baird, Bob Hopkins, Jean Porter, Glen Langan, Dick Gordon, Bobby Barber, and Milt Bronson

Lou accidentally lands roles for himself and Bud in a Civil War melodrama, "South of Dixie," presented at The Little Theater.

35. "From Bed to Worse"
With: Sidney Fields, Gordon Jones, Lucien Littlefield, Dick Wessel, Joe Devlin, Charles E. Delaney, and Shirley Tegge

The Boys become green thumbs as they attempt to plant a beautiful backyard garden and win a cash prize offered by a civic group.

36. "$1000 TV Prize"
With: Sidney Fields, Gordon Jones, Bob Hopkins, Ray Walker, Ralph Sanford, and Milt Bronson

Bud and Lou are supposed to have the landlord's television repaired professionally, but attempt to do it themselves. While in Fields' apartment, Lou answers the telephone and correctly provides the answer to a question on the *Money To Burn* television quiz show.

37. "Amnesia"
With: Sidney Fields, Gordon Jones, Jack Mulhall, Charles Cane, Adele Jergens, Paul Bryar, Kathryn Sheldon, and Milt Bronson

Lou is in love with Edna, a girl with whom he has only corresponded. With some old friends, Bud pulls a gag to break up Lou's silly romance. He convinces Lou that he already married the girlfriend. The woman posing as Lou's wife makes him miserable.

38. "Efficiency Experts"
With: Sidney Fields, Jean Willis, Lucille Barkley, Theodore Von Eltz, Herbert Hayes, Lillian Bronson, Frank Scanell, Joe Ray, and Bobby Barber

Bud and Lou are hired as efficiency experts instructed to restrain their client's daughters from spending money. The adult daughters, however, realize what is happening and decide to teach Bud and Lou a lesson, "turn on the charm, and take the shirts right off their backs."

39. "Car Trouble"
With: Sidney Fields, Gordon Jones, Emory Parnell, Horace Murphy, Percy Helton, Charles Williams, Milt Bronson, Ted Stanhope, Bobby Barber, and Sid Saylor

Lou wins an automobile from the Jeepers Creepers Baby Food Company. When The Boys realize the car is a lemon, they decide to drive to Flint, Michigan, to purchase a new automobile.

40. "Wife Wanted"
With: Sidney Fields, June Vincent, Frank Jara, Tracy Roberts, Claudia Barrett, Connie Cezon, and Jerry Pattison

Lou will get ten thousand dollars from his grandfather, "Sourdough Costello," if he is married. The Boys comb the town in search of a spouse for Lou. Lou wants to marry his former girlfriend, Agnes, who is dating a wrestler, Bone-Bender Brodsky.

41. "Uncle from New Jersey"
With: Sidney Fields, Gordon Jones, Ralph Gamble, Tim Ryan.

continued on page 268

Abbott & Costello in (North) Hollywood

In late 1953, after completing two seasons of *The Abbott and Costello Show,* their *Dr. Jekyll and Mr. Hyde* picture, a stint in Las Vegas, and a second tour of London, Lou wanted to spend a little time at home. His life was exploding. Daughter Paddy had suddenly eloped, which crushed Anne and him—for the moment. The IRS nightmare was complicating both his and Bud's lives to an unbearable degree. Lou found no alternative but to move his family to the ranch

property in Canoga Park and sell his beautiful white home in the San Fernando Valley on Longridge Avenue. As Lou made the deal to sell his home and all of its furnishings, he asked the buyer if he and his family could have one last holiday in the Longridge home before handing over the keys. According to Chris Costello, it was "a Christmas to remember."

"At the stroke of midnight on Christmas Eve, we all congregated in the theater, where the pool table was piled to the ceiling with brightly wrapped packages."

These rare photographs, taken just before Lou painfully relinquished the dwelling, were shot in and around the Longridge property. The clowning and celebrating were winding down. At this point, "Bud's drinking had him bloated until he actually looked pudgier than my father," said Chris Costello. Lou had lost weight, maintained his tan, and even slowed down on the cigars a bit. He actually appeared healthier than he had in years. But not happier.

(All images courtesy of Archive Photos)

continued from page 265

Mr. Fields is about to evict Bud and Lou; however, Bud convinces Fields that Lou's Uncle Ruppert is a millionaire and Lou is the sole heir. Mike the Cop begins to believe that the visiting Uncle Rupert (impersonated by Costello) has been murdered.

42. "Private Eye"
With: Sidney Fields, Gordon Jones, Lyn Thomas, Bill Varga, Frank Richards, Bobby Barber, Keith Richards, Harry Clexx, Lou Krugman, and Paul Stader

Lou receives his diploma from "The Watchdog Correspondence School" and helps a friend locate $50,000 in bonds, which are hidden in an old haunted house.

43. "The Tax Return"
With: Sidney Fields, Gordon Jones, Thurston Hall, Bennie Bert, Al Hill, Richard Powers, Ray Walker, and Bobby Barber

Lou receives a tax refund check for one million dollars. He takes the check to the bank, demands cash, and is followed home by crooks.

44. "Public Enemies"
With: Sidney Fields, Gordon Jones, Joe Sawyer, Claire Carleton, Mike Ross, Veda Ann Borg, and Robert Bice

Because of an inaccurate newspaper report bearing his photograph, Costello is mistaken for a crook known as "Dapper Dan." A group of safecrackers, who have moved into the boardinghouse, force Costello to assist in a robbery.

45. "Bank Holdup"
With: Sidney Fields, Gordon Jones, Douglas Fowley, Ed Dearing, Emmett Vogan, Milt Bronson, Bobby Barber

Bud and Lou are unwittingly hired as armed bodyguards for hoodlums Joe and Lefty Lucas, and assist in a bank robbery. They pay rent with their share of the money, then attempt to recover the stolen money from the landlord's safe.

46. "Well Oiled"
With: Sidney Fields, Gordon Jones, Connie Cezon, William Fawcett, Wild Red Barry, Richard Norris, and Grace Hale

The Boys help Mr. Fields, who is being threatened with a breach of promise lawsuit. Lou poses as a Texas millionaire (with Bud as his chauffeur) and courts the woman, who is threatening Fields, in order to discredit her.

47. "The Pigeon"

With: Sidney Fields, Gordon Jones, Gloria Henry, Ted Hecht, Ray Montgomery, Harry Clexx, Hank Patterson, and Bobby Barber

Bud and Lou's beautiful next-door neighbor, Ruby Norton, uses Costello as a decoy in an attempt to finally break off her romance with mobster Steve Terry.

48. "Honeymoon House"

With: Sidney Fields, Karen Sharpe, George Chandler, Renie Riano, Danny Morton, and Tommy Farrell

With the aid of Abbott and Mr. Fields, Lou constructs a prefab house for his fiancée, Sally. The new house is sabotaged by Sally's former boyfriend. Sally's parents arrive to inspect the dwelling and are almost killed.

49. "Fencing Master"

With: Sidney Fields, Gordon Jones, Fortunio Bonanova, Byron Folger, Harry Clexx, Robert Karnes, Roy Lennart, and Bennie Burn

Abbott involves Costello as a human guinea pig in a zany experiment performed by a mad scientist, Dr. Bluzak. Lou thinks he's indestructible until he challenges a fencing ace to a duel.

The entire collection of The Abbott and Costello Show episodes was released on home video from Shanachie Entertainment.

Bud has just received a disasterous rubdown in the hilarious, final episode of The Abbott and Costello Show. *(Courtesy of Joe Glaston)*

50. "Beauty Contest Story"
With: Sidney Fields, James Flavin, Sandra Spence, Claudia Barrett, Dick Wessel, Ralph Gamble, Charles Halton, and Jan Kayne

Bud and Lou judge the "Miss Mud Turtle" beauty pageant for the Fraternal Order of Mud Turtles. Pressure is applied to sway their votes.

51. "Fall Guy"
With: Sidney Fields, Walter Catlett, Noreen Nash, Charles Hall, Gloria Saunders, Frank Marlowe, Joe Haworth, Ruth Lee, John Bernadino, Bobby Barber, and Milt Bronson

Bud and Lou have no luck selling "No Peddlers Allowed" signs. Eventually, The Boys get involved in a scheme to take two sisters out on a date, but when they arrive at the house, their dates' father has Bud and Lou install a new television antenna on the roof.

52. "Barber Lou"
With: Sidney Fields, Renie Riano, and Bobby Barber

After helping Mrs. Bronson with her amateur theatrical, tired Bud wants Costello to give him a relaxing rubdown. Costello is supposed to follow the instructions of a radio masseuse, but mistakenly utilizes directions for painting a car at home. (Note: This hilarious episode was written by Sid Fields and Lou Costello. The voice of the radio announcer is that of Sid Fields.)

Animated Antics

Bud and Lou's manager, Eddie Sherman, remained constantly on the lookout for projects involving his former clients—even after Lou's death and Bud's retirement. The team was his whole existence, some say. They were his "baby," his income, and his claim to fame.

In 1965 Sherman noticed *The New Three Stooges* cartoons produced by Cambria Productions, and a similar idea involving the likenesses of Bud and Lou struck him. Sherman sold the idea of a color animated version of Abbott and Costello to Lee Orgel, president of Jomar Productions.

Orgel was the first to introduce an animated cartoon commercial on network television in 1949 with his innovative spot on Dodge dealers of America. He went on to produce several cartoon series, as well as the classic *Mr. Magoo's Christmas Carol*, the first made-for-television animated special in 1962.

"I wrote the Abbott and Costello cartoon pilot and sold the show to Hanna-Barbera," Orgel says. He approached Hanna-Barbera studios with his rough artwork, script and sample storyboards. He chose this particular studio not only because they were one of the leading animation mills churning out cartoons for TV, but also because they had recently produced a series of Laurel and Hardy cartoons. "We were financed by the General Tire and Rubber Company in a joint venture with RKO Pictures. Hanna-Barbera handled the actual production of the cartoon."

Hanna-Barbera Studios had already struck gold with the networks and home viewers with *Huckleberry Hound, Yogi Bear, The Flintstones,* and *The Adventures of Jonny Quest,* among many other animated series on prime time and slotted on Saturday mornings.

According to Orgel, originally Joe Barbera did not relish the idea of hiring Bud Abbott to supply the voice of his character, thinking a younger, more vibrant actor would be more practical. Orgel convinced Bill Hanna and Joe Barbera that recognizing the actual voice of Abbott would lend the series a worthy element of authentici-

ty. Orgel also had to fight for Stan Irwin, a friend of his, as a casting choice for Costello. (Barbera's choice was Vegas stand-up comic, Shecky Greene, who also had an adept Costello impression in his repetoire.)

Finally, the cartoon moguls concurred with Orgel's plan. However, for some reason, the studio's original press releases introducing the new series to syndicators did not make much mention—or any hype—of Bud's involvement in the production. Also unusual was the name Barbera over the name Hanna in the tag credits for most of the series, although their hands-on involvement of the series was minimal.

The series was a positive thing for Abbott, a now fully retired comedian. Not only was it welcomed income and activity for him, but it was especially valuable for his morale, says his family. Old Bud was anxious to dress up a bit, shave and slick the hair back for work at a studio again. Maybe gruff-voiced Bud still felt the residual impairments of a stroke and his trademark staccato delivery had begun to rust, but he was anxious. Because he never manned an automobile, the elder comedian had to be driven in to the studio on Cahuenga Boulevard in North Hollywood for the tapings.

How the studio managed to mispell the name of Bud's costar on the series is anyone's guess. The first half of the series credits the voice of Costello as provided by Stan *Erwin.*

"It started as Er, and when I saw it and told them, the studio advised me what it would cost to correct it, so I asked them to put Ir when they possi-

bly could. The later episodes have it right," says Stan Irwin from his office in Beverly Hills. "Afterall, I'm not going to criticize their inefficiency. It really didn't make a difference. Just doing the cartoons was a kick to me."

Stan Irwin, who didn't resemble Costello and topped the comedian by a few inches, was in his mid forties when he stepped up to the mike to supply that perfectly high-pitched squeal for the cartoon Costello. As it turned out, Irwin had already had a smidgen of a history with the comedy team. As a former stand-up comic, he had performed a Lou Costello impression, which Costello himself enjoyed.

In the 1950s, while working as the executive producer at the Sahara Hotel in Las Vegas, it was Irwin who booked Bud and Lou in a show called "Miltown Revisited," which ended up being their final engagement as a team in late 1956. Months later, fol-

Stan Irwin was the voice of Costello in the Hanna-Barbera cartoons.

lowing the team's split, Lou Costello asked Irwin to perform "Who's On First?" with him at a couple of charity engagements at the Biltmore Theater in Los Angeles.

"I never immitated Bud," Irwin was quick to point out. "I just did the feed and it went marvelously."

Irwin recalled his preparation for the bit. "I bought the record and transcribed 'Who's On First?' and learned it," he says. "Then I went backstage and told Lou, 'OK. Nothin' to worry about. Got it down word-for-word.' Lou looked at him. "You've got *what* down?"

"'Who's On First?' I took it off the record."

Lou shook his head and calmly explained to Irwin: "That's not how Bud and I would do it. What Bud and I would do is try to trick each other, or try to trap each other to keep it good and fresh."

As a fan of Abbott and Costello, Irwin was thrilled about providing the voice for one of them in a cartoon series. "I would fly in from Las Vegas on the days of recording and drive to Bud's small house in the Valley," he says, "and sometimes we'd sit for a while and reminisce. He'd talk about the good times. Bud would have me look in his closets and I saw a collection of everything Abbott and Costello did. He saved a lot. I remember looking at a picture of Bud Abbott's former bar in one of his estate homes, and the bar was bigger than the entire house in which he was now living."

Irwin drove Bud into the studio, recalling that Bud's health was "deteriorating tremendously," he said,

"and at times I'd have to help him in and out of the car." Abbott walked with a cane, slowly, and once he made his way down the corridor of Hanna-Barbera's main building and into Studio B, he'd sit for a while and rest. Although Bud smoked cigarettes heavily at the time, Irwin said he does not recall the comedian lighting up in the car or while working—which was commonplace at the time.

"We would all stand in the studio during the session, but Bud would sit. He was more comfortable that way," Irwin says. Everyone at the studio was accomdating of Bud, and patient with him, and in some cases, in downright awe of the man sitting quietly right there in the studio with them. The sound technicians and director, Art Scott, were "beautiful," Irwin recalls. "Whenever Bud started slurring—you know, it was his teeth—the director would say, 'Bud, we had a little problem with the sound in here. Mind if we take it over?,' or a technician would say, 'Our fault, Bud, our fault. We weren't ready. Mind doing it again?'"

Some of the studio's voice-over veterans joined Bud and Stan Irwin to enact the supporting characters on the series: Hal Smith, Don Messick, John Stephenson, Mel Blanc, Janet Waldo, and Alan Reed.

"The hardest thing for director Art Scott was trying to maintain Bud's vitality," remembers Don Messick. "Scott tried to keep Bud's energy up."

Messick, best known for creating the voice for some of Hanna-Barbera's best (Scooby-Doo, Mutley, Bamm Bamm of *The Flintstones*, Astro on *The Jetsons*, Yogi Bear's pal, Boo Boo,

among them), recalled driving Bud home from the studio once. "I helped him walk up to the door and he invited me into his home one late afternoon," Messick says. "I remember his doctor only allowed him an ounce of whiskey, and we laughed about that. He gave me a 78 RPM record of 'Who's On First?,' which I've kept all these years."

During the final dozen episodes or so, a special arrangement was made for Stan Irwin. He explains: "I was pulled into New York to produce *The Tonight Show* with Johnny Carson, so I directed the cartoons myself out of New York. "The studio would send me the storyboard, the script, and the

pre-recorded material with openings for my lines," Irwin says. "In New York I would go to the studio which they set up and I completed the episodes under my own directions and then send the tapes back."

If Bud Abbott ever objected to the cartoon's content, quality, overall production—or even Irwin's impression of his former partner, he never let his opinion be known. Those cartoons were made so rapidly, no one really pressed for artistry, proper continuity, or snappy writing. Much more attention, in those days, was payed to deadlines and budgets. After performing such captivating dialogue exchanges like this next beaut, one wonders whether Bud just sat there in front of his mike, still and silent, thinking, "My God, what am I *doing* here?"

ABBOTT: Ah, the African Congo. Land of mystery and adventure. And land of Momba Zimba.

COSTELLO: Is that anything like the Watusi, Abbott?

ABBOTT: No! Momba Zimba is native for "white rhino." And that's what we've come to Africa to catch.

COSTELLO: And sell it to a zoo and make a thousand bucks, hey Abbott?

ABBOTT: Right!

Stan Irwin noted, "Bud really seemed to like to work. He never said a word about how I did Costello. I knew I was good. For a cartoon, it was good. I wasn't looking for confirmation."

Between 1966 and 1968, the studio pumped out a total of 156 five-minute Abbott and Costello cartoons. The unique, blasting theme song was composed by Hoyt Curtin, once labeled "the king of television cartoon music." Curtin was the maestro responsible for most of Hanna-Barbera's cool cartoon themes—including "Top Cat," "The Flintstones," "The Jetsons," "Josie and the Pussycats," and "Scooby-Doo."

Curtin not only composed the "Abbott and Costello Theme" but also composed and conducted the underscoring for each episode employing an eighteen-piece orchestra.

According to Lee Orgel, an original budget of $6,680.00 was allotted for each episode, which was tawdry even for the time. The quality of the syndicated cartoon series is not as bad as that of some television productions in the mid-Sixties. Although the series was produced in "limited animation" (some might describe it as barely animated), the storylines and gags are cute—albeit most are vacant of any traditional Abbott and Costello routines and verbal wordplays that viewers might expect. (Maybe that was their point?) Costello's tired "I'm a Baaaaad Boy" phrase, was about as close as the scripts came.

Admittedly, it's occasionally fun to see The Boys cast as Space Private Eyes, cavemen, exotic animal poachers. You name it. Sometimes they were just plain lunkheads caught up in outlandish binds. But the saving grace throughout all of them, without a doubt, was Bud's gravely voice ordering his little pal around, just like old times.

"How did you get us mixed up in this, Costella!"

Robert Easton on Abbott & Costello

In 1951, Robert Easton was in his early twenties when he played the cornbread-chompin' hillbilly Luke McCoy in *Comin' Round the Mountain* with Bud and Lou. Easton, a tall and lanky Texan, has been no stranger to bucolic roles in countless TV shows (including *The Beverly Hillbillies,* of course) and dozens of films (even a "Ma and Pa Kettle" flick for good measure). Easton also whittled out a

spoke a Russian tongue with impressive command. His professional services ("The Henry Higgins of Hollywood, Inc.") as a dialect doctor are continually sought today. Among his clients / students: Robin Williams, Anthony Hopkins, Jane Fonda, Tom Cruise, Gregory Peck, Charlton Heston, Laura Dern, Sir Lawrence Olivier and Ben Kingsley. Here, Easton—possibly the only surviving cast member from *Comin' Round the Mountain,* discusses his work with Bud and Lou.

Q: What scenes do you vividly recall shooting?

A: In the film there is a sequence which had each of us entering the shack and getting into bed. Finally we're all in the bed. Some of this was cut out of the final release, I think, because we shot this scene in a tank-like setup where the payoff had to do with a flood. They built it technically so the water got so high it lifted the bed, which floated, and Lou wound up somewhere else.

Q: You met John Grant—Bud and Lou's writer—didn't you?

Costello with Shaye Cogan and Robert Easton in Comin' Round the Mountain. *(Courtesy of Robert Easton)*

perfect niche in Hollywood as one of the most respected dialect coaches in the business, assisting, for instance, actor Al Pacino with his Cuban dialect in *Scarface.* On several popular *Tonight Show* appearances with Johnny Carson, the master dialectician rippled off a Scottish brogue and

A: Oh yes. I had a very interesting talk with John Grant about how they did this film. He and the other writers, Lees and Rinaldo, screened every film they could get hold of which dealt with hillbillies. Specifically I remember they had looked at *Sergeant York, Tobacco Road,* and *Roseanna McCoy.*

And then they got ideas about what they could parody. The original title for this film was *The Real McCoy* and they later switched it to *Comin' Round the Mountain.*

Q: I know you had some film experience at this time, but how did you approach this hillbilly character?

A: I had worked out this minimalist, underplayed character, with the dull eyes and all of that. It worked very well. I played the entire film barefoot—that was part of my character and some of the days it was pretty cold. If I remember correctly, it was done in January and February on the stages and backlot at Universal. We had one sequence in the house with animals and everyone was dancing.

I was eating cornbread and my eating all the time was something I brought to the character. Costello didn't really like that. One of the scenes in the house, I was sitting and a female goat urinated on my foot. Everybody thought it was hysterical. And on another take, a chicken defacated on my foot. That became a running gag. People would ask me if I had washed my feet.

In one of the scenes where I had bare feet, Costello was wearing the hobnail boots. During the scene—it was a fairly close two-shot—he stood on my foot which was painful. I didn't say anything because if this was a longshot and the camera picks it up, it might be funny, as well as my lack of reaction to it. Well, after the take, the director said, "Bob, I don't know what happened but your timing was

off." I told him, "That's because Mr. Costello was standing on my foot." He said, "Lou, Lou, c'mon, don't do that."

Q: How was your relationship with Costello during all of this?

A: Not easy. You see, Ida Moore, who was a very kindly, grandmotherly figure, she came to me and said, "When you work with a comedian, you have to be very careful that you're not too funny yourself. They don't like that." Now that had not been my experience with comedians in the past. I had worked with Jack Benny, who was known for his generosity. I had also worked with Milton Berle, who was extremely kind and unselfish, even though he wasn't known for that type of attitude. When I worked with Red Skelton many many times over the period of twenty years, I found him to be incredibly unselfish. And Ida Moore told me, "You watch it, because if you're not careful, your part may get cut down because Lou doesn't like you being funny."

"Squeeze over, Squeeze Box." The hillbillies hit the sack in a scene from Comin' Round the Mountain. *(Courtesy of Joe Wallison)*

Q: What was Bud and Lou's working relationship like at this time?

A: As you know, there was a rivalry between Bud and Lou. One time, in between scenes, as we were lining up, Bud said very loudly, "This kid is very funny," and he looked at Costello and said, "I think I'm gonna get myself a new partner." Bud came over to me and he started doing the "Who's On First?" routine. I thought, oh boy, better to screw this up. It was complimentary, but I pretended like I didn't know the routine, like I never heard of it, and I think I said something like, "Well, I don't really know anything about baseball." If I had gone into the routine with him, I might have gotten laughs on the set, but it was dangerous. This was the first time I had run into the problem of "don't be too funny."

Q: They say the star of the film sets the tone during the shoot. What kind of tone did Bud and Lou set?

A: It was a very pleasurable experience. A learning experience for me. I felt that Bud was very professional and always gentlemanly and friendly. Lou, he was unpredictable, moody. Some days he was in a good mood and jolly and other days he was in a bad mood. I know in the first edition of your book you quote Lucille Ball who said he was child-like without being childish. I've gotta say, I saw both sides of that.

Robert Easton, the leading dialect coach in Hollwood today. (Courtesy of Robert Easton)

Especially when his pal Bobby Barber was around.

Q: Was Bobby Barber around a lot?

A: He had him there all the time, just to run stupid, meaningless errands. And the way Lou treated him was very disturbing. On one hand, it was very kind of him to provide employment for this man, keep him on the payroll. But there was a kind of sadistic thing there. For instance, he had Bobby wearing this outlandish outfit with the coat that went way down to his ankles and a hat that Costello kept pulling down over his eyes. If he walked passed, Costello would trip him. There was a lot of physical horseplay, which I know Bobby could handle, but there was a little sadistic edge to it. Maybe Bobby didn't feel that way at all and was more than willing. If he felt demeaned by all this, he never showed it. It may have been something that I felt more for him.

Q: Have you ever resisted playing bucolic characters?

A: No. I've loved it. When I played them, it was always sympathetic. They weren't guys loaded with intelligence, but they were sympathetic and good-natured. Years ago, I suddenly started getting offered these southern parts that I didn't want to do. The scripts all called for the characters to be racists, bigots, rapists...and I didn't want to do that. And that's when I began learning all these other dialects—to break out of the typecasting. And it worked for me.

CHAPTER 13

Abbott & Costello Cartoons

Program Synopses
(Courtesy of Hanna-Barbera Productions, Inc.)

1. "Go Go Goliath"
Abbott gets Costello to fight the giant Goliath for a million bromin. After whipping the big guy with a slingshot, The Boys find out that a million bromin equal thirty-five cents.

2. "Dog Gone Dog"
Abbott feeds a pup Fast-Grow Plant Food by mistake. The dog becomes a gigantic pup, larger than a house.

3. "In the Soup"
Abbott & Costello are cooking in prehistoric times. They try to get a bone for their soup but have to fight a tiger for it, and the bone falls into a volcano.

4. "Cops and Saucers"
A flying saucer invades earth and meets Abbott & Costello, as cops. The pilot is a Martian robot who tries to capture them for examining purposes. Costello turns the tables on the Martian and frightens him away.

5. "There Auto Be a Law"
Abbott & Costello have a super cop car with all kinds of gadgets. A crook steals their car, and they have a duel with him in another super car. They apprehend him by converting the stolen car into a jail.

6. "Tiny Terror"

Abbott & Costello are maintenance men who get involved with a professor and his miniaturizing machine. They get shrunk to mouse size. After battling cats, rats, and birds, they change back to normal, but Costello gets in another machine and is regressed to a baby.

7. "The Cloud Monster"

An evil genius in a rocket ship uses a cloud monster to do his thievery. Detectives Abbott & Costello set out to capture him, using various weird and scientific gimmicks. Costello foils the crook by pretending to drink a high-explosive liquid that makes him a human bomb.

8. "Gravity Grabber"

A crook has a de-gravity gun that he uses to get people up in the air while he robs the bank. Abbott & Costello are do-gooder super sleuths in flying suits. They land on the crook's satellite ship and meet his assistant, a space monster. The Boys trick the crooks into de-gravitizing themselves and zooming into space.

9. "Big Bird Breakout"

A professor in prison hatches a monster bird, who breaks him out. Guards Abbott & Costello chase them. Abbott puts Costello in a helicopter bird-suit, and the propeller cuts the feathers off the giant bird, causing it to crash.

10. "The Vikings"

Abbott & Costello get carried back in time and wind up with the Vikings. Costello accidentally becomes chief and has to fight a battle. By accident, he wins and must marry an ugly princess. Instead, he gives up his crown and rushes back to his own time.

11. "Sahara You"

Lost on vacation, Abbott & Costello wind up as foreign legionnaires. They get out only after capturing a desert villain. As hero, Costello signs an autograph that turns out to be enlistment papers in the Mongolian air force.

12. "Going Buggy"

Abbott makes Costello spray their garden for bugs. Costello finishes and takes a nap in a hammock. He wakes up and finds that all the bugs have grown into monsters. After a big battle, in which Abbott & Costello take a beating, Costello discovers it was all a bad dream.

13. "Eskimo Pie-Eyed"

Northwest Mounties Abbott & Costello are out to get the giant King Kong Kanuck of the North.

14. "The Forty Thieves"

Abbott & Costello fall from a flying carpet and land next to the Forty Thieves' caves.

15. "Lube a Tuba"

Costello practices his tuba and blasts Abbott out of the house. The horn falls over Costello, and he gets stuck in it. Driving to the doctor, Costello finds himself alone riding through traffic. He crashes into Abbott and the motorcycle cops who are chasing him.

16. "Down in the Dumps"

A villain builds a mechanical monster out of junk. Abbott & Costello, as cops, are sent to catch the marauding menace. After they fight and chase the monster around town, it runs out of power. They convert the junkyard into a police department "junkenstein" playground.

17. "Wizard Land"

Abbott & Costello are magicians. They are vanished into Wizardland, where they get involved with a genie in a magic contest.

18. "Frail Whale"

Abbott & Costello go to sea with Captain Ahab to capture Moby Dick.

19. "Tooth or Consequences"

Abbott & Costello, as veterinarians, are called to an alligator farm to pull a bad tooth from an alligator. After a big hassle with the alligator, they finally get the tooth pulled, but from the wrong reptile.

20. "Sitting Pitty"

Abbott & Costello hire themselves out as baby sitters to a giant. The baby giant takes The Boys over as toys.

21. "Mark of El Zap"

Abbott & Costello are the Masked Avenger's assistants. They get involved in riding and dueling. The finale is in a bullring, with Costello fighting the bull.

22. "Catman on a Hot Tin Roof"

A real cat burglar is chased by policemen Abbott & Costello. They arrest a wildcat by mistake.

23. "El Fantasy"

Abbott & Costello are sent to repossess an elephant from a circus. They run into trouble with the owner, a gorilla, a lion, and an elephant.

24. "Shutter Bugged Sea Serpent"

As magazine photographers, Abbott & Costello go to sea in search of a sea serpent. After a big fight, the serpent turns out to be a big ham and poses for pictures.

25. "Super Lou"

A good fairy godmother makes Costello a superhero, and he goes to a masquerade party where he takes care of a couple of jewel thieves.

26. "Stand-In, Stand-Off"
Costello is a movie stuntman. He gets things so mixed up, the director becomes a stuntman himself to keep out of Costello's way.

27. "Mouse Route"
A witch turns Abbott & Costello into mice.

28. "Kooks and Spooks"
Costello has inherited a castle that he must spend one night in before he can claim it. If something happens to him, the castle goes to the lawyer. If something happens to the lawyer, the castle goes to Lou's uncle's dog, Fang.

29. "Dinosaur Dilemma"
Abbott & Costello fall from a plane into a prehistoric world and are involved with giant beasts, birds, and cavemen. The site turns out to be an amusement park.

30. "Indestructible Space Suit"
The army hires Abbott & Costello to test an indestructible space suit. The Boys go through all kinds of violence while testing the outfit. The suit finally disintegrates when Abbott pulls a loose thread.

31. "Frigid Fugitive"
Abbott & Costello are guarding a professor's abominable snowman in a freezer cabinet. The snowman gets out and wreaks havoc. The Boys finally capture the thing and put it in a steam cabinet by mistake, which shrinks the beast to a miniature monster.

32. "Astro-nuts"
Abbott & Costello are in a space capsule and get involved with a Martian invader in his flying saucer.

33. "Mighty Midget Mustang"
Abbott & Costello hunt for a circus's escaped miniature mustang. They chase it into the desert and into a secret canyon, and wind up with a whole family of performing mustangs.

34. "The Bouncing Rubber Man"
Abbott & Costello are guarding a scientist's new formula for rubber. While keeping it from a spy, Costello swallows some formula and becomes a rubber man. He bounces about, fighting the spy and his big assistant, the Crusher.

35. "Galoots in Armored Suits"
Abbott & Costello are tailors in days of old. They build a suit of armor, and Costello has to battle a champion knight to rescue the fair maiden-in-distress.

36. "The Purple Baron"

A World War I ace is outfought by blundering Costello in an old-fashioned dogfight.

37. "The Two Musketeers"

Abbott & Costello are swordsmen who are out to save the queen from the evil duke.

38. "In Blunderland"

Abbott & Costello chase a rabbit and fall into Blunderland. They meet a giant rabbit, a glad hatter, a marching hare, a sliding-door mouse, and the queens of spades, diamonds, clubs, and hearts.

39. "Skyscraper-Napper"

A villain in a weird robot spaceship from another planet descends on New York and steals buildings. Abbott & Costello are detectives assigned to stop the villain, which they do by getting his thought-control helmet.

40. "Going to Pot"

Abbott & Costello are on the island of Boola-Boola as members of the Friendship Corps. Their task is to make friends with the formerly savage natives. One cannibal in particular keeps grabbing Costello and trying to cook him.

41. "A Creep in the Deep"

Neptune's nephew, an evil reincarnation of the legendary undersea ruler, has created an underwater kingdom. With his army of obedient sharks, octopuses, sawfish, etc., he raids passing cargo ships for their valuables. Abbott & Costello, as the world's foremost underwater agents, are sent to capture him.

42. "Crying High"

Abbott & Costello accidentally get involved in a parachute contest.

43. "Germ Squirm"

Abbott & Costello get shrunk to germ size in order to catch a bad- guy germ.

44. "Weird Neighbors"

A distraught woman stops Abbott & Costello's patrol car to complain that her new neighbor's pet is trampling her flower bed. The new neighbor is from the planet Venus, and the pet is a tremendous freak animal. The pet resists all attempts to remove him from the flower bed and tramples the squad car before being won over by a peanut-butter sandwich from Costello's lunch box.

45. "Pigskin Pickle"

Abbott is the coach of a football team, and Costello is the water boy. It's the day of the big game, and Abbott's team is being trimmed by the opposing team. Clams Arrenganto, the big gambler, has bet $10,000 on Abbott's team and threatens to rub him out if they lose. Costello gets propelled into the game by accident, and things look worse than ever. Clams is about to rub out Abbott, when Costello inadvertently scores a touchdown, winning the game and sending Clams to jail.

46. "Two on the Isle"

This episode is a Robinson Crusoe takeoff, in which Abbott & Costello are marooned on a desert island, with Costello taking the part of Friday. His assignment is to hunt for food among the wildlife, but each attempt ends with Abbott getting clobbered. The Boys finally escape the island when a piece of it breaks off. Costello improvises a set of oars and oarlocks, and The Boys row off into the sunset.

47. "The Mole Man Mine"

Prospecting for the Lost Dutchman Gold Mine, Abbott & Costello are kicked down a deep shaft by their burro. They are confronted by a giant mole man, who clobbers them with solid-gold nuggets. The Boys are blasted back to the surface when the mole man, through ignorance, sets off their dynamite supply. Costello saves the day by hanging on to a million-dollar nugget, but uses it to knock the mole man back down the shaft.

48. "Lashed but Leashed"

Abbott & Costello, as bank maintenance men, get involved with a crook who uses a whip to do his dirty deeds. The Boys confuse him enough to take away his whip, and send him to jail.

49. "Space Toy Tyrants"

Patrol-car partners Abbott & Costello are unsuccessful in thwarting a robbery of the gold vaults at Fort Knox by a small spaceman. A chase leads to a toy factory, where The Boys discover that toy spacemen have taken over the factory and intend to take over the world. Abbott & Costello manage to capture the ambitious toys. The police chief, however, cannot be convinced that the toys are dangerous, and they use his lax attitude to escape again.

50. "The Little Fat Boy Who Cried Wolf"

Abbott & Costello are sheepherders, and Costello naturally draws the first watch. He vows not to cry "wolf" but does cry "hippo," "rhino," "lion," "giraffe," and "kangaroo." Abbott refuses to believe the outlandish claims, saying "seeing is believing." Costello replies "very well," and he determinedly rounds up the animals. But, before he can show the proof to Abbott, a circus man shows up and pays him a $1,000 reward for recapturing the escaped animals. When asked by Abbott how he came by the money, Costello simply explains that as long as there were no animals, then there is no money either.

51. "Wacky Wax Work"

Abbott & Costello, trapped in a wax museum overnight, have a bad time with wax monsters who come to life. The monsters turn out to be crooks using the museum as a hideout.

52. "Werewolf Whimwham"

Abbott's malady is one passed on to him from his Uncle Wolfgang, who would turn into a werewolf if ever a beam from a full moon should shine on him. It's bedtime, and there's a full moon out that night. Costello is up the entire time trying to prevent the light of the moon from hitting Abbott.

53. "The Monsterkeet"

Costello is experimenting with his Junior Atomic Scientist Kit. His pet parakeet drinks a concoction Costello mixed up, and grows to tremendous size. The monsterkeet wrecks the house and gives Abbott & Costello a hard time. Costello decides to fight fire with fire, and drinks some of the concoction. Costello grows and is able to tie up the monsterkeet. The concoction wears off, and they return to normal size. Abbott pours the offending concoction down the sink, and the germs in the drain all grow to tremendous size and throw a party.

54. "Invader Raider"

Huge tubes from space, pulled by rockets, plummet into the Hudson River and Central Park Lake, and pump them dry. Abbott & Costello, as space detectives, sever one of the tubes with their helicopter blades, and are sucked into the tube and transported to a distant planet. They battle and subdue the strange villain in his hideout. Costello tries to shut off the tremendous pump but reverses it instead, and the three of them are shot back to earth through the tube.

55. "A Goose Misuse"

Abbott & Costello are assigned to guard the king's priceless goose, which lays golden eggs. The goose is filched by a giant, but his huge footprints allow The Boys to track him to his castle. After a series of futile attempts to

regain the goose, Abbott hits upon the only logical plan. He dresses Costello in a goose costume, switches him for the real McCoy, and scurries off with the real goose safely under his arm, while Costello is left in the unenviable position of trying to produce a golden egg for the giant in order to avoid detection.

56. "Monster Muddled"

Abbott & Costello are patrolmen assigned to quiet down a masquerade party. Costello finally realizes it's no masquerade, but a monsters' shindig. He's saved when the clock strikes twelve and the ghouls disappear. Abbott enters and congratulates him on a job well done.

57. "Who Needs Arrest"

Patrolling in a Ben Hur-type chariot, Abbott & Costello receive orders to arrest Costello's friend Hercules. The huge Hercules gives Costello a terrible clobbering, until Costello accidentally rips the mask and beard off him, revealing that the villain is the circus strongman masquerading as Hercules.

58. "Paddleboat Pirate"

Abbott & Costello are disguised as Southern gentlemen aboard a Mississippi riverboat. In actuality, they're riverboat detectives assigned to nab the notorious river pirate, Jean Le Feedback. Instead, Le Feedback captures them and plans to use the riverboat to attack an ocean liner. The ocean liner turns out to be a navy battleship that nearly blasts them out of the water. The story ends with Abbott & Costello bringing the chastised Jean Le Feedback back to port, tied above the revolving paddles of the riverboat for the spanking of his life.

59. "Going, Going, Gun"

Abbott & Costello are western sheriffs who have to bring in Gruesome Galloot, the stagecoach robber. Gruesome is too much for Bud and Lou, and they wind up behind bars.

60. "Road Race Ruckus"

Abbott & Costello get in a sports-car race in Italy and use a tricky car to defeat the champ.

61. "Gone Ghosts"

Abbott & Costello are hired to haunt a castle, but they get spooked themselves when they meet a real ghost.

62. "Baby Buggy"

Abbott & Costello are garbagemen. They find a baby in a garbage can. Only, unbeknownst to them, it's actually a Martian baby, dropped from a passing spaceship. While The Boys try frantically to locate its parents, the baby makes them even more frantic with its powers of levitation, invisibility, self-transformation, etc. The Martian parents come back to earth and finally retrieve him.

63. "Hey, Abbott!"

Costello takes the place of a test pilot in order to test a new one-man, all-jet helicopter.

64. "Drumsticks Along the Mohawk"

Abbott & Costello are Pilgrims back in the 1600s. They've decided to celebrate their first year in the New World with a turkey dinner, to which they've invited Chief Leaping Lizard and his tribe. Costello is sent out to prepare the turkey, which, meanwhile, has eaten some baking yeast and grown to the size of a two-story building. Costello makes many unsuccessful attempts to capture the giant bird, until the chief threatens to scalp The Boys for having promised the tribe a nonexistent turkey dinner. At the last moment, the giant turkey crashes into their cabin, and the frightened Indians take off in a panic.

65. "A Car Is Born"

Abbott & Costello work for a scientist who has invented a special liquid that brings their car to life. The liquid gets spilled onto a line of motor scooters, which come to life and chase them all over town.

66. "Teeny-Weeny Genie"

The setting is ancient Persia. Abbott & Costello own a junk shop, where Costello finds an old lamp and rubs it. Out pops a baby genie who is too young to perform any miracles, but is old enough to escape into the ancient city and create all sorts of mischievous damage—ripping up buildings, stealing rides on flying carpets, etc. They finally get him back into the lamp, but Costello accidentally rubs it again, and the baby genie reappears, along with his forty-foot older brother.

67. "Lumbering Lummoxes"

Abbott & Costello are up in the North Woods working as lumberjacks. Their nemesis is Big Pierre, the giant lumberjack boss who's out to get them due to Costello's costly and constant bumbling. He threatens to fire The Boys unless they can clear the entire hill of trees before sundown, which Costello inadvertently manages to do, thus saving their jobs.

68. "Professor Uncle's Ants"

Abbott & Costello are space detectives who chase the sinister Professor Uncle and his diabolical Astro-Ants. Bud and Lou outsmart the professor and turn the ants against him.

69. "High-Wire Lion"

Policemen Bud and Lou get into a high-wire act while trying to catch a runaway circus lion.

70. "Fish Hooked"

Abbott & Costello are arctic fishermen who get into a big struggle with a hungry polar bear over a fish.

71. "Magic Monster"

While surfing, Abbott & Costello find a magic lamp. A genie appears and gets out of hand.

72. "The Planet Plant"

A small planet in our galaxy explodes, and some of the debris reaches earth in the form of a weird plant that makes itself at home in Lou's flower garden. The plant gives Lou a hard time and starts growing and eating everything in sight, including Abbott's car. Abbott doesn't believe Lou until the plant starts eating The Boys' house. They try to dynamite the plant's roots, but succeed only in blowing the plant into a number of smaller plants, which take root and start growing. Abbott cuts out to the ballpark and leaves Lou to cope with his problem garden.

73. "Spacebeard"

When space detectives Abbott & Costello tangle with Spacebeard aboard his Space Shark, they are quickly captured. Before making them walk the space plank, Spacebeard forces them to bury his treasure on his Island in the Sky. Costello tries to dig deep enough to escape, and punctures the helium sac that supports the Island in the Sky. When everything plummets and crashes onto earth, The Boys are saved by the thrust of the escaping helium.

74. "Marauding Mummy"

Abbott & Costello, as museum guards, have the job of guarding a fabulous ruby stone that is supposed to have a curse on it. Costello has a bad time with a mummy that is trying to do away with him. The mummy turns out to be a notorious jewel thief who is trying to steal the ruby.

75. "Baby Shoo"

Abbott & Costello are private eyes on the track of Jack of All Crimes. Costello disguises himself as a baby and gets into Jack's house. He encounters Jack's giant gorilla, Grunto. Costello subdues both of them with his baby bag of tricks.

76. "The Long, Long Camper"

Abbott & Costello are enjoying a vacation in the national park until a huge bear moves into their camper. The bear thwarts all of Costello's attempts to evict him. He rips the camper off the truck and takes it into a cave to hibernate. When The Boys try to break into the cave to retrieve their camper, they get into trouble with the ranger.

77. "Puppet Enemy Number One"

Bud is a wood-carver who decides to carve himself a wooden boy that would be like a son to him.

78. "Phantom of the Hoss Opera"

Abbott & Costello are sheriffs in a Western ghost town when the ghosts of Billy the Kid, Black Bart, and Jesse James come to life and begin shooting up

the town. Costello finally subdues them by inadvertently starting a desert whirlwind, which blows them back into their tombs.

79. "Fumbled Fable"

This episode is a takeoff on the "Little Red Riding Hood" story. Costello delivers the basket of goodies instead of Little Red Riding Hood, and is trapped alone with the Wolf/Grandma, who's out to eat him. Abbott is the woodsman who finally saves the day.

80. "Rabbit Grabbers"

Bounty hunters Bud and Lou try to collect $500 for capturing the pesky varmint Texas Jack. They set all kinds of lures, including a girl rabbit as a trap, but she runs off and elopes with the love-smitten Jack.

81. "Vacuum Villain"

Abbott & Costello pose as bank guards in order to capture the diabolical Vacuum Villain. Costello gets hit on the head, and he thinks he's a bank robber. Poor Abbott gets caught in the middle when his befuddled pal teams up with the real crook.

82. "Big Cannon Caper"

Bud and Lou are the king's musketeers who have to fight the evil duke. They are so inept at battle that the kingdom is reduced to a royal junkyard.

83. "Throne for a Loss"

Costello inherits a kingdom from a long-forgotten uncle. Along with the castle, he inherits an evil prime minister (Basil Ratfink), who's out to destroy Costello and take over the kingdom himself. Fortunately, Ratfink's booby traps backfire.

84. "Phony Express"

Pony Express riders Abbott & Costello run into Indian trouble when they meet Chief Nasty Bear.

85. "Concrete Evidence"

Abbott & Costello are cops assigned to stop Captain Marble, an arch criminal with the ability to change himself into a statue at will. Costello captures him by accidentally knocking him into a park fountain and washing away his magical powers. Captain Marble ends up as a permanent statue in the park.

86. "The Lava Monster"

Explorers Abbott & Costello are out to snap a picture of the dreaded Lava Monster. The beast turns out to be an unwilling subject and gives Bud and Lou a bad time as he makes it hot for them inside his active volcano home.

87. "Glass Reunion"

This episode is a takeoff on the "Cinderella" fairy tale. Costello is the poor, ragged chimney sweep, and Abbott is the fairy godfather who sends him to the ball, where Lou is pursued by the adoring and beautiful princess.

88. "A Guest in the Nest"

Abbott & Costello are high atop a mountain crag, with Costello in a bird costume. They're out to get photos of the rare Giant Mountain Buzzard in its natural habitat. Lou slips and falls into the nest, causing the eggs to hatch. The mother buzzard thinks Lou is one of her newborn chicks and proceeds to teach Lou how to fly, eat, etc.

89. "Gone Like the Wind"

Bounty hunters Bud and Lou try to capture the wily rabbit Texas Jack. They try all kinds of tricky rabbit catchers, but Jack turns everything about and foils their schemes.

90. "Gadzooka"

Cops Bud and Lou protect their city from the gigantic monster Gadzooka. After wrecking most of the city, the beast is tamed when Costello pulls a thorn from his foot. New problems develop when Gadzooka's whole family wants to move in with nice guys Abbott & Costello.

91. "Merry Misfits"

Bud and Lou are seeking to become members of Robin Hood's Merry Men. They attempt to rescue Robin from an evil sheriff, but they botch up the job.

92. "Broom Gloom"

Abbott & Costello are door-to-door broom salesmen who try to sell a new model broom to a reluctant witch.

93. "The Hound Hounders"

Dogcatchers Bud and Lou get involved in a bank robbery when a crook disguises himself as a dog.

94. "Rescue Miscue"

Bud and Lou are mountain ski patrolmen. They meet a friendly but monstrous Saint Bernard dog. The three of them go out on a rescue mission, and their clumsy efforts call for them to be rescued instead.

95. "Fighting the Clock"

Abbott & Costello are crime fighters assigned to stop the Clock, an arch villain whose hideout is in an abandoned watchtower and whose gimmicks are built around clocks, time bombs, etc. He and his henchman, Big Ben, end up as the bell ringers, striking the hours high atop the Hall of Justice building.

96. "Sinister Professor Sinister"

An evil professor builds a diabolical weapon to help capture the world. Unluckily for him, Abbott & Costello get on his trail. Costello becomes the strongest man in the world when Abbott sprays him with an energy ray. Lou then takes all the professor's toughest devices and puts them to useful purposes.

97. "Ship Ahooey"

Sailors Abbott & Costello are AWOL from their naval ship. In trying to catch up with the ship in a small motorboat, The Boys take a shortcut through the target area, and get bombarded by their own ship.

98. "Pigs in a Panic"

The Three Little Pigs call on detectives Bud and Lou to help them get rid of the Big Bad Wolf. The only problem is, Abbott & Costello mess things up worse than the pesky wolf.

99. "Underworld Whirl"

Super Terror strikes the nation's capital and runs off with military plans. Space sleuths Abbott & Costello give chase and wind up deep underground. Costello goes after Super Terror as the Invisible Man, except he becomes visible at embarassing times. The Boys capture the crook, but Costello's nowhere to be seen.

100. "Bully Billy"

Abbott & Costello are pushed into saving a mountain village from a menacing monster. Then they find that their deed goes unrewarded.

101 "Dragon Along"

This medieval story finds Abbott & Costello as royal dragon slayers. The king offers the hand of his daughter as a reward to the one bold enough to battle the dragon. Abbott first cons Costello into fighting the beast, and then into letting Abbott claim the reward. But, as things turn out, Abbott gets his just desserts; the daughter is by far the homelier "dragon."

102. "Password to Panic"

The Chief of Panic, head of a worldwide crime syndicate, has a giant judo wrestler as his strong-arm man. Abbott & Costello accidentally fall into the clutches of this evil pair, but they bumble around so much that they get the crooks fighting among themselves.

103. "Mounty Bounty"

Mounted policemen Abbott & Costello have to bring in Mighty Maurice the outlaw. He proves to be big, rough, and tough, but Bud and Lou remain true to the Northwest Mounty tradition. They do things the hard way, but they finally get their man—after he gets them a few times.

104. "Super Terror Strikes Again"

Abbott & Costello track Super Terror to the jungle, where they have to use special crime-fighting equipment to battle the super crook. A shrinking-and-growing machine makes them very big men on the job.

105. "No Place Like Rome"

The setting is ancient Rome. Abbott & Costello are hot-dog vendors outside the Colosseum. They sneak inside to sell their franks, but Costello finds himself in a gladiator's costume, and in mortal combat against the Mad Mongolian, a thirty-foot-tall gladiator. Lou finally defeats him by donning a pair of winged sandals belonging to the Roman god Mercury.

106. "Texas Jack"

Abbott & Costello set all kinds of tricky traps to snare the fastest rabbit in the world, Texas Jack. But no matter what they try, he outruns their best devices.

107. "Follow the Bouncing Blob"

Abbott dumps Costello's chemistry experiment into the kitchen sink, and it starts bouncing higher and higher. The least angle deflects it in a new direction. It makes a shambles inside the house and soon is all over the neighborhood. A motorcycle officer becomes involved and takes a beating. Abbott dynamites the super blob. But this action does not solve the problem; it merely turns it into many, many small ones.

108. "Not-So-Sweet Sioux"

Abbott & Costello, the owners of a messenger service in the middle of the Mojave Desert, are called to deliver a vital message to Garcia. They run up against a series of setbacks due to the presence of Super Chief, a giant Indian, who refuses to let them cross his territory. Costello finally defeats him, only to discover that Garcia owns Garcia's Taco Stand and the message is an order for a dozen enchiladas.

109. "Queen of Diamonds"

A native island queen thinks Costello is the mighty spirit Gadoola Bong. Abbott cons Lou into going along with the gag. This ploy results in a wild battle in which Lou must prove to be the true spirit by fighting a giant gorilla.

110. "Picture Frame-Up"

The crook Super Terror steals art treasures from a museum by bringing pictures to life and having the subjects do his bidding. Abbott & Costello, space private eyes, get into the case and brush up on their painting. They learn Super Terror's secret and turn the subject against him.

111. "Luna Tricks"

Super Terror has a secret moon-based lab from which he directs his sinister schemes. Space detectives Abbott & Costello blast off for the moon and put

Super Terror into a new orbit. They use all kinds of exotic weapons to overcome the fantastic machines in Super Terror's lab.

112. "Pearl-Diving Perils"

Abbott & Costello, out fishing, are captured by the notorious pirate Greenbeard and are forced to dive for a sea chest filled with giant black pearls. After numerous undersea misadventures, Bud and Lou come up with the sea chest and drive Greenbeard off the ship with cannon fire. They think they are millionaires until Lou reveals that he used the giant black pearls as cannonballs.

113. "Booty Bounty"

Cowboys Abbott & Costello get jobs as bounty hunters. They have to hunt down Old Saw Tooth, the mountain lion. They find that Old Saw Tooth doesn't take too kindly to folks capturing him, and he gives The Boys a good runaround for their money.

114. "G.I. Jokers"

Army training becomes no joke for Bud and Lou when they encounter invaders from space who don't understand that the war games are all in fun.

115. "Tasmanian Terror"

Abbott & Costello are zoo attendants who receive a wild beast that runs amok.

116. "Dangerous Buck"

Bud and Lou are a couple of unlucky prospectors who run into a hip Indian who drives a sports car and uses James Bond-type Indian weapons. The Indian turns The Boys loose and hunts them down like buffalo.

117. "The Gadget King"

A huge, gadget-laden robot runs amok when the inventor's control box is accidentally smashed. Officers Abbott & Costello try to stop him. Costello gains entry to the robot's engine room, but only makes matters worse with his switch-throwing and wire-pulling. The robot then flies off with Costello. The inventor, via TV screen, locates Costello on a strange planet and orders him to fly the robot back. The robot won't leave the new planet, however, because everyone there is a gadget robot and he's making time with a cute female.

118. "The Fiendish Farmer"

An arch criminal known as the Fiendish Farmer drops special seeds that grow into terrorizing things. These things interfere with Abbott & Costello's golf game, so The Boys proceed to drive the intruders from their course and the Fiendish Farmer gets trapped by his own devices.

119. "The Ice-Tronauts"
On space patrol, Abbott & Costello investigate an invading icetronaut spacecraft. They discover that they have to fight an ice king, his ice warriors, and ice lizards. Bud and Lou find a way to make things hot for these intruders, and their invasion plans melt away.

120. "Gator Baiter"
A wrestling alligator attaches itself to Abbott & Costello, and they have a rough time getting rid of it.

121. "Rabbit Rouser"
Abbott & Costello develop a mechanical hound with which to capture the pesky rabbit Texas Jack. The hound gives chase, but the rabbit outsmarts the mechanized mutt. Texas uses a mirror to reflect the hound's laser rays, and they break him up. Not to be outdone, Texas Jack builds a forty-foot rabbit from the parts and sends it after Abbott & Costello.

122. "Save a Cave"
Cavemen Bud and Lou meet a dragon-a-saurus who drives them from their cave. Bud gives Lou a dragon-a-saurus club and sends him to fight the beast, but he's no match for the monster. The Boys discover they can tame him with hot lava soup, but his appetite is so great it's a never-ending job keeping him fed.

123. "Wild Man Wild"
Bud and Lou open a circus with a wild man as a main attraction. The wild man escapes, and Bud makes Lou take his place in the cave. The real wild man returns to confuse Abbott, and the excitement begins as Bud tries to give him orders, thinking he's Costello.

124. "Which Witch Is Which"
Abbott arouses the ire of a witch, and she changes him into a frog. Costello performs difficult and dangerous tasks as the price for getting Abbott restored to manhood. When the witch reneges on her promise, Costello gets mad. He grabs the witch's wand and does some wild, uncontrolled changes on his own. When he accidentally transforms the frog back into Abbott, and the witch into a beautiful woman, he decides to quit while he's ahead and breaks the wand over his knee.

125. "Super Knight"
Abbott & Costello are court buffoons who are forced to fight the villainous Black Knight. Merlin gives Costello a magic spell to help him in battle. He does pretty well, until the magic wears off.

126. "Son of Konk"
Abbott & Costello are deliverymen. They go to pick up a cute little monkey to be taken to the circus, only to find it's really a huge gorilla. Trying to sub-

due Konk, the gorilla, is quite a job, and he escapes. There's a mad chase that leads across town to a circus, and Costello and Konk end up as a circus act.

127. "Shooting the Works"

As policemen, Bud and Lou are assigned to stop Zucchini, the Human Cannonball, who has turned to a life of crime. They are equipped with a James Bond-type super car, but it's hardly a match for Zucchini's trick cannon, which frustrates their every capture attempt.

128. "Doggies by the Dozen"

Abbott & Costello are running a delivery service. While making a delivery, Costello is confronted with the problem of getting past a huge, homely canine prankster. No matter what he tries, Costello cannot seem to evade the shaggy menace. The dog seems to always be in eight places at the same time. Costello waves the white flag and has a powwow with the bowwow. It is then that he discovers that the dog has a dozen canine cousins to aid him in his watchdog duties.

129. "Rhino Riot"

Abbott & Costello are in Africa hunting rhino with a tranquilizer gun. Costello keeps shooting himself with the gun and going to sleep. The rhino gives them a bad time and finally chases both of them out of Africa.

130. "Bully for Lou"

The notorious crook Rock-A-Bye Baby hypnotizes the superhero Mighty Much into doing his dirty deeds for him. Abbott & Costello try to stop their hero from wrongdoing. Costello puts dynamite under his hat and uses his head to bring Mighty Much to his senses.

131. "Cherokee Choo Choo"

The Iron Horse has trouble getting through Indian territory. But when Abbott & Costello take charge, things go too far, and they run the train into Eskimo country.

132. "Hotel Suite and Sour"

Super Terror uses a hotel as a hijacking ruse to steal scientists and take them to another planet. Abbott & Costello are space detectives who become victims of Super Terror but manage to unravel his web of intrigue.

133. "Shoo Shoes"

Costello, the inventor, develops flying jet-propelled shoes. Abbott tries them on, and the shoes go wild, flying him all over the country. Lou lassos Bud and finally pulls him down, but Bud takes off again when Lou comes up with another invention.

134. "Teensy Versus Weensys"

Abbott & Costello are castaways on a desert island and get tied up by little people.

135. "Tragic Magic"
Bud and Lou are working backstage at a magic show where the Great Hamboni is performing his famous "Levitating an Elephant" trick. When Big Max, the famous gangster, shows up, Hamboni makes himself disappear. Max thinks Lou is Hamboni and forces Lou to help him levitate a bank safe to his hideout by using his magic wand.

136. "Carnival of Menace"
The Ruthless Ringmaster, a vicious villain who travels about in a flying circus tent, is in the midst of stealing all the gold from Fort Knox, when Bud and Lou drive up with an armored-car delivery of gold.

137. "Hullaba-Lou"
In the days of Camelot Bud and Lou find themselves as attendants to a mean little prince. The king sends them off to get the prince a flying horse. Bud and Lou put on a horse suit and attempt to lure the flying horse in close so they can capture it.

138. "Get 'im Tiger"
Tiger hunters Abbott & Costello catch a giant tiger by the tail, but Costello manages to tame the beast, and he becomes a real, live, tiger-skin rug.

139. "Mountain Mischief"
Abbott & Costello are hired to serve an eviction notice on a hillbilly. Unfortunately, Costello strongly resembles the hillbilly's archenemy feuding family, the McStellos. Costello takes quite a beating, but finally succeeds in serving the notice fair and square. The Boys are relieved to be home again, until they learn the hillbilly has moved into the apartment across from theirs.

140. "The Drastic Driller"
Abbott & Costello, private eyes, chase the low-down crook, Drastic Driller, who is about to steal valuable secret machinery. They go deep underground in their pursuit, and hit a geyser that results in the Driller getting into hot water.

141. "Turkish Daffy"
The Sultan of Istanbul hires Abbott & Costello as guards to watch over a gem, the Star of Shishkabar. The Thief of Badguy swipes the jewel from under their noses, but an Arabian knight's chase through Istanbuli results in the return of the priceless bauble. Costello sadly finds out that this valuable stone is not to be sneezed at.

142. "Yankee Doodle Dudes"
On desert sands, Bud and Lou ride a tired camel who suddenly panics at the sight of Ali Ben Sikh, the outlaw slave trader. The outlaw captures Bud and Lou, and takes them to market. He sells them in the bargain basement to a mysterious buyer.

143. "Gorilla Thriller"
Abbott & Costello are street musicians. Bud plays the organ, and Lou wears a monkey suit. Konga, the circus gorilla, escapes to look for her baby. She picks up Costello, and so begins a simian mix-up.

144. "The Eighth Dwarf"
Snow White is captured by an evil giant, and Abbott & Costello pester the monster until he gives her up. The Seven Dwarfs honor Costello by making him the eighth dwarf, and present him with his own broom and eight dirty rooms to clean.

145. "Super Car"
Abbott talks Costello into becoming a stunt driver in order to test a new super car. The car holds up through most of the tests, but Costello manages to reduce it to junk.

146. "Desert Danger"
A motion-picture crew shooting a space picture in the desert goes into town for lunch. Abbott & Costello, who are lost, wander onto the spaceship and think aliens have landed. Abbott makes Costello stay and guard the ship, while he goes to notify authorities. When the motion-picture crew returns, Costello won't let them near the ship. Before Abbott gets back, Costello manages to wreck the spaceship, the company car, and the nerves of everyone involved.

147. "Rodeo Rumpus"
Abbott talks Costello into riding a bucking horse for a big-money prize. When Costello accidentally wins, he decides to spend all the money on the horses, and winds up going around in circles.

148. "The Sinister Stinger"
A diabolical genius called the Sinister Stinger threatens an entire city. Supersleuths Abbott & Costello use their most fantastic weapons to invade the Stinger's beehive and make him behave.

149. "Magic Mix-up"
Princess Sleeping Beauty is rescued by Abbott & Costello's super magic after she is captured by the evil wizard. However, in a face-to-face contest with the wizard, Abbott discovers he's run afoul of the Fastest Wand in the West.

150. "Bad Day at High Noon"
Sheriffs Abbott & Costello meet up with the outlaw the Star-Spangled Bandit, who likes to steal badges from lawmen.

151. "Shock Treatment"
Policemen Abbott & Costello pull a switch on the Voltage Villain and charge him with power purloining.

THE ABBOTT
AND COSTELLO
STORY

BY DREW FRIEDMAN

THE TEAM OF BUD ABBOTT AND LOU COSTELLO FIRST RECEIVED NATIONAL EXPOSURE ON THE KATE SMITH RADIO PROGRAM.

IN 1941, HOLLYWOOD BECKONED, AND THE DUO WAS MORE THAN EAGER TO OBLIGE.

ABETTED BY THE ANDREWS SISTERS IN A SERIES OF WAR COMEDIES, THEIR SUCCESS WAS ASTOUNDING.

HEY, ABBOTT, WHERE DO ALL THE LITTLE BUGS GO IN WINTER?

SEARCH ME.

NO, THANKS. I JUST WANTED TO FIND OUT.

WE'RE MOVIN' UP.

YET BEHIND THE SCENES THERE WAS HEATED TENSION BETWEEN THE TWO, AGGRAVATED BY LOU'S STUBBORNNESS.

IN 1943, LOU COSTELLO BRAVELY FACED THE GREATEST TRAGEDY OF HIS LIFE... THE DROWNING OF HIS BABY SON, LOU, JR.

THEIR FILMS, NEVER FAVORITES WITH THE CRITICS, KEPT ON COMING, HIGHLIGHTED BY ABBOTT AND COSTELLO MEET FRANKENSTEIN.

GODDAMIT, LOU, WHAT ARE YOU TRYIN' TO PULL?!

"COSTELLO AN' ABBOTT." DAT'S TH' WAY I WAN' IT! DAT'S TH' WAY IT'S GONNA BE!

MONSTERS... DON'T BE SILLY.

IN THE EARLY FIFTIES, BUD AND LOU MOVED TO TELEVISION WHERE THEIR TRIED-AND-TRUE ROUTINES CONTINUED TO BRING JOY AND LAUGHTER TO THEIR FANS.

THE BOYS WOULD EVENTUALLY BREAK UP IN 1957 AND NEVER SPEAK AGAIN. LOU DIED IN 1959 AND BUD, HAVING BEEN WIPED OUT BY THE I.R.S. IN 1960, LIVED ON A MODEST PENSION UNTIL HIS DEATH IN 1974.

THE FELLOW'S NAME ON BASE?

WHO.

THE GUY ON FIRST BASE.

WHO IS ON FIRST BASE.

HAH! HAR! HA! HAW!

MY POOR LITTLE BUDDY. I DIDN'T EVEN KNOW HE WAS SICK.

250 Flee Buckling L.A. Apartment

FUNMAKER LOU COSTELLO DIES OF HEART ATTACK

©1984

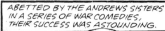

152. "Tom All Thumbs"

The cobbler Abbott and his assistant Tom Thumb Costello become heroes when they capture Sir Robalot and return the king's stolen crown.

153. "Star Light, Star Fright"

Movie producer Abbott puts stuntman Costello through some slam-bang screen tests, and one unscheduled scene takes Costello way out of this world.

154. "Private General Nuisance"

The World War I army antics of Private Costello and Sergeant Abbott turn the battlefield into a series of disasters. Even when the war ends, Costello is too mad to stop fighting.

155. "Trigger Tricks"

Western bad guy Cactus Clyde holds up the train. He doesn't know that the two famous Slinkerton detectives, Abbott & Costello, are on his tracks. Wearing cactus disguise suits, The Boys attempt to pin the crime on Cactus Clyde.

156. "Pinocchio's Double Trouble"

Wood-carver Abbott tries once more to carve a puppet. Again it looks just like Costello. This time a fairy princess bestows life on the wooden boy. The boy tries to be good, but he gets swindled by an evil magician and tells a few fibs, which causes his nose to grow. After the wooden boy has more dealings with the magician and another whale of an adventure, the good fairy turns him into a real Pinocchio Costello. Happy Abbott carves him a wooden puppy, who has a few nose problems of his own.

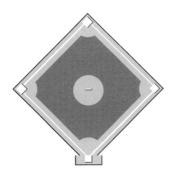

Extra Innings: Postscript 1997

Marooned on a desert island with just a water purifier and a video player, I'd hope to find these ten movies buried in the sand: *Modern Times, Casablanca, Dr. Strangelove or How I Learned to Stop Worrying and Love the Bomb, Play It Again Sam, Nashville, Bull Durham—two* copies in case one wears out, *The Wild One, A Night at the Opera,* and most important . . . *Buck Privates.*

Why *Buck Privates?*

So I can laugh, that's why. So I can laugh with all my heart whether the sun comes up or the moon fails to rise. So I can laugh without pretension, without irony, without pathos, without satire, without care.

I have probably watched *Buck Privates* more times than any other human being not related to the Abbotts or the Costellos. That's because I watch it every semester with at least one group of students, sometimes more. I have continued to use Abbott & Costello films in my classes since we wrote this book sixteen semesters ago. I sit in the back of the room behind the students and

I laugh every time. So do they. Despite themselves.

Bud Abbott and Lou Costello were enormously successful in their time. Students today are somewhat surprised by this, as were the critics of the 1940s and the 1950s. Read reviews of their films and you are left with the impression critics were completely confounded by The Boys' popularity. After all, Abbott & Costello lacked the physical grace of Chaplin and the intellectual power of the Marx Brothers, their nearest comedic competitors. Yet huge audiences were attracted to their increasingly improbable titles. Why?

We worked hard to answer that question when we wrote this book almost a decade ago, and I think we were partially successful. They were good at what they did. They played the underdog chord beautifully. They were in the right place at the right time. But the whole answer remained elusive.

Now I know that answer; it was under my nose all along. I arrived at it in a roundabout way. You see, I

actually use their movies—more specifically their routines—to illustrate how much more literate American humor was before television. That's right, more literate. I borrow my point from Neil Postman, then play "Who's on First?" followed by a seven-minute car chase from *The Blues Brothers* in which less than a dozen words are said. I ask which is more dependent on the ability of the audience to read. Of course, "Who's on First?" is *totally* dependent on a literate audience. The car chase from *The Blues Brothers* may actually be funnier without the sound.

The students nod their heads respectfully when I turn on the lights and make my point, but I can tell they think I'm nuts.

Then I use the "Boogie Woogie Bugle Boy" number from *Buck Privates* to illustrate the nature of racism in popular films. I point out that *Buck Privates* wasn't *meant* to be racist; it obviously reflected a socially acceptable sentiment of the times. Acceptable racism is probably more dangerous than overt racism, I argue. The students look at me dutifully concerned, then stare at their shoes.

I use other comic films to teach: Chaplin, Marx Brothers, Woody Allen, Spike Lee. I show *Modern Times* and preface it by telling the students I think this is the best American comedy ever. They scribble what I say in their notes but when Chaplin walks off into the California sunset and I turn on the lights, they seem to be thinking, *What's up with this guy? Did he miss* Spaceballs?

However, when I show them an Abbott & Costello film, and I don't say anything teacherly, just put the film on and get out of the way, one thing always happens. They laugh. It starts with a chuckle that a guy in the first row tries to swallow, but can't. Then it spreads across to the window side of the room and roars to the back. Every time, without fail, laughter rolls. Good, from-the-gut laughter. Uninhibited laughter.

For example, a scene we nearly overlooked when we wrote this book, the musical number with Lou Costello and Shemp Howard in *Buck Privates,* always leaves the students in stitches.

The point is, Abbott & Costello are funny. That's the whole reason why they were so popular in their time. They made people laugh—without thought, without guilt. And America needed laughter more than anything else between Pearl Harbor and Elvis.

Their time may come again. We're still waiting for Abbott & Costello, like Humphrey Bogart, to be rediscovered.

Rediscovery will be easier now than when we put this book together. Since then, nearly every one of their films has become available on videotape and laser disc. So has the complete history of *The Abbott and Costello Show* from television, as well as live television that was preserved on kinescope. Their Al Hirschfeld likenesses have been released on U.S. postage stamps. (Hirschfeld himself was lionized in the 1996 Oscar-nominated documentary, *The Line King.*) And the hottest comedian in the world, Jerry Seinfeld, paid tribute to The Boys in a highly rated prime-time special on NBC titled, "Abbott and Costello Meet Jerry Seinfeld."

"I grew up on these two guys," Seinfeld says at the beginning of the special. At the end, he concludes:

"Without them, we wouldn't even know how some of these wonderful routines were performed. They are the only ones who preserved an entire era of American entertainment. These were the roots of virtually every contemporary comedian working. And Bud and Lou are still getting laughs today."

Abbott & Costello also met *Biography* on A&E since we wrote this book. The segment included comments from Tom and Dick Smothers, John Landis, Henny Youngman, and Steve Allen. Like the Seinfeld special, it was full of sidesplitting clips, interviews with family members, and snippets of home movies. Both specials remind us how likable these two men were, how warm they were to the camera, how just-like-us they were in film and life.

Finally, we must say good-bye to several persons who contributed memories and wonderful photographic images; sadly, these folks are no longer around:Bob Cummings, Sheldon Leonard, Vic Parks, Maxene Andrews, Bud Abbott Jr., and Eddie Forman. We're glad we talked with them when we did. Each was gracious and kind about our inquiries.

The Boys' timing was always right on cue, from burlesque to television. We've got to believe the time will be right someday for their rediscovery and another generation will be introduced to the laughter of the innocent.

—John Lofflin
May 1997

Me? I'd prefer a few great (yes, *great!*) episodes of *Gilligan's Island* at my side if I were stranded on that deserted isle—if for nothing but sheer hope. Remember, *they* got rescued. For the stormy nights, I'd like to watch *Abbott and Costello Meet Frankenstein,* and for the blistering tropical noon, maybe *Pardon My Sarong.*

To assure some hard laughs, the kind that induces a snort, a video "must" would be some of Bud and Lou's TV episodes—with Joe Besser, of course. And a few vintage Three Stooges shorts for insurance. With Shemp to be precise.

Actually, I hope that anyone who reads this has the opportunity to be stranded with this book for several hours to absorb it all. The wonderful part of assembling a book like this, is the hunt, the search for unseen Abbott & Costello. I think we've unearthed a few gems for ourselves, and for any other curious fan of vintage comedy who may breeze through this. Possibly there's a surprise or two in here for the families of Bud and Lou as well. This scrapbook, of sorts, may provide a clearer picture of who these guys were, hopefully without appearing iconoclastic.

Personally, there has been an edgy side to this assignment. Throughout all the research and interviews and laughs and ultimate deadlines, a ghostly image of Bud and Lou seemed to materialize around corners, in dreams; at the strangest moment, their names would pop up in unrelated conversation. The whole thing makes me wish I could have met these guys, or watched them work, even just once. Especially Bud, because I love gentle souls.

—Stephen Cox
May 1997

Mr & Mrs M.J. Dutta
211 Goodrich Street
Hayward CA 94544-3407

About the Authors

Stephen Cox graduated in 1988 from Park College in Kansas City, Missouri, with a B.A. in journalism and communication arts. He has written several books on film and television, including: *The Beverly Hillbillies, The Addams Chronicles, Here's Johnny!, Here on Gilligan's Isle* (with Russell Johnson), *The Hooterville Handbook: A Viewer's Guide to Green Acres,* and *The Munchkins of Oz.* Cox is a freelance writer and an occasional contributor to the *Los Angeles Times.* He lives in Los Angeles.

John Lofflin, a reporter since 1971, holds a master's degree in political science. His research interest is the relationship between media and American culture. Lofflin teaches journalism, media theory, and film humor at Park College in Kansas City, Missouri. He has reported on business and finance for *The New York Times, The Kansas City Star, Money* magazine, *Institutional Investor, Veterinary Economics,* and *Newsreach.* Lofflin is currently completing a novel and working on a book about minor-league baseball in Iowa. He lives in Kansas City, Missouri.